THE CATHOLIC UNIVERSITY OF AMERICA
CANON LAW STUDIES
No. 175

The Local Religious Superior

AN HISTORICAL CONSPECTUS AND COMMENTARY ON THE RIGHTS AND DUTIES OF THE MINOR LOCAL SUPERIOR IN RELIGIOUS ORDERS OF MEN

BY

PATRICK M. J. CLANCY, O.P., S.T.Lr., J.C.L.
Priest of the Province of St. Albert the Great

A DISSERTATION

Submitted to the Faculty of the School of Canon Law of the Catholic University of America in Partial Fulfillment of the Requirements for the Degree of Doctor of Canon Law

THE CATHOLIC UNIVERSITY OF AMERICA PRESS
WASHINGTON, D. C.

1943

Revisores Ordinis:

JOANNES E. MARR, O.P., S.T.LR., S.T.D.
JOANNES J. McDONALD, O.P., S.T.LR., S.T.D.

Imprimi Potest:

PETRUS R. O'BRIEN, O.P., S.T.LR., PH.D.
Prior Provincialis.

Nihil Obstat:

HIERONYMUS D. HANNAN, A.M., LL.B., S.T.D., J.C.D.,
Censor Deputatus.

Washingtonii, die 24 maii 1943.

Imprimatur:

✠ MICHAEL J. CURLEY, D.D.,
Archiepiscopus Baltimoriensis-Washingtoniensis.

Baltimorae, die 25 maii 1943.

Printed by
THE PAULIST PRESS
New York, N. Y.
51

TABLE OF CONTENTS

PAGE

FOREWORD ix

PRELIMINARY NOTIONS

CHAPTER I

THE AUTHORITY OF RELIGIOUS SUPERIORS 1

ARTICLE I. RELIGIOUS SUPERIORS 1

ARTICLE II. JURISDICTION AND DOMINATIVE POWER ... 2
A. Power of Government 2
B. Jurisdiction 3
1. History 3
2. Present Meaning 4
3. Division 6
C. Dominative Power 7
1. Meaning 7
2. Division 9
D. Distinction Between Jurisdiction and Dominative Power 9

HISTORICAL DEVELOPMENT

CHAPTER II

THE MONASTIC ABBOT 12

ARTICLE I. THE EARLY PERIOD OF MONASTICISM 12

.TICLE II. THE PERIOD OF GENERAL MONASTIC EXEMPTION 15

PAGE

ARTICLE III. LEGISLATION IN THE COUNCILS OF THE LATERAN 20

CANONICAL COMMENTARY

PART ONE

RELIGIOUS SUPERIORS AND THEIR POWER OF GOVERNMENT

CHAPTER III

RELIGIOUS SUPERIORS IN THE CODE OF CANON LAW 24

CHAPTER IV

THE AUTHORITY OF THE LOCAL SUPERIOR IN THE CODE OF CANON LAW 26

ARTICLE I. HISTORICAL NOTES 26

ARTICLE II. THE JURISDICTIONAL AND DOMINATIVE POWER OF CANON 501, § 1 27

ARTICLE III. THE EXTENT OF THE POWER OF JURISDICTION 30

A. Prelates 30

B. Ordinaries 36

C. Subjects of the Local Superior 38

PART TWO

RELIGIOUS SUPERIORS AND THEIR LEGISLATIVE AND JUDICIAL POWER

CHAPTER V

LEGISLATIVE POWER 40

ARTICLE I. HISTORICAL NOTES 40

ARTICLE II. THE EXISTENCE OF LEGISLATIVE POWER... 41

PAGE

Article III. Jurisdictional Precepts 44
A. *"Praecepta singulis data"* 45
B. Common Precepts 46

Article IV. The Power of Dispensation 47
A. Historical Notes 47
B. The Present Law 47
C. Jurisdiction Involved 50

CHAPTER VI

JUDICIAL POWER 51

Article I. Historical Notes 51

Article II. Present Legislation 52
A. The Judge of First Instance in the Religious Tribunal. 52
B. Other Rights and Duties Involved in Ecclesiastical Trials 54
C. The Process of Beatification and Canonization 55

PART THREE

RELIGIOUS SUPERIORS AND THEIR EXECUTIVE POWER

CHAPTER VII

RIGHTS AND DUTIES UNDER THE LAW *DE RELIGIOSIS* 56

Article I. Residence 56

Article II. Decrees of the Holy See—Catechetical Instruction 58

Article III. The Canonical Visitation 62

Article IV. The Council 63

Article V. Temporal Goods 66
A. Acquisition 66

PAGE

B. Administration 69
1. The Procurator of the Convent 69
2. Acts of Ordinary Administration 71
C. Alienation 73
1. Historical Notes 73
2. Present Legislation 74
D. Investments 77
E. Responsibility for Debts and Obligations 78
F. Donations 79

ARTICLE VI. THE POSTULANCY 80

ARTICLE VII. THE NOVITIATE 82
A. Admission 82
B. Training of the Novices 83
C. The Novice Master 84

ARTICLE VIII. ADMISSION TO AND RECEPTION OF RELIGIOUS PROFESSION 87

ARTICLE IX. THE *Studium* 91

ARTICLE X. OBLIGATIONS OF RELIGIOUS 93
A. The Retreat, Daily Spiritual Exercises, Weekly Confession, Frequent Holy Communion 95
B. The Religious Habit 100
C. The Cloister 101
D. Parochial and Diocesan Work 106
E. The Religious Pastor 108
F. The Religious Subject as Pastor or Vicar 112
G. Choral Obligation and Conventual Mass 116

ARTICLE XI. EGRESS AND DISMISSAL OF SUBJECTS 122
A. Historical Notes 122
B. Present Legislation 123

CHAPTER VIII

THE SACRAMENTS 128

ARTICLE I. BAPTISM AND CONFIRMATION 128

PAGE

ARTICLE II. THE HOLY EUCHARIST AND EXTREME UNCTION 130
A. The Sacrifice of the Mass 130
1. The *Celebret* 130
2. The Obligation of Celebrating Mass 133
3. Mass Stipends 135
B. Holy Communion and Extreme Unction 136
1. Administration *devotionis causa* 136
2. Administration of Viaticum, and Extreme Unction. 138

ARTICLE III. PENANCE 144
A. Legislation Previous to the Code 144
1. Members of the Community 144
2. Women Religious 146
3. The Laity 149
4. Reservation of Sins 153
5. Special Faculties 154
(a) To Absolve from Reserved Sins 154
(b) To Absolve from Reserved Penalties 156
B. Present Legislation 157
1. Ordinary Jurisdiction 157
2. Delegation of Jurisdiction 158
3. The Local Ordinary 161

ARTICLE IV. HOLY ORDERS 163

APPENDIX—MATRIMONY 164

CHAPTER IX

OTHER RIGHTS AND DUTIES UNDER THE LAW *DE REBUS* 165

ARTICLE I. CHURCHES AND ORATORIES 165

ARTICLE II. ECCLESIASTICAL BURIAL 166
A. Cemeteries 166
B. Funeral Rites 168

PAGE

Article III. Custody and Worship of the Blessed Sacrament 170

Article IV. Images, Relics, Processions 171

Article V. Preaching 171
A. Legislation Before the Code 171
B. Present Legislation 174

Article VI. Censorship and Prohibition of Books.. 177

CHAPTER X

COERCIVE POWER 178

Article I. Legislation Before the Code 178

Article II. Present Legislation 180
A. The Existence of Coercive Jurisdiction 181
B. The Extent of Coercive Jurisdiction 191

CONCLUSIONS 199

BIBLIOGRAPHY 201

ABBREVIATIONS 208

ALPHABETICAL INDEX 209

BIOGRAPHICAL NOTE 219

CANON LAW STUDIES 221

FOREWORD

THE Code of Canon Law often refers to religious superiors, frequently without determining the type of superior meant. This study will concern itself with the legislation in the Code which refers to the minor local superior in religious Orders of men. An attempt will be made to list his rights and duties, and to comment upon them. Since the local superior is presupposed in the following pages to be constituted in office, no attempt will be made to consider the legislation governing his appointment to the office or his removal therefrom.

A word of explanation is due the reader as to the arrangement of the material. A brief article concerning religious superiors in general, followed by a treatment of jurisdictional and dominative power and of the difference between them introduces the study. A chapter dealing with the monastic abbot and his authority serves as a foundation for the proper understanding of the jurisdictional and dominative authority of the minor local superior in religious Orders, since historically the abbot may be regarded as the forerunner of the minor local superior in religious Orders, even though the abbot is considered a major religious superior in the present legislation.

Following the two preliminary chapters, the canonical commentary is begun immediately, as it was thought better to present the basic historical matter underlying each of the rights and duties of the local superior in conjunction with the commentary on each right or duty, rather than in a separate section of the work apart from the commentary. The body of the study is divided on the basis of the division of jurisdictional power into its legislative, judicial, and executive functions, with a subdivision of executive power into administrative and coercive.

The writer wishes to express his gratitude to his Provincial, the Very Reverend Peter O'Brien, O.P., S.T.LR., PH.D., for the opportunity of advanced study in Canon Law; to the faculty of the School of Canon Law of The Catholic University of America for their guidance and for their patience; to his brethren of the Dominican House of Studies, Washington, D. C., and River Forest, Illinois, for their aid and encouragement; to those who helped in the preparation of the manuscript; and finally to the conventual priors of his own Order who have been the inspiration for what is written in the following pages.

Preliminary Notions

CHAPTER I

THE AUTHORITY OF RELIGIOUS SUPERIORS

Article I. Religious Superiors

Careful direction is needed to attain any end. All the more is direction needed to reach the end of the religious vocation.[1]

The Church as founded by Christ was placed under the care of Peter as its head. Even the minor societies in that perfect society from the very beginning of monasticism were placed under the care of a superior who would rule them and lead the members to the end of their religious profession, as may be seen in the *Codex Justinianus*.[2] Throughout the centuries the different religious bodies have been governed by various types of superiors. Some have been governed more monarchically than others, while some have chosen a very democratic system of government in which many of the members share the burden of government. Nearly all, however, are ruled by a local superior whose power is confined to a definite place, whether that place be called monastery, convent or religious house, and whether the local superior himself be known as abbot, prior, guardian or rector. Very often this local superior is himself subject to a higher superior or superiors within the same religious institute.

[1] *Sancti Thomae Aquinatis Doctoris Angelici Opera Omnia Iussu Impensaque Leonis XIII, P. M. Edita* (Romae: 1882—); *Summa Theologica* (Romae: 1888-1906), IIa IIae, qu. CLXXXVI, art. 5. Hereafter cited as *Summa Theologica.*

[2] "Sancimus, ne quis duobus monasteriis praesit, sed ut ea sint quidem sub religiosissimo episcopo ejus territorii in quo sita sunt, unumquodque vero proprium habeat antistitem, quo de institutione et factis antistitis respondeat episcopus, de monachis antistes: eoque modo bona disciplina servabitur nec quicquam deinceps turbulenter vel per superbiam potissimum ab iis fiet qui hunc sanctum ordinem amplexi sunt; quae nunc et in posterum perpetuo observari oportet." (1.3) 39.

Article II. Jurisdiction and Dominative Power

A. *Power of Government*

The mere fact that any society has a director will not prove sufficient to attain the purpose of the union. Such a leader must be able to exercise authority by which he can officially direct his subjects to the attainment of the aims of the society. Without this authority each member would be left to act for himself exclusively according to his own judgment as to what means are best fitted to attain the end, a procedure directly contrary to the very purpose of the community as a social entity in which all the members aim by common means to attain a common end.

Authority to govern or rule arises from the character of the society. Often authority is found *ex natura,* as in a perfect society. Sometimes it is conferred upon a ruler by a higher legislator, or by the will of those who wish to band themselves together for some common purpose. In general the kind of authority exercised in any society will depend upon the nature of the society itself, flowing from that society as a necessary attribute.[3] If the union is a natural one the authority of its ruler will be natural, as is the authority of the father of a family. If the union depends upon some positive determination, the power of its rulers will also depend upon the same positive determination, whether the determination be of a higher legislator or of equals who wish to entrust the direction of their activity to another. Viewed from this angle of origin, authority may be said to be either natural or positive. The same authority viewed from the nature of the society in which it is exercised belongs either to a perfect society or to an imperfect one. That power which is essentially characteristic of a perfect society is known as jurisdiction or *potestas perfecta.* The power which is exercised in an imperfect society is known as dominion.

[3] "Inde fluit imperandi ius seu auctoritas, unde orta est societas."—Ottaviani, *Institutiones Iuris Publici Ecclesiastici* (2 vols., Romae: Apud Aedes Facultatis Iuridicae ad S. Apollinaris, 1925), I, n. 29.

B. *Jurisdiction*

1. History[4]

Jurisdiction, or the authority found as an essential characteristic of a perfect society, has been understood in various ways throughout history. Its present meaning is a result of the development of the Roman law concept of jurisdiction taken in its literal meaning of *ius dicere,* and restricted to the judicial forum. In two of the Novels of Justinian[5] one finds the word *iurisdictio* used in the sense of *potestas publica regendi communitatem,* a concept which included not only the judicial order, to which jurisdiction had been confined throughout early Roman law, but which included also the notion of authority in general.[6] In the Church from the time of St. Gregory the Great (590-604) the term was used in its later Roman law signification of the power of general administration both spiritual and temporal.[7] However, Van de Kerckhove shows that in the latter half of the twelfth century when canonists made frequent use of the terms *lex iurisdictionis* and *lex diocesana,* the *lex iurisdictionis* referred only to administration in the spiritual order to the exclusion of any direction over temporal affairs.[8] The *lex iurisdictionis* was to be further limited even in the spiritual order, for after 1215 it was clearly distinguished even from the power of Orders, and given the signification of public power of

[4] This section is for the most part a summary of the following articles: M. Van de Kerckhove, "De Notione Jurisdictionis in Jure Romano,"—*Jus Pontificium,* XVI (1936), 49-65; *Idem,* "De Notione Jurisdictionis apud Decretistas et Priores Decretalistas,"—*Jus Pontificum,* XVIII (1938), 10-14. Hereafter cited as *JP.*

[5] N. (131.3); N. (120.6).

[6] "Itaque iurisdictio facta est synonimia vocabuli 'potestatis,' non sensu romano classico, sed potestatis in genere, vocabulum proinde omnino genericum et qua tale omnibus ramis ordinis administrativi applicabilis (*sic*)"—M. Van de Kerckhove, "De Notione Jurisdictionis in Jure Romano,"—*JP,* XVI (1936), 62.

[7] Cf. Hilling, "Über den Gebrauch des Ausdrucks iurisdictio im kanonischen Recht während der ersten Hälfte des Mittelalters,"—*Archiv für katholisches Kirchenrecht,* CXVIII (1938), 165-170. Hereafter cited as *AKKR.*

[8] "Notio Jurisdictionis apud Decretistas et Priores Decretalistas,"—*JP,* XVIII (1938), 12.

ruling a perfect community.[9] This is notable because only a few years earlier (1188) the *lex iurisdictionis* included the *ordinatio ecclesiarum et altarium, virginum consecratio, crismatis, et generaliter omnium sacramentorum collatio.*[10] Canonists of the thirteenth century, however, considered jurisdiction as a *potestas publica regendi communitatem perfectam,* embracing legislative, judicial, and coercive power.[11]

As jurisdiction will frequently pertain to the "power of the keys," it is interesting to note that the early Decretists did not refer to the authority of the Church in the internal forum by using the word *iurisdictio.* This usage, so common in present day theological and canonical works, was first employed by Joannes Teutonicus (+ c. 1244-1245) in his *Summa ad Decretum* written about the year 1210. The employment of the word *iurisdictio* as referring to the power of the keys is also found in the writings of Saint Raymond of Pennafort (1175-1275) [12]

Canonists, referring to the power of jurisdiction in the Church, from the time of the thirteenth century onwards have used the term *iurisdictio* in the sense of public authority to govern and rule the Church, thus continuing the usage employed after the IV General Council of the Lateran (1215). Larraona cites the following definition as the classical definition of jurisdiction in pre-Code doctrine: *Potestas publica circa regimen animarum."* [13]

2. Present Meaning

Canon 196 [14] of the Code of Canon Law describes the power of jurisdiction principally from the aspect of its extent to both the external and internal forum, but the explicative words of the defini-

[9] *Ibidem,* p. 13.

[10] *Ibidem,* p. 12.

[11] *Ibidem,* p. 13.

[12] *Summa* (ed. nova, Veronae, 1744), lib. III, tit. XXIV, § 5, pp. 451-452.

[13] "De Potestate Dominativa Publica in Iure Canonico."—*Acta Congressus Iuridici Internationalis* (5 vols., Romae: Apud Custodiam Librariam Pont. Instituti Utriusque Iuris, 1935-1937), IV, 147. Henceforth cited as *ACII.*

[14] "Potestas iurisdictionis seu regiminis quae ex divina institutione est in Ecclesia, alia est fori externi, alia fori interni, seu conscientiae, sive sacramentalis sive extra-sacramentalis."

tion *seu regiminis* contain a clue to the very extensive meaning of the power of jurisdiction as including legislative, judicial, and coercive authority. It has already been noted [15] that the Decretalists understood *iurisdictio* to be an authority or power proper to a perfect society, and therefore embracing legislative, judicial, and coercive power, as distinct from the power of Orders. This same meaning is implied in the present legislation of the Code, which identifies *iurisdictio* and *regimen*.[16] Kearney notes this as follows: "The Code has seized upon the extensive meaning of the term, denoting the most ample power of government in all its functions. In order that this intention of the legislator might be manifest, it is called *potestas iurisdictionis seu regiminis*; the particle *seu* denotes the identity of the concept, while the term *regimen* is explicative of the preceding word and reveals its extension." [17]

Authors seek to include all the Code implies in Canon 196 by giving various explanatory definitions. Prummer [18] defines jurisdiction in general as *potestas legitima ad societatis regimen ordinata,* and ecclesiastical jurisdiction as *potestas regendi fideles in ordine ad salutem aeternam et includit potestatem docendi, iudicandi, coercendi, leges ferendi, sacramenta administrandi etc., uno verbo: per modum regiminis exhibendi fidelibus, i.e. baptizatis omnia media a Christo instituta pro salute aeterna obtinenda.* Such a definition would be more satisfactory were it to indicate the source of the power of jurisdiction. Wernz [19] does so in the definition which he gives: *Iurisdictio vero ecclesiastica est publica potestas*

[15] *Supra,* pp. 3-4.

[16] Cf. I. Chelodi, *Ius de Personis iuxta Codicem Iuris Canonici* (ed. altera a Sac. Ernesto Bertagnolli recognita et aucta, Tridenti: Libr. Edit. Tridentum, 1927), n. 125. Hereafter cited as *Ius de Personis.* Maroto, *Institutiones Iuris Canonici ad Normam Novi Codicis* (2 vols., Matriti, 1919), I, n. 573. Hereafter cited as *Institutiones.*

[17] *The Principles of Delegation,* The Catholic University of America Canon Law Studies, n. 55 (Washington, D. C.: The Catholic University of America, 1929), p. 45.

[18] *Manuale Iuris Canonici in Usum Scholarum* (6. ed., Friburgi Brisgoviae: Herder, 1938), qu. 86, r. 1. Hereafter cited as *Manuale I. C.*

[19] *Ius Decretalium ad Usum Praelectionum in Scholis Textus Canonici sive Iuris Decretalium* (6 vols. in 7, Romae-Prati, 1898-1913), II, n. 3. Hereafter cited as *Ius Decretalium.*

regendi homines baptizatos directe in ordine ad salutem supernaturalem a Christo vel ab Ecclesia per injunctionem sive missionem canonicam alicui concessa."

This indication of the origin of ecclesiastical jurisdiction is of value in distinguishing it from civil jurisdiction, for though civil authority sometimes arises from the will of the people, true ecclesiastical jurisdiction never arises from the will of the people, but must always be a participation in that *potestas regiminis* given to the Church by her Divine Founder.[20] Only the Church can give such power to others, since the Church alone possesses it essentially. Her jurisdiction is an authority divinely bestowed primarily upon the Head of the Church, the Pope, and upon the bishops, and through them upon the other rulers in the Church. Well, therefore, does Wernz define the power of jurisdiction as derived *"a Christo vel ab Ecclesia per injunctionem sive missionem canonicam alicui concessa."* [21]

In the following pages, therefore, jurisdiction in its complete signification will be regarded as the *potestas regendi seu legislegendi, judicandi, et coercendi subjectos religiosos ut fideles in ordine ad salutem aeternam ab Ecclesia Superiori Religioso concessa.*

3. Division

In canon 196 ecclesiastical jurisdiction is divided into jurisdiction of the external and internal forum. Jurisdiction of the external forum has reference to that authority which is accompanied by public juridicial consequences and is directed primarily to the good of the Church, while authority or power in the internal forum is exercised in the domain of conscience, and therefore is primarily of a moral nature, whether this domain be reached by the channels of sacramental administration and grace, or by means other than sacramental but still directed primarily to the good of the individual.[22]

Jurisdiction is either attached by law to an office, in which case it is known as *ordinary,* or it is committed to some person, in which

[20] Cf. canon 196.

[21] *Op. et loc. cit.* Cf. canon 109.

[22] Cf. canon 196; I. Chelodi, *Ius de Personis,* n. 125.

case it is known as *delegated*. If the incumbent exercises the power inherent by law in his office in his own name, the jurisdiction is *ordinary* and *proper*, if in the name of another, the jurisdiction is *vicarious*, though still *ordinary* because attached by law to an office.

The division of jurisdiction into *contentious* and *voluntary*, is based on the manner of its exercise, that is, whether judicially or non-judicially. *Universal* jurisdiction is exercised by the Supreme Pastor of the Church alone, while the authority of all those inferior to the Pope is of a particular nature. *Territorial* jurisdiction will point out the geographical nature of the superior's power, while *personal* jurisdiction refers to the subjects over whom the power will be exercised.

C. *Dominative Power*

1. Meaning

To jurisdiction as a necessary attribute of a perfect society may be compared the authority which is exercised by the ruler of an imperfect society. Such authority may arise naturally, as the power of the head of a family, or it may arise through an agreement by which one person subjects himself to the rule of another. The subject then obligates himself to be guided by the determination of another in the choice of means to the end of the society. The nature of the authority which the director of an imperfect society possesses will be judged by the nature of the society in which it is exercised.[23]

As an imperfect society the authority within it will also be imperfect, that is, imperfect in comparison to the power exercised in a perfect society.

The authority of an imperfect society, known as dominative power or authority, is a characteristic of all human societies; it has existed in religious communities from the beginning, and is generally understood to arise from the agreement which a religious makes when he enter the religious state, and in virtue of which he subjects

[23] "Potestas respondet adaequate ex iure naturali et respondere debet ex iure positivo naturae ac characteribus societatis ad quam regendum ordinatur." —Larraona, "De Potestate Dominativa Publica in Iure Canonico,"—*ACII*, IV, 148-149.

himself to the dominative authority of those who will be appointed to direct him to the end of the religious institute.[24]

Canonical writers usually define dominative power in relation to jurisdiction as an imperfect authority private in nature and based on the authority exercised by the master over his slave. Blat [25] traces the development of dominative power from an original condition of master and slave to the *societas herilis* in which servants freely contracted to give their services to a master. From this institution the authority which the superior of an imperfect society exercises over his subjects received its name dominative power, inasmuch as the master was regarded as having dominion over his servant.

Dominative power as exercised in religious institutes may therefore be defined as *that authority which a superior has over his subjects in virtue of their enrollment in the community, and by reason of which he governs their actions, within limits defined by the Code of Canon Law and the particular Constitutions of the institute, to the attainment of the end or purpose of the society.*

The Code, as a compilation of the laws of the perfect society which is the Church, devotes all of the title V of the second book, with the exception of canon 210, to the power of jurisdiction, and frequently makes reference to it throughout the remainder of the Code. No definition of dominative power is given in the Code, however, and reference is made to it explicitly only in canon 501, § 1, and in canon 1312, § 1. The absence of any formal treatment of dominative power in the Code is not surprising when it is remembered that jurisdiction is essentially an attribute of the perfect society with which the Code is primarily concerned, while dominative power is an attribute of an imperfect society, the legislation for which the Code leaves in great power to particular enactment.

[24] Cf. F. Suarez, *Opera Omnia* (ed. nova, 28 vols., Parisiis, 1856-1878), *De religione*, tr. VII, lib. II, cap. XVIII, n. 5. Hereafter cited as *De religione*. *Dictionnaire de Droit Canonique* (Tom. I-II, publié sous la direction de R. Naz, Paris—VI: Librairie Letouzey et Ané, 1935-1937), s. v. "Abbesses," I, 67.

[25] "De Potestae Superiorum in Religionibus secundum Codicem I. C.,—*Commentarium pro Religiosis et Missionariis*, XVI (1935), 324. Hereafter cited as *CpRM*.

Mention is made throughout the Code, however, of authoritative acts of superiors which are certainly acts of dominative power even though not expressly referred to as such in common law.

2. Division

The division of dominative power into public and private made by Larraona is worthy of note.[26] Usually authors refer to dominative power as a *potestas privata*. This is certainly proper in comparison with the *potestas publica* which is jurisdiction. Yet when certains acts of dominative power, such as the admission and dismissal of religious, the prohibition of a superior forbidding a subject to receive Orders or to exercise an Order received, are considered, they are seen to exhibit a social and juridical character. At least they are not acts as evidently private as those exercised by the heads of domestic societies, or even by those superiors of non-juridical societies recognized by the Church. For this reason, as well as for doctrinal and exegetical reasons, Larraona advocates a division into *dominativa publica et dominativa privata*. The division, he maintains, would help to point out the true nature of both jurisdictional and of dominative power inasmuch as it would clarify the authority of the superiors of clerical non-exempt religious institutes.[27] The division, while not changing in any way the true nature of the authority of such superiors, provides a clearer concept of their power and is worthy of adoption.

D. Distinction Between Jurisdiction and Dominative Power

Jurisdiction, embracing all power necessary for the attainment of the end of a society, is a *potestas perfecta regiminis*. It is this element of complete legislative, judicial, and coercive power exercised by the ruler of a perfect society which principally distinguishes his power of jurisdiction from the less extensive and imperfect dominative power of the head of an imperfect society.

Dominative power and jurisdiction both spring from the nature of the societies in which they exercise their influence. Essentially,

[26] "De Potestate Dominativa Publica in Iure Canonico,"—*ACII*, IV, 148.

[27] *Art. cit.*, pp. 179-180.

before any designation of a subject who will administer it, dominative power resides in an imperfect society. The same is true of jurisdiction in relation to a perfect society, since one cannot conceive of any society without some authority. But how is one to know whether the authority in a society is dominative or jurisdictional? One way of solving the problem will be to examine the nature of the society which exercises the authority. If the society is a perfect society it will have perfect authority or jurisdiction. If it is an imperfect body, dominative power alone will be found to reside essentially in its rulers. From such an analysis only two societies, the Church and the State essentially exercise jurisdiction. However, a participation in the jurisdictional power of the perfect society may be given to the rulers of those imperfect societies which are also parts of a perfect society. Thus by a positive determination of the supreme ruler of the higher body the superiors of an imperfect society may exercise jurisdiction, not essentially as rulers of the imperfect societies, but as superiors of an officially recognized part of a perfect society.

This concession of jurisdiction to rulers of those societies which are recognized as parts of the perfect society does not imply that these rulers always exercise jurisdictional power whenever they govern their subjects. On the contrary, their jurisdictional power will always retain its essential nature of a participated power, subject to the limitations placed upon it by the one who concedes it. Therefore if the supreme legislator declares that a particular act is to be regarded as an act of jurisdiction, the act mentioned is undoubtedly jurisdictional. The difficulty remains therefore only in regard to those acts which have not been explicitly designated by the legislator as jurisdictional, either because he is silent in regard to them, or because he has conceded jurisdiction only in a general way, to be exercised by the recipient in those matters which demand the use of jurisdictional authority.

Therefore some criterion is needed to determine whether the performance of a right or duty by a superior of an imperfect society is to be regarded as an act of jurisdictional or of dominative power.

Presupposing that a superior has been granted a limited participation in the jurisdictional power of a perfect society, and presupposing the definition of jurisdiction as ***potestas legitima ad societatis regimen ordinata,*** the writer presents the following as a norm for determining whether a particular act of a superior of an imperfect society is jurisdictional or not: If the act tends directly to the attainment of the end of the perfect society and only indirectly to the good of the imperfect society, the act is jurisdictional; if the act is primarily directed to the end of the imperfect society, and only secondarily to the end of the perfect society, the act indicates the use of dominative power alone. In the opinion of the writer, therefore, the only time the superior uses his jurisdictional power is in acting as an officially recognized minister of the *Church,* for in matters which pertain directly to the good of the *religious institute* there is no need for the use of the Church's official power, but only of that power which is inherent in the imperfect society as such, namely, dominative authority.

If it is remembered that this principle is not meant to decide whether or not an individual superior has jurisdiction, but only to determine whether a superior, recognized as having jurisdiction, is actually using it, it should be of aid in determining the character of the acts of superiors in clerical exempt religious institutes. These superiors are recognized in law as capable of exercising jurisdiction [28] but it does not follow from this that they make use of jurisdictional power every time they exercise authority. Indeed even these superiors use dominative power and not jurisdiction in most of their administrative acts, for as a general rule a superior is employed in ruling his subjects more frequently as religious than as members of the Church. Consequently, since jurisdiction as understood in relation to religious can be defined as the power of ruling subjects as members of the Church,[29] it may be said that superiors use that power only when they are ruling their subjects as members of the Church and not primarily as members of a religious institute.

[28] Cf. canon 501, § 1.

[29] Cf. Fanfani, *De Iure Religiosorum ad Normam Codicis Iuris Canonici* (2. ed., Taurini-Romae: Marietti, 1925), n. 51. Hereafter cited as *De Iure Religiosorum.*

Historical Development

CHAPTER II

THE MONASTIC ABBOT

Article I. The Early Period of Monasticism

Prescinding from the eremitical form of monasticism in which some local authority at least was also recognized, one discovers the local superior of the early monastic foundations as the abbot of the monastery. In the Pachomian form of monasticism the abbot of the principal monastery was the superior-general of the whole multitude, and he named the superiors of the other monasteries.[1] Saint Benedict described the office of the abbot in the second chapter of his Rule, and in the sixty-fourth chapter gave a list of the qualities which the abbot should possess. Cardinal Gasquet makes reference to the abbot's authority as follows: "The whole government of every religious house depended upon the abbot . . . He was the main-spring of the entire machine, and his will in all things was supreme. All the officials from the prior downwards, were appointed by him, and had their authority from him; they were his assistants in the government of the house."[2] In the original plan of St. Benedict the abbot could be assisted by a prior, or by deans, but these minor officials were always only assistants.[3] In later centuries when smaller communities were founded they were attached to a neighboring monastery as filial houses, and their superior was known as a prior, though distinct from the prior or assistant of the abbot of the principal monastery. The priors of the filial houses

[1] Butler, *The Lausiac History of Palladius* (Texts and Studies, VI, 2 vols., Cambridge, 1898), I, p. 235.

[2] *English Monastic Life* (2. ed. rev., New York, 1904), p. 50.

[3] Cf. Butler, *Benedictine Monachism* (2. ed., London: Longmans, Green and Co., 1924), p. 216; Delatte, *The Rule of Saint Benedict* (New York: Benziger Bros., 1921), pp. 194-199.

exercised dominative power over their subjects, but appear to have been entirely subordinate to the abbot of the principal monastery in all matters of jurisdiction, as may be seen from a study of the Cluniac system in which the prior of the filial house was only "the shadow of the abbot of Cluny, and no house, not even the greatest monastery, had any inherent principle of life."[4] However, in English Benedictine monasteries which were attached to cathedral churches, "the priors ruled with an authority equal to that of an abbot, and whatever legislation applies to the latter would apply equally to the former."[5] The monastic abbot certainly possessed jurisdiction taken in its widest sense of the power of governing subjects toward an end. But contrasting strict jurisdictional power with dominative authority, one must be led to the conclusion that the early abbot possessed the latter and not the former. Moreover, it is worthy of note that not many of the early abbots were priests at all, nor were the monks. Consequently, they were subject to the spiritual jurisdictional power of the local ordinary and clergy. Gradually as the needs of the monasteries grew, some of the monks were ordained to the priesthood. Others received Sacred Orders at the request of the bishop and with the consent of the abbot, that they might aid in the work of the salvation of souls, under the jurisdiction all the time, however, of the local ordinary.

This power of the local ordinary over the monks was often insisted upon in the Councils of this period. In the IV General Council of Chalcedon (451), the power of the bishop over the monks was clearly indicated, and from the wording of the fourth canon of this Council, little jurisdiction would seem to be left for the local superior.[6] This legislation of the Council of Chalcedon

[4] Cf. Butler, *Benedictine Monachism*, p. 238.

[5] Cf. Gasquet, *English Monastic Life*, pp. 40-41.

[6] ". . . It is decided that no one shall build or found a monastery . . . without the consent of the bishop of the city. It is decided furthermore that all monks in every city and country place shall be subject to the bishop . . . that they shall not leave their monasteries and burden themselves either with ecclesiastical or worldly affairs or take part in them unless they are commissioned to do so for some necessary purpose by the bishop of the city. . . . The bishop of the city, moreover, shall exercise a strict supervision over the monasteries."—c. 12, C. XVI, q. 1; Mansi, *Sacrorum Conciliorum Nova et Amplissima Collectio*

remained the canonical norm governing the jurisdictional power of the local ordinary over the monasteries for centuries.[7] In later centuries this canon of Chalcedon was often pointed out as affirming the bishop's right of jurisdiction over the monasteries in his diocese.

Particular Councils likewise pointed out the subjection of the abbot and monks to the local bishop. In the III Synod of Arles (455) it was enacted that the bishop alone should consecrate the oils, and confirm the newly-baptized.[8] The I Council of Orleans (511) ruled that the abbot was to be subject to the bishop, and to be corrected by the bishop when he failed in the observance of the rule.[9] The III Council of Orleans (538) decreed that the abbots and priests had to have the permission of the bishop to alienate ecclesiastical goods.[10] A Council held in Paris in 614 forbade the monks to baptize or to say Mass for deceased lay persons.[11]

On the other hand, some of the first traces of jurisdictional power seem to be in evidence when one reads in canon 27 of the Council of Agde (506) that the abbot was given complete charge over the lay-monks, none of whom, according to canon 3 of the Council of Lerida (546), were to be ordained by the bishop without the consent of the abbot.[12] Canon 2 of the Council of Tarragona (516) prohibited the monk from presuming to undertake any work of the ministry except at the command of the abbot, and also prohibited him from engaging in forensic matters.[13] A *dictum* following c. 25,

(53 vols. in 59, Paris, Leipzig, Arnhem, 1901-1927), VI, 1226. Hereafter referred to as Mansi. Schroeder, *Disciplinary Decrees of the General Councils*, Text, Translation, and Commentary (St. Louis: Herder, 1937), p. 92. Hereafter referred to as Schroeder, *Disciplinary Decrees*.

[7] Cf. Hüfner, "Das Rechtsinstitut der klösterlichen Exemtion in der abendländischen Kirche,"—*AKKR*, LXXXVI (1906), 304. Hereafter this article will be referred to as Hüfner, "Klösterlichen Exemtion."

[8] Hefele-Leclerq, *Histoire des Conciles* (Paris: Letouzey et Ané, 1907-1938), II (2), 583. Hereafter referred to as Hefele.

[9] C. 16, C. XVIII, q. 2; Hefele, II (2), 1013.

[10] C. 41, C. 12, q. 2; Hefele, II (2), 1161.

[11] Hefele, III (1), 71; cf. Hüfner, "Klösterlichen Exemtion,"—*AKKR*, LXXXVI (1906), 305.

[12] Cc. 33, 34, C. XVI, q. 1.

[13] C. 35, C. XVI, q. 1; Mansi, VIII, 543.

C. XVI, q. 1, sums up several previous canons ascribed to this period: "*. . . monachos posse poenitentiam dare, baptizare, et cetera sacerdotalia officia licite administrare. Quod vero populi electione, episcoporum institutione, et abbatis consensu potestatem suam exsequi valeant Ieronimi, Gelasii, et Gregorii auctoritate probatur.*"

From these examples of the relative position of both bishop and abbot, one can easily see that the local superiors of this period were very much under the jurisdiction of the bishop in whose diocese their monastery was located. Occasionally, however, the bishops were too exacting or too harsh in their dealings with the monks, and consequently, when St. Gregory the Great (590-604), a former Benedictine monk himself, became Pope, many papal letters were sent to bishops, especially regarding the freedom of election for the office of the abbot. He and many of the Popes before him gave protection to the monks, but hesitated to depart from what was considered the traditional practice of the Church, the subjection of the monks to their diocesan bishop.

Thus the early local superior's power was certainly dominative, though some slight traces of what we would today term "ordinary jurisdiction" appear. This dominative power was sufficient for the internal needs of the slowly rising institutes, and since as yet they, as religious bodies, were not called upon to undertake any immediate direction of the faithful other than their own members, they were more the passive rather than active subjects of jurisdiction. In the next period, during which the first real exemptions from episcopal authority were granted, the local superiors obtained for themselves some of the jurisdiction formerly exercised by the diocesan bishop.[14]

Article II. The Period of General Monastic Exemption

As monasticism progressed, the internal government of the monasteries demanded greater personal direction, and less interference

[14] It is generally admitted that some of the monasteries in Ireland were governed by local superiors who exercised the power of jurisdiction. In some of the monasteries there, the abbot exercised jurisdiction over a resident bishop, whose duty it was to perform only the pontifical functions. Cf. Haddan and Stubbs, *Councils and Ecclesiastical Documents Relating to Great Britain and Ireland* (3 vols. in 4, Oxford, 1869-1873), I, 143.

from without. It was to guarantee greater freedom in following out the monastic life, and to preserve a uniformity of government as well as of purpose, that exemption from episcopal control was first conceded. The question of jurisdiction among religious superiors is very much bound up with the history of monastic exemption in the Church. It would seem to follow naturally that upon securing freedom from the control of the bishop, the monks should be subject to the jurisdictional power then given by the Church to the superior of the monastery, unless the Papal grants decreed otherwise. Though the religious frequently claimed direct subjection to the Pope this could only be true in relation to exemption from the local bishop's authority. Certainly it would not be possible for the Pope to exercise direct control over each of the exempt communities, nor would it be to the advantage of the religious communities to be subject still to delegates of the Pope who were not at the same time members of the religious community. Thus arose the jurisdictional power of the local superior.[15] In 628 the monastery of Bobbio in Italy secured what is generally believed to be the first grant of exemption from episcopal authority. Pope Honorius I (625-638) in that year exempted the monastery from all external authority except that of the Pope himself: " . . . et ideo omnem cujuslibet Ecclesiae sacerdotem in praedicto monasterio ditionem qualibet auctoritate ne extendere . . . omnino prohibemus."[16] The wording of the privilege offers no direct proof that any episcopal or quasi-episcopal jurisdiction was conferred upon the abbot of Bobbio, but it would appear that as abbot of a monastery now exempt from all external jurisdiction, he would have obtained at least part of that power formerly exercised by the bishop. This deduction, however, cannot be substantiated by any

[15] Cf. Suarez, *De religione*, tr. VIII, lib. II, cap. I, n. 6. Bouix, *Tractatus de Jure Regularium* (3. ed., 2 vols., Parisiis, 1883), II, 378. Hereafter cited as *De Jure Regularium*. Wernz, *Ius Decretalium*, III, pars 2, n. 683.

[16] Epist. *"Si semper,"* 11 ian. 628—Jaffé, *Regesta Pontificum Romanorum* (2. ed., 2 vols. in 1, correctam et auctam auspiciis Gulielmi Wattenbach curaverunt S. Loewenfeld, F. Kaltenbrunner, P. Ewald, Lipsiae, 1885-1888), n. 2017. Hereafter the letters L, K, and E will be joined with the letter J to designate the editor of the document cited from Jaffé's work in its second edition. The letter of Honorius I is designated thus: JE, n. 2017.

direct or positive reference to the power of the abbot in the Papal letter.

About the year 674 the monastery of St. Martin of Tours also received exemption. Pope Adeodatus II (672-676), writing to all the bishops of France, proclaimed the monastery free from episcopal power, except as regards the ordination of priests and the consecration of the sacred chrism.[17] This document is worthy of special note inasmuch as jurisdiction, as understood to include administrative power over temporal goods, was certainly given to the abbot.

Various Papal concessions were also granted to the monastery of Fulda. In the original grant of exemption, the bishop was permitted to celebrate Mass there only upon invitation of the abbot.[18] The abbot of Fulda was later commanded and given power to preach the word of God "auctoritate Sancti Petri." [19] Pope Stephen IV (816-817), in 817, bestowed Papal exemption upon the monastery of Farfa. The Pope placed all the possessions of the monastery under the temporal jurisdiction of the abbot and his successors,[20] a grant renewed by Pope Paschal I (817-824) in the same year and with even greater jurisdictional power for the abbot, for the Pope writes: "Nullus autem Episcopus audeat synodare vel excommunicare monachum vel clericum ipsius monasterii, quos praedicto abbati suisque succesoribus concedimus monendos et constringendos." [21] Whether the Pope actually by this letter gave the abbot power to excommunicate is not certain, but the power to warn

[17] Epist. *"Aequitatis nos admonet,"* date uncertain, but between 672-676—JE, n. 2105; Mansi, XI, 103; *Bullarum Diplomatum et Privilegiorum Sanctorum Romanorum Pontificum Taurinensis Editio* (24 vols. et Appendix, Augustae Taurinorum, 1857-1872), I, 208. Hereafter cited as *BRT*. Migne, *Patrologiae Cursus Completus, Series Latina* (221 vols., Parisiis, 1844-1864), LXXXVIII, 1141. Hereafter cited *MPL*.

[18] Pope Zacharias (741-752), epist., *"Quoniam semper,"* 4 nov. 751—JE, n. 2293; *MPL*, LXXXIX, 954; Mansi, XIII, 349; *BRT*, I, 238.

[19] Leo VII (936-939), epist. *"Summam gerentes sollicitudinem,"* 13 maii 936—JE, n. 3596; *MPL*, CXXXII, 1065.

[20] Epist., *"Cum magna nobis,"* 23 ian. 817—JE, n. 2544; *BRT*, I, 262; *MPL*, CXXIX, 973.

[21] Epist., *"Cum magna nobis solicitudine,"* 1 febr. 817—JE, n. 2546; *BRT*, I, 266; *MPL*, CXXIX, 977.

and to correct the monks was certainly given. The Pope would seem at least to have been referring to some greater power of warning or correcting them than that which the abbot in virtue of his position always held, even when the monks were subject to the jurisdiction of the local ordinary.

Pope Paschal (817-824) also conceded to the abbot of the monastery of St. Vincent, situated near the river Volturno in Italy, the privilege of inviting any bishop whatsoever for the consecration of the church and for the ordination of clerics and priests.[22]

In a letter to the bishops and people of France Gregory IV (827-844) bestowed extensive jurisdiction on the abbot of Fleury. Without his permission no archbishop, bishop, or cleric was to come to the monastery to perform any ordination, or even to celebrate Mass. The monk elected as abbot was empowered to choose any bishop he pleased to bestow the abbatial blessing. If the abbot was accused of any crime, he was to be tried not by one bishop, but by a provincial council, or, if he desired, by the Pope himself.[23]

In 855 the privileges of the monastery of Corbie were confirmed, and it was stated "that no bishop or archbishop shall come to the monastery unless called there by the abbot or one of the monks." If asked by the abbot, the bishop was permitted to consecrate or bless the altars of the monastery.[24]

In 863 Pope Nicholas I (858-867) confirmed previous privileges of the monastery of Carilef, granting the abbot power over all the temporal goods of the monastery, "ut quidquid secundum ipsius monasterii utilitatem regulariter et canonice voluerint agere, in eorum (sc. abbatis et fratrum) situm sit potestate." [25]

Pope John XI (931-936) ruled that the abbot of Cluny could

[22] Epist., "*Divinis praeceptionibus,*" iul. 819—JE, n. 2552; *BRT*, I, 269; *MPL*, CXXIX, 980.

[23] Epist., "*Quoniam ex Apostolica,*" apr. 829—JE, n. 2570; *BRT*, I, 280; *MPL*, CXXIX, 995.

[24] Benedict III (855-858), epist., "*Cum Romanae sedis,*" 7 oct. 855—JE, n. 2663; Mansi, XIV, 118; *BRT*, I, 295; *MPL*, CXV, 693.

[25] Epist., "*Regum corda,*" apr. 863—JE, n. 2735; Mansi, XV, 346; *BRT*, I, 315.

receive under his jurisdiction any group of monks who cared to seek greater perfection.[26]

By a provision of Pope Gregory V (996-999), no bishop could presume to consecrate or to ordain at Cluny unless invited by the abbot.[27]

In 970 Pope John XIII (965-972) granted the abbot of St. Vincent of Metz extensive privileges: "Si vero Episcopus defuerit liceat abbati in festivis diebus ad sedem episcopalem accedere, ibique . . . missas celebrare." [28]

The following is the jurisdiction given (992) to the newly elected abbot of the monastery of Our Saviour at Aniane: " . . . licentiam donandi poenitentiam, undecumque ad se humiliter concurrentibus, excommunicandique perversos potestatem habeat, et solvendi satisfacientes auctoritate apostolica indulgemus." [29]

This is the clearest grant of coercive power so far noticed, and it would seem to have extended beyond his own subjects, particularly so during the time of interdict.

In 996, Gregory V (996-999) permitted the monastery of St. Martin of Tours to have its own resident bishop: "et quaecumque emendanda et corrigenda sunt cum consensu abbatis sui canonica institutione et secundum ordinem cuncta peragat." [30]

The same Pope granted (999) the monastery of St. Andrew at Avignon the right to bury anyone who chose to be buried there.[31]

Thus Pope after Pope granted privileges of exemption, which, since they gave the local superior power of administration both spiritual and temporal, in some instances even beyond his own

[26] Epist., "*Convenit apostolico moderamini*," mart. 931—JL, n. 3584; *MPL*, CXXXII, 1055.

[27] Gregory V, epist., "*Desiderium quod*," 998-999,—JL, n. 3896; *MPL*, CXXXVII, 932.

[28] Epist., "*Cum in exarandis*," 29 sept. 970—JL, n. 3741; *MPL*, CXXXV, 980.

[29] John XV (985-996), epist., "*Convenit apostolico moderamine*," iun. 992—JL, n. 3844; *MPL*, CXXXVII, 835.

[30] Epist. "*Innotuit satis*," 29 sept. 996—JL, n. 3870; *MPL*, CXXXVII, 907.

[31] Gregory V, epist., "*Cum summus apostolicae*," ian. 999—JL, n. 3898; *MPL*, CXXXVII, 937.

monastery, can be considered as having given him jurisdiction.[82]

So many of the grants during this period are alike that it would be almost needless repetition to list them, and to point out words and clauses which seem to confer jurisdiction on the local superior. A point worthy of note, however, is that with the reign of St. Gregory VII, (1073-1085), Urban II, (1088-1099), and Paschal II (1099-1118), the Popes began to exempt whole Orders, whereas before only single monasteries had been granted the privilege. Urban II declared the whole Order of the Vallombrosians exempt,[83] a privilege later (1169) confirmed by Alexander III (1159-1181).[84]

In an earlier chapter,[85] it was stated that beginning with the last quarter of the twelfth century (1188), the notion of jurisdiction was restricted to the spiritual realm alone. Henceforth only the examples of spiritual administration will be noted as evidence of the local superior's jurisdictional power. This concept of jurisdiction remained current until after the IV General Council of the Lateran (1215), when it was further distinguished even from the power of Orders.

Article III. Legislation in the Councils of the Lateran

The I General Council of the Lateran (1123) found it necessary to legislate for the monks. In canon 17 they were forbidden to administer Extreme Unction, and to sing public Masses. The chrism and holy oils were to be obtained from the bishops in whose dioceses they resided, and it was his exclusive right to consecrate their altars and promote their subjects to Orders. Likewise, they were forbidden to impose public penances and to visit the sick.[86]

[82] Cf. the meaning of the term *iurisdictio* in the early ages of the Church as described above, pp. 3-4; also M. Van de Kerckhove, "De Notione Jurisdictionis apud Decretistas et Priores Decretalistas,"—*JP*, XVIII (1938), 10-14.

[83] Epist. *"Cum universis,"* 6 apr. 1090—JL, n. 5433; *MPL*, CLI, 322.

[84] Epist. *"Desiderium quod,"* 14 febr. 1169—*MPL*, CC, 569; JL, n. 11596; cf. also Epist., *"Desiderium quod ad,"* 20 apr. 1176—*MPL*, CC, 1067; JL, n. 12695.

[85] *Supra*, chap. I, art. II, p. 3.

[86] Cf. c. 10, CXVI, q. 1; Hefele, V (1), 381; Mansi, XXI, 285; Schroeder, *Disciplinary Decrees*, p. 189.

Schroeder, commenting on the canon, writes: "The reason for the prohibition is to be found in the ever increasing encroachment of the monks on parochial ministrations, and much more so in their frequent and flagrant invasion of the episcopal rights and privileges." [37] Canon 6 of the III General Council of the Lateran (1179) forbade monks or any religious to presume to appeal against the discipline of their superiors.[38]

The IV General Council of the Lateran (1215) considered in detail many of the problems of exemption, and not a few of the problems of the monasteries. Canon 10 imposed upon the bishop the obligation of securing specially trained priests to help in the work of preaching and of the hearing of confessions.[39] This canon was to be the basis for the work of the mendicants in assisting bishops in pastoral work, and much controversy was to be provoked regarding the question as to who was to give jurisdiction to the priests chosen. Canon 12 of the same Council ordained that provincial chapters consisting of abbots and priors were to be held every three years by every religious Order that had not been in the habit of holding them. The presiding officers of these chapters were to be two Cistercian abbots, together with two others chosen from the members of the provincial chapter, all four of whom would have coercive jurisdiction to impose ecclesiastical censures upon those who would presume to molest the monasteries either in the person of their subjects or in their properties.[40] Thus the abbot or prior chosen to preside would have penal jurisdiction, but not primarily as local superior in virtue of his office, but *ex officio* as a presiding officer of the chapter.

Canon 57 dealt with the burial of members of an Order and of those who had left their possessions to an Order during life. Under certain conditions, these were permitted to be buried from the

[37] *Disciplinary Decrees*, p. 190.

[38] Cf. c. 26, X, *de appellationibus*, II, 28; Schroeder, *Disciplinary Decrees*, p. 220.

[39] Cf. c. 15, X, *de officio iudicis ordinarii*, I, 31; Hefele, V (2), 885; Mansi, XXII, 998; Schroeder, *Disciplinary Decrees*, p. 251.

[40] Cf. c. 7, X, *de statu monachorum et canonicorum regularium*, III, 35; Hefele, V (2), 886; Mansi, XXII, 998; Schroeder, *Disciplinary Decrees*, p. 254.

church of the Order. Jurisdiction would seem to have been conferred here upon the superior of the monastery to which the church was attached.[41]

Canon 60 of the Council forbade abbots to interfere in matters pertaining to the bishops. It enumerated the handling of matrimonial cases, the imposition of public penances, and the granting of letters of indulgence as matters which concerned the episcopal office exclusively, unless the abbots by a special concession or by other legitimate reasons could defend their assertion of rights in matters of this kind.[42]

The IV General Council of the Lateran (1215) marks a divisional point in this study. Up to this point the jurisdiction of the abbot of a monastery has been considered almost exclusively, since the abbot was the first local superior among the religious. With the founding of the mendicant Orders the individual monasteries or convents of the mendicants were governed each by its own superior, who was subordinate to the provincial superior or head of the province of which his convent formed a part. The local prior held supreme authority in the government of his own convent. It will be shown that the local superior of the mendicants had jurisdiction and authority to rule his subjects in one way very similar to the monastic abbot, but in another different from it both in character and in extent.

It is with the jurisdiction of the local superior of the mendicants that this study is primarily concerned. All that has been written up to this point concerning the jurisdiction of the abbot has been presented primarily as a foundation for the understanding of the jurisdictional power of the local superior among the mendicants.

Up to this point also the treatment has followed a chronological order, but, as has been pointed out in the Foreword,[43] both the basic historical matter underlying each of the rights and duties of

[41] Cf. c. 24, X, *de privilegiis,* V, 33; Hefele, V (2), 897; Mansi, XXII, 1043; Schroeder, *Disciplinary Decrees,* p. 284.

[42] Cf. c. 12, X, *de excessibus praelatorum et subditorum,* V, 31; Hefele, V (2), 897; Mansi, XXIV, 1047; Schroeder, *Disciplinary Decrees,* p. 285.

[43] *Supra,* p. ix.

the local superior and the canonical commentary will be treated together in the remainder of the work, not according to a chronological order, but on the basis of the division of jurisdictional authority into its legislative, judicial, and executive functions.

CANONICAL COMMENTARY

PART I

RELIGIOUS SUPERIORS AND THEIR POWER OF GOVERNMENT

CHAPTER III

RELIGIOUS SUPERIORS IN THE CODE OF CANON LAW

Throughout the entire Code and especially in the second part of the second book entitled "De Religiosis," the Code makes frequent reference to the religious superior.[1]

Sometimes he is referred to simply as "Superior,"[2] or qualified as "supremus Moderator,"[3] "Superior major,"[4] "Superior provincialis,"[5] Superior localis,"[6] "domus Superior,"[7] "Superior minor localis,"[8] or "Superior regularis."[9]

In a religious Order excluding the monastic Orders, a threefold division of government is usually found, each with a superior at its head. The superior who has charge of the entire Order is usually referred to as the "Superior General," the "Master General," or under some similar title. The second division of government is found in those Orders which are divided into provinces, and the provincial superior is usually referred to as the "Provincial Superior" or the

[1] Cf. Larraona, "Commentarium Codicis,"—*CpR,* IV (1923), 39, note 268; 40, note 269.

[2] Canon 509, § 1.

[3] Canon 502.

[4] Canon 504.

[5] Canon 516, § 1.

[6] Canon 516, § 1.

[7] Canon 472, 2°.

[8] Canon 505.

[9] Canon 506, § 2.

"Prior Provincial." Thirdly, there are the superiors of the individual houses within a province of an Order, and these are usually known as the local superiors, the "Guardians," the "Priors" or the "Superiors of the house." The titles vary slightly in different Orders but generally the rights and duties of the superiors in this threefold division of the government are the same.

The subject of this study is not the supreme moderator of an Order, or the superior of a province within it, but the local superior of a community of men, whatever be his title. However only the *minor* local superior will be considered. Any local superior who is recognized as a major superior, e. g., an abbot of a monastery, or the conventual prior of monasteries which are *sui iuris,* will be excluded, since such superiors are major superiors, and consequently religious ordinaries.[10] It is not the purpose of the writer to treat of religious ordinaries. Excluded also will be those local superiors who are not recognized as such in canon law, e. g., the superior of filial houses in monastic Orders.[11] Furthermore, officials within a religious house, such as the procurator, the *magister spiritus,* or the novice master, are also excluded, even though these officials are sometimes referred to as superiors. However, the assistant superior, or the superior recognized *ex officio* as the substitute or vicar of the minor local superior will be included in the study, if he is recognized as the local superior possessing, during the time that he is in charge of the house, ordinary jurisdiction and not merely delegated power. This would have to be determined from the Constitutions of the Order.

Even though the minor local superior is to form the exclusive subject of this study, he will frequently be referred to simply as "the local superior" in the following pages.

[10] Cf. Schaefer, *De Religiosis ad Normam Codicis Iuris Canonici* (3. ed., Romae: S.A.L.E.R., 1940), n. 103. Hereafter cited as *De Religiosis.*

[11] Cf. S. C. de Religiosis, 1 febr. 1921—*Acta Apostolicae Sedis, Commentarium Officiale* (Romae 1909—), XVI (1924), 95. Hereafter cited *AAS.*

CHAPTER IV

THE AUTHORITY OF THE LOCAL SUPERIOR IN THE CODE OF CANON LAW

Article I. Historical Notes

Canon 501, § 1 is a fundamental canon in which the Code recognizes the dominative power which has always resided in religious superiors. Innocent III (1198-1216) refers to the dominative power of the abbot and claustral prior to direct their subjects to the goal of perfection,[1] and the Council of Trent (1545-1563) reaffirms the power of superiors to demand the observance of all the means to that end.[2]

The affirmation of the dominative power of the superiors, therefore, is not new, but authors believe that the jurisdictional authority of clerical exempt religious superiors is here expressly stated for the first time, even though this doctrine was commonly held to be an effect of exemption even before the present legislation.[3]

With the foundation of the mendicant Orders and their system of provinces, and of houses within a province, each province and house came to have its own superior. Unlike the superiors of dependent monasteries who ruled their houses only in the name of the abbot of the principal monastery, the local superior of the mendicants was supreme in his own convent. Though his subjects were exempt from the jurisdiction of the local bishop, it was inexpedient that they should be governed directly by the Pope, inadvisable and against the purpose of exemption that they should be governed by delegates of the Holy Father, and often inconvenient that they should be directed immediately by their provincial superior. It is

[1] C. 6, X, *de statu monachorum et canonicorum regularium,* III, 35.

[2] Sess. XXV, *de regularibus,* c. 1—Schroeder, *Canons and Decrees of the Council of Trent* (St. Louis: Herder, 1941), pp. 217, 485. Hereafter cited as *Canons and Decrees.*

[3] Cf. Chelodi, *Ius de Personis,* n. 252; Schaefer, *De Religiosis,* n. 105.

not extraordinary therefore that ecclesiastical jurisdiction should have been conferred upon the local superiors directly.

The abundant legislation passed by the Council of Trent does not very often make explicit mention of the local superiors. The Council generally refers to the "superiores" without any qualifying word.[4] However, general terms are to be taken in a general sense, and where the legislator does not distinguish, neither ought another. One can lawfully conclude that when the Council used the general term "superior" it intended to include all religious superiors, minor as well as major, unless the nature of the power granted, or the context clearly pointed out that the minor local superiors were not referred to.

As will be evident from the historical matter presented in the following chapters both the jurisdictional and the dominative power of the local superiors are recognized in the decrees of the Popes[5] and of the Sacred Congregations between the Council of Trent and the Code. Canonical writers of this period commonly held that the local superior was a prelate.[6]

Article II. The Jurisdictional and Dominative Power of Canon 501, § 1

The Code recognizes the dominative authority of all superiors and the jurisdictional power of the superiors of clerical exempt religious institutes, and states that their authority is to be regulated according to the common law and the Constitutions.

The office of local superior does not essentially demand jurisdictional power. Jurisdiction essentially belongs only to the Pope and to the bishops. If any other superiors have this power it is only because they have received it as a participation in the supreme authority of the Church. The Code of Canon Law should therefore be consulted to determine whether the local superior has any juris-

[4] An exception to this rule is found in sess. XXV, *de regularibus*, c. 6, where explicit mention is made of *provinciales, abbates,* and *priores.* Cf. Cc. 20 and 22 of the same session.

[5] Cf. S. Pius V, Const. *"Romani Pontificis,"* 21 iul. 1571—*BRT*, VII, 931.

[6] Cf. *infra,* chap. IV, art. III, p. 30.

dictional power at all, and to learn the extent of his jurisdiction, once it is recognized to exist.

Canon 501, § 1 states that in clerical exempt communities the superiors exercise jurisdiction. The local superior even though a minor superior is not excluded from this canon, for he is a true superior and must therefore be included under the general term "Superiores" used in the canon. One can conclude that the local superior has jurisdiction in all its fulness, unless the Code in individual canons, either in text or context, limits the fundamental jurisdiction granted in this canon or unless it is restricted by the Constitutions.[7]

Actually the jurisdiction of the local superior has been limited in the Code, and is often restricted in the individual Constitutions. Certain acts of jurisdiction are reserved in the Code to the higher superiors. For example, the power of acting as judge in first instance in a process involving religious of his own institute is reserved to the provincial superior,[8] and the power to reserve sins is limited to the supreme moderator.[9] In other canons the Code leaves the determination of the competent superior to the Constitutions, both generally, when it states that the jurisdiction of the religious superior is to be exercised *ad normam constitutionum et iuris communis,* and specifically, e. g., in canons 875, § 1, and 1338, § 1.

In view of the wording and punctuation of canon 501, § 1, one might doubt whether the Constitutions may limit the jurisdictional power of religious superiors. It is evident that the dominative power of religious superiors is to be exercised *ad normam constitutionum et iuris communis,* but one might ask whether or not these words are also to be carried over into the latter half of the canon, along with the words *Superiores et Capitula,* subject of the verb, *habent.* The solution of the problem is of some importance in determining whether or not the local superior is to be included as one of those superiors to whom jurisdiction is given in those canons of the Code

[7] Cf. Schaefer, *De Religiosis,* n. 103; Berutti, *Institutiones Iuris Canonici* (6 vols., vol. III, *De Religiosis,* Taurini-Romae: Marietti, 1936), III, n. 23. Hereafter cited as *Institutiones.*

[8] Canon 1579, § 1.

[9] Canon 876.

which do not define what particular superior can exercise the jurisdiction given, or which do not state explicitly that the competent superior is to be determined by the Constitutions. The question involved may therefore be stated: Does canon 501, § 1 give the Constitutions general power of limitation over only the dominative power of superiors or is it at least implied that the words *ad normam constitutionum et iuris communis* are to be understood as modifying also the jurisdictional power given in the canon?

Berutti affirms that the Constitutions may limit both the dominative and the jurisdictional power of superiors.[10] Schaefer is of the same opinion.[11]

The writer likewise believes that the general grant of jurisdiction given to religious superiors is to be regulated *ad normam constitutionum et iuris communis,* both from the fact that it is possible to consider the phrase as modifying the latter half of canon 501, § 1, without doing violence to the text,[12] and also from the fact that generally the Code leaves specific determinations of the general laws of the Code for religious to the Constitutions of the various institutes. It is true that some of the canons make explicit reference to the power of the Constitutions to determine further a general grant of the power of jurisdiction given to religious superiors,[13] but this does not seem to militate against the granting of such power generally to the Constitutions in canon 501, § 1, at the very beginning of the legislation for religious. The explicit granting of the power of limitation in other canons makes for greater clearness, even though not necessary.

[10] *Institutiones,* III, n. 23.

[11] "Constitutiones iurisdictionem a iure Superioribus concessam, moderari et definire valent, non autem auferre."—*De Religiosis,* n. 105.

[12] The position of the phrase at the beginning of the canon set off by commas, seems to indicate that it also belongs, as do the words *Superiores et Capitula,* to both parts of canon 501, § 1.

[13] Cf. canons 875, § 1; 1338, § 1.

Article III. The Extent of the Power of Jurisdiction

The extent of the religious superior's jurisdiction is expressed in canon 501, § 1, where it is stated that his authority extends to both the external and the internal forum.

A. *Prelates*

Pre-Code authors commonly recognized as prelates the conventual prior, the guardian, and others having authority similar to these, "Quia hi Patres [Generales, Provinciales et Priores Conventuales] habent curam animarum cum potestate et iurisdictione ordinaria in utroque foro. . . ."[14]

Under the law of the Code the local superior of clerical exempt communities also enjoys the status of a prelate, for canon 501, § 1 gives him ordinary jurisdiction in the external forum, and canon 110 declares that in proper legal terminology prelates are those who exercise ordinary jurisdiction in the external forum.[15]

[14] Donatus (+1661), *Rerum Regularium Quadripartita Praxis Resolutoria* (4 vols. Neapoli, 1652-1661), tom. II, pars III, tr. IX, qu. 4, n. 1. Hereafter cited as *Rerum Regularium.* Suarez, *De religione,* tr. VIII, lib. II, cap. II, nn. 1-2; Passerinus (+1677), *Tractatus de Electione Canonica* (ed., post Romam prima in Germania, Coloniae Agrippinae, 1694), cap. VI, n. 8; Ascanius Tamburini (+1666), *De Jure Abbatum et Aliorum Praelatorum* (3 vols. in 2, Coloniae Agrippinae, 1691), tom. II, disp. I, qu. II, n. 2. Hereafter cited as *De Jure Abbatum.* Bouix, *De Jure Regularium,* II, 379; Wernz, *Ius Decretalium,* III, n. 683.

[15] Cf. Larraona, "Responsa Minora,"—*CpR,* II (1921), 114; *idem,* "Commentarium Codicis,"—IV (1923), 76; VI (1925), 427; Schaefer, *De Religiosis,* nn. 102, 105; Vermeersch-Creusen, *Epitome Iuris Canonici cum Commentariis ad Scholas et ad Usum Privatum* (3 vols.; vol. I, 3. ed., Mechlinae-Romae: Dessain, 1927), I, n. 573. Hereafter cited as *Epitome.* Wernz-Vidal, *Ius Canonicum ad Codicis Norman Exactum* (7 vols. in 8, Romae: apud aedes Universitatis Gregorianae, 1923-1938), III, n. 95. Hereafter cited as *Ius Canonicum.* Prümmer, *Manuale I. C.,* qu. 186, 2; De Meester, *Juris Canonici et Juris Canonico-Civilis Compendium* (ed. nova, 3 vols. in 4, Brugis, 1921-1928), II, n. 954. Hereafter cited as *Compendium.* M. Coronata, *Institutiones Iuris Canonici ad Usum Utriusque Cleri et Scholarum* (5 vols., Taurini [Italia]: Marietti, 1928-1936), I, n. 506. Hereafter cited as *Institutiones.* Ferreres, *Institutiones Canonicae* (2. ed., 2 vols., Barcinonae, 1920), I, n. 809. Hereafter cited as *Institutiones.*

Ojetti[16] and Chelodi[17] maintain that in the new law of the Code the regular local superior cannot be called a prelate, though both authors would admit that the major religious superiors are prelates. Writing in 1928 before the Pontifical Commission's response as to whether or not privileges communicated before the Code were still enjoyed by religious institutes,[18] Ojetti admits that the local superior of the Mendicants was a prelate in virtue of a privilege given to the conventual prior of the Order of Preachers by St. Pius V (1566-1572).[19] He asserts that the local superior's right to the title of "prelate" was based principally upon this privilege, and admits that all those superiors who shared in it had quasi-episcopal jurisdiction.[20]

Since it is now certain that all privileges of religious acquired by communication and peacefully enjoyed by religious institutes before the promulgation of the Code of Canon Law were not revoked in view of the wording of canon 613, § 1, *exclusa in posterum qualibet communicatione,*[21] local religious superiors of those religious Orders which communicated in the privileges of the constitution, *"Romani*

[16] *Commentarium in Codicem Iuris Canonici* (4 vols., Romae: apud Aedes Universitatis Gregorianae, 1927-1931), III, 25-27. Hereafter cited as *Commentarium. Idem,* "Praelatus in Codice I. C. quisnam sit?"—*Periodica de Re Canonica et Morali utile praesertim et Missionariis* (Brugis: 1905—), XVIII (1928), 229*-231*. Hereafter cited as *Periodica.*

[17] *Ius de Personis,* n. 252, p. 419, note 1.

[18] *Pontificia Commissio ad Codicis Canones Authentice Interpretandos,* 30 dec. 1937—*AAS,* XXX (1938), 73. Hereafter the replies of this Commission will be referred to by the abbreviation *PCI.*

[19] Const. *"Romani Pontificis,"* 21 iul. 1571—*BRT,* VII, 931.

[20] Pre-Code authors were not in agreement as to whether the local superior exercised quasi-episcopal jurisdiction. Donatus (*Rerum Regularium,* tom. I, pars II, tr. IX, qu. 12, nn. 2-3) and Reiffenstuel (*Jus Canonicum Universum,* 5 vols. in 7, Parisiis, 1864-1882, lib. V, tit. VII, n. 418) admitted that he was a prelate, but denied that he had quasi-episcopal jurisdiction. Suarez (*De religione,* tr. VIII, lib. II, cap. II, n. 10), Passerinus (*Tractatus de Electione Canonica,* cap. XXVI, n. 14), Bouix, (*De Jure Regularium,* II, p. 382), and Bachofen (*Compendium Juris Regularium* [New York, 1903], p. 226 [hereafter cited as *Compendium*]) taught that he had quasi-episcopal jurisdiction. Ojetti (*Commentarium,* III, 27) agrees that the local superior had this power *before* the present law.

[21] *PCI,* 30 dec. 1937—*AAS* (1938), 73.

Pontificis," still exercise quasi-episcopal jurisdiction, since this privilege remains in force even after the Code.[22]

It appears equally clear that the local superior enjoys the title of prelate from the law of the Code, even though such a dignity could not be based on privilege. Canon 110 requires only ordinary power in the external forum. It does not distinguish, nor demand that this power be proper or vicarious, much less quasi-episcopal,[23] and consequently since every local superior of clerical exempt religious institutes has ordinary jurisdiction in the external forum in virtue of canon 501, § 1, he is to be considered a prelate.

Furthermore, if as Ojetti states, the jurisdiction of prelates according to the law of the Code is quasi-episcopal, the local superior must still be classed as a prelate, for his jurisdiction is in part at least quasi-episcopal, even though he is not an ordinary in the sense of canon 198.[24] This seems to be evident from the fact that many functions ordinarily reserved to the bishop of a diocese over his subjects and denied to a pastor, are exercised in a religious Order by the local superior, e. g., the power to delegate jurisdiction to other priests, even those not of his own Order, to hear the confessions of his subjects,[25] and to preach to them.[26] Though the quasi-episcopal nature of the jurisdiction of the major religious superiors is more clearly evident than that of the local superior, yet in view of the jurisdiction given in the Code, e. g., in canons 875, § 1, and 1338, § 1, there seems to be ground for considering the local superior's jurisdiction as quasi-episcopal. However, Maroto, writing of the quasi-episcopal jurisdiction of major superiors, points out that this division of jurisdiction into episcopal and quasi-episcopal was drawn up to distinguish secular prelates, and therefore is better not employed when considering the jurisdiction of religious prelates.[27] It is only given

[22] Cf. canon 4.

[23] Cf. Wernz-Vidal, *Ius Canonicum,* III, n. 95, note 15.

[24] Cf. Larraona, "Commentarium Codicis,"—*CpR,* IV (1923), 107, note (339); Blat, "De Potestate Superiorum in Religionibus secundum Codicem I. C.,"—*CpRM,* XVI (1935), 329-330; Prümmer, *Manuale I. C.,* qu. 186, 2; qu. 212, 2, b); Schaefer, *De Religiosis,* n. 50, 6, E).

[25] Canon 875, § 1.

[26] Canon 1338, § 1.

[27] *Institutiones,* I, 673, note (1).

here in consideration of Ojetti's objecting to local superiors being called prelates, because, as he maintains, they do not exercise quasi-episcopal jurisdiction. Without therefore adopting his terminology for general use, the writer holds that the jurisdiction of the local superior is of a quasi-episcopal nature, a power frequently equivalent to the power of a bishop over his subjects.

Chelodi offers a similar objection to considering local superiors as prelates.[28] He expresses suprise that it should be held that quasi-episcopal jurisdiction should be given to all minor religious superiors. It would be of help to have a definition of quasi-episcopal jurisdiction from the works of those authors who frequently refer to it. Chelodi gives none in his work, *Ius de Personis*. However in pre-Code doctrine the definition given by Suarez (1548-1617) seems to have been accepted commonly. He defines it as that jurisdiction which extends "ad actus qui communi et ordinario jure sunt proprii jurisdictionis Episcoporum." [29] It was called "quasi" episcopal because it gave the superior exercising it authority similar to that exercised by a bishop over his subjects, in some ways inferior to the episcopal power, and in others superior to it.

If Chelodi refers to quasi-episcopal jurisdiction as of a nature superior to ordinary jurisdiction in the external forum, one may answer that such jurisdiction is not demanded in canon 110 as a qualification of those who are to be known as prelates under the law of the Code. If Chelodi means by quasi-episcopal jurisdiction that which extends to acts which by common and ordinary right belong to bishops, as Suarez understood it, one may answer that every minor superior in clerical exempt religious institutes, "even those of a very small house," [30] can exercise quasi-episcopal jurisdiction, since all of these superiors are able to perform acts, ordinarily belonging to bishops.[31]

[28] *Ius de Personis*, p. 419, note 1.

[29] *De religione*, tr. VIII, lib. II, cap. II, n. 13.

[30] Cf. Chelodi, *Ius de Personis*, p. 419, note 1.

[31] E. g., the right to delegate others to hear confessions of his subjects (canon 875, § 1), and the right to give others jurisdiction to preach to the religious (canon 1338, § 1), as well as the power to impose precepts to which canonical penalties may be attached (canon 2220, § 1).

This concession of jurisdiction granted to all superiors in clerical exempt religious institutes should not appear extravagant, for in declaring it to be the right of the religious superiors, the legislator was inserting in the common law of the Code what had been previously recognized by privilege as the prerogative of the conventual priors of the Dominican Order and of others who participated in the privilege of St. Pius V, *"Romani Pontificis,"* which declared that the conventual prior in the Order of Preachers had the same authority over his subjects as bishops had over the clergy and laity "tam quoad absolvendi et dispensandi hujusmodi quam alias quascumque facultates." [32]

Toso maintains that *ex jure communi* local superiors exercise jurisdiction only in the internal forum.[33] This he attempts to sustain by stating that the words "Superiores et Capitula" are not to be understood in the same sense in the second part of canon 501, § 1, as they are in the first, and says that to possess jurisdiction in the external forum the local superior would have to have ordinary power like the power of abbots of monasteries, and thus should have been included among those enumerated in canon 198 as ordinaries. Toso also states that jurisdiction in the external forum cannot be understood without legislative power, and since no local superior has such power, neither can he exercise jurisdiction in the external forum.

The writer believes that all three reasons are based on false assumptions. First of all, Toso freely states, without adducing any proof, that the word "Capitula," the subject together with the word "Superiores" of the verb "habent" in the second part of canon 501, § 1, does not refer to every class of religious chapter. One may ask, what is the reason for such a statement? The canon does not distinguish between general, provincial, or local chapters. When it uses the word "Capitula" without modification, it must be understood to include all chapters of clerical exempt religious institutes. For the same reason all superiors are included in the word "Superiores."

Secondly, as is freely maintained in this work, the jurisdiction of the local superiors is ordinary jurisdiction "ex officio quod gerunt,"

[32] 21 iul. 1571—*BRT,* VII, 931.

[33] *Ad Codicem Juris Canonici Commentaria Minora* (5 vols., vol. II, Romae, 1922), II, 31-32. Hereafter cited as *Commentaria Minora.*

but, as was pointed out before,[34] it does not follow from this that their power is the same or even similar in many respects to the power of an abbot, nor that the local superior should have been included as an ordinary. The legislator has seen fit to regard religious ordinaries as only those who are major superiors in clerical exempt religious institutes, and not all who exercise ordinary jurisdictional power.[35] The local superior is not a major superior because he does not exercise authority *ad instar provincialium,* and he is not an ordinary because he is not a major superior.

Finally in answer to Toso, it may be said that though jurisdiction often includes legislative power, and certainly does so when it is possessed in its perfection, yet the Church in conceding a participation in her jurisdictional power is not obligated to bestow it in its perfection upon all those whom she wishes to exercise jurisdictional authority. Still it does not follow that because a superior does not possess legislative jurisdiction, he has no jurisdiction at all in the external forum. If it were true that one exercising jurisdiction must of necessity exercise or be able to exercise legislative power this would be so either from the nature of jurisdiction itself, or from some positive legislation in the Code. But surely there is nothing in the nature of jurisdiction to prevent the exercise of its functions separately, nor is there any canon in the Code which requires religious superiors to be able to exercise jurisdiction in its perfection before they are permitted to exercise it in the external forum. On the contrary the Code often restricts the jurisdiction of those to whom it has given a participation in this power. The power of the vicar general, to give an example outside of the legislation for religious, is ordinary, and yet, though fundamentally complete, is restricted in the Code and may be restricted by the bishop himself.[36]

Therefore one cannot admit Toso's conclusion that the local superior has no jurisdiction in the external forum. On the contrary it is asserted here that the local superior has jurisdiction in both the external and internal forum, as may be seen from canon 501, § 1, which is not to be limited to major religious superiors, but is to be

[34] *Supra,* chap. III, p. 25.

[35] Cf. canons 198; 488, 8°.

[36] Canon 368, § 1.

taken literally as including all those who are true religious superiors, whether supreme, provincial or local.[37]

B. *Ordinaries*

Canon 198 enumerates those who are referred to under the general term *ordinarius* as used in the Code. Included among them are the major superiors of clerical exempt religious institutes. To determine who are major superiors canon 488, 8° must be consulted. In view of the fact that the local superior exercises ordinary jurisdiction one might ask, whether or not he is to be considered as a religious ordinary. The solution of such a problem depends not on whether or not he has ordinary jurisdiction, as Augustine[38] and Toso[39] seem to imply, but on whether or not he is a major superior.[40]

Included among those listed as major superiors in canon 488, 8°, are the abbot of a monastery which is *sui iuris*, and others who have power *ad instar provincialium*.[41]

The abbot of a monastery *sui iuris* is a local superior, but since he is also a major superior, he is rightly designated as a major local superior, and as an ordinary. As such he is not included in this study, which limits itself to the *minor* local superior.

The minor local superior's right to inclusion under the term *ordinary* will also be determined on whether or not he has power *ad instar provincialium*.[42] However it is not apparent that any local superior has the power necessary to qualify as a major

[37] "Si in Codice vox Superior non habeat notam specificationis vel determinationis, ex. gr. Superior major, generalis, provincialis, localis, comprehendit omnes qui hoc nomine gaudent in iure, nisi ex textu, vel ex contextu patet vocem sese referre ad Superiorem majorem."—Schaefer, *De Religiosis*, n. 103.

[38] *A Commentary on the New Code of Canon Law* (8 vols., Vol. III, 3. ed., St. Louis: Herder, 1922), III, 105. Hereafter cited as *Commentary*.

[39] *Commentaria Minora*, II, 31-32.

[40] Cf. canon 198, § 1, and canon 488, 8°. Pejška, *Ius Canonicum Religiosorum* (3. ed., Friburgi Brisgoviae: Herder, 1927), p. 231.

[41] The conventual priors of monasteries which are *sui iuris* may also be considered major superiors, and consequently ordinaries. (Cf. Vermeersch-Creusen, *Epitome*, I, n. 546.)

[42] Cf. canon 488, 8°, and canon 198, § 1.

superior. The legislator in speaking of power *ad instar provincialium* undoubtedly refers not to any power which though similar essentially to that of a provincial, e. g., ordinary jurisdiction, is nevertheless exercised only in favor of the members of a particular community, and not of several houses within the same province.[43] The legislator has in mind superiors who exercise authority which is provincial in character, such as vicars of a province, or provincial visitators. The latter, though not provincials, do nevertheless exercise power which is *ad instar provincialium,* and are therefore major superiors, and religious ordinaries. No such power is exercised by the local superiors of houses which are not *sui iuris.*

Under pre-Code law, and under Constitutional provisions based upon the old law, the jurisdiction of the local superior was much more extensive than it is under the present law, and in many cases was certainly as extensive as the jurisdiction of the provincial superior is now under the present law. In the law of the Code, much of the power of government over religious subjects is reserved to the provincial superior *ex officio.* He may freely delegate his ordinary jurisdiction to the local superior, but as such the latter cannot be said to have power *ad instar provincialium* but only delegated power. This delegated provincial power is not sufficient to give the conventual prior or guardian in religious Orders the status of a major superior, and consequently he cannot be called an ordinary.[44]

Augustine holds that the local superior is a major superior, and consequently an ordinary, basing his opinion on the fact that the superiors of clerical exempt religious Orders have ordinary power. "The power of the superiors of clerical exempt religious Orders is called *ordinary* because given in virtue of their office. For the same reason the Code states that these superiors are to be considered under the name Ordinary."[45]

[43] Cf. Berutti, *Institutiones,* III, n. 7, (g).

[44] Cf. Coronata, *Institutiones,* I, n. 280.

[45] *Commentary,* III, 105; in another place (*Commentary,* IV [2. ed., St. Louis: Herder, 1921] 259, note 29) he considers the conventual prior of the Augustinians as a major superior. Such a conclusion cannot be retained for the Constitutions of the Order state: "Praeter superiores locales seu minores, adsunt in Ordine Superiores maiores . . ." (n. 42).

As has been shown, therefore, the religious superior will not be called an ordinary on the ground that he has ordinary power, but only on the ground that he is a major superior. But he is not a major superior, because he is not mentioned among those enumerated in canon 488, 8°, and consequently he is not an ordinary.

C. *Subjects of the Local Superior*

Canon 501 states that the local superior's jurisdiction is to be exercised ***in subditos.*** The subjects are the professed members of his community. Novices during their novitiate are subject to the dominative power of the local superior in all that pertains to the general government of the house, but their special training is under the direction of the novice master.[46] For the most part the novices are also subject to the jurisdictional authority of the local superior, even though they do not lose their proper diocese until perpetual profession,[47] and have the right of choosing their place of burial beforehand, should death occur during the period of novitiate.[48] Postulants in virtue of an agreement, implicit or explicit, which is made when they come to the community are also subject to the dominative power of the local superior, and to his jurisdictional power as provided for in the law.

The jurisdiction of the local superior may be exercised also over the religious of his own Order who are not assigned permanently to his community, but who are actually present as visitors, if the Constitutions so prescribe. Such visitors become subject to the jurisdiction of the superior of the house in which they are, but at the same time remain subject to the jurisdiction of their own local superior.

The Code often makes mention of the subjection of nuns, "moniales," to regular superiors,[49] but it seems to leave the determination of the particular superior, whether local, provincial or general to the Constitutions of each Order. Though in practice the

[46] Canon 561.

[47] Canon 585.

[48] Canon 1221, § 1.

[49] Canons 506, § 2; 512, § 2, 1°; 525; 527; 533, § 1, 1°; 534, § 1; 535, § 1, 1°, 2°; 549; 552; 603, § 2; 652, § 2.

subjection is to the provincial or general superiors, or to their delegates, *per se* there is nothing to prevent the nuns from being under the jurisdiction of the local superior. However, the very name of *local* superior seems to imply that his authority is to be exercised only over those who are members of his own community, or who are living either permanently or temporarily within the confines of the monastery or convent.[50]

The jurisdiction of the local superior over those who live in the house as servants, students or guests, or who are cared for there during infirmity is also recognized.[51]

Since the jurisdiction of the local superior over all of his subjects is annexed by law to his office in canon 501, § 1, it is *ordinary*, and since it is exercised in his own name as superior of the community it is *proper* and not *vicarious*. Finally, it is *personal*, in that it extends to his subjects wherever they are, either in the house or outside of it.

[50] A careful search of Papal documents and of pre-Code authors, especially in the matter dealing with the confessors of nuns, has failed to reveal any definite information as to what regular superior, local, provincial or general, usually governed the nuns who were subject to an Order. Both the documents and the authors consistently refer to the "regular prelates" or to the "regular superiors" without determining what particular one. As far as the writer has been able to ascertain, at the present time, in the United States at least, there are no nuns subject to regular local superiors. It was not thought advisable to comment on the canons listed in the previous footnote (49), in view of the fact that to do so would seem to be without practical purpose.

[51] Canons 514, § 1; 850, § 1; 938, § 2; 1338, § 1.

Part II

Religious Superiors and Their Legislative and Judicial Power

Having considered the jurisdiction of the local superior in a general way, the writer will now treat of legislative and judicial power. This will be done in Chapter V and in Chapter VI, where it will be shown what rights and duties the local superior has in relation to the exercise of these functions of jurisdiction.

CHAPTER V

LEGISLATIVE POWER

The Sovereign Pontiff has supreme and full power of jurisdiction over the universal Church.[1] Other superiors have jurisdiction only in a partial way. One of the principal functions of jurisdictional power is legislative authority, which in its perfection implies the power to enact law. A law is defined by St. Thomas Aquinas as "an ordinance of reason for the common good, made by him who has care of the community, and promulgated." [2] If, therefore, the local superior has jurisdiction, has he also legislative power?

Article I. Historical Notes

The local superior of the Mendicants was never considered a lawgiver in the strict sense of the term. Canon 12 of the IV General Council of Lateran (1215) refers to the legislative power of the general chapters,[3] but no indication of the local superior's ability to

[1] Canon 218.

[2] *Summa Theologica*, Ia IIae, qu. XC, art. 4.

[3] C. 7, X, *de statu monachorum et canonicorum regularium*, III, 35. Cf. Schroeder, *Disciplinary Decrees*, pp. 253, 567.

legislate for his entire community seems to be given in the Decretals. Neither could he bind his entire community at once by giving what is known as a common precept,[4] for these precepts take on the nature of a law, and have the force of law. Donatus sums up the common teaching as follows: "Reliqui autem inferiores Praelati nequeunt leges ferre, sed tantum praecepta, et mandata, quae exspirant morte mandantis . . . et hoc ideo, quia hujusmodi Praelati non habent publicam auctoritatem, nec jurisdictionem universalem in ordine ad totam Religionem, quam professi sunt, prout requiritur, ad ferendam leges, pro communi bono, tum etiam, quia haec potestas condendi proprie leges, est de reservatis principi in signum supremi potestatis."[5] Authors taught the same doctrine even up until the promulgation of the Code, either by directly denying any legislative power to the local superior, or by attributing it only to the general chapter of an Order.

Article II. The Existence of Legislative Power

Since the local superior has been given jurisdiction in virtue of canon 501, § 1, it may be asked whether he can legislate for his subjects, since the power of legislation is one of the principal functions of jurisdictional power, though separable from it, and not necessarily connected with it.

It is not stated explicitly anywhere in the Code that the local superior can enact ecclesiastical law in the strict sense of the term taken as an "ordinatio rationis ad bonum commune Ecclesiae, ab eo qui communitatis ecclesiasticae curam habet, promulgata."[6] On the other hand, his power of dispensation is not as extensive as is the power of religious ordinaries,[7] and consequently it may be said to have been restricted from that aspect at least. Moreover it is generally held that local superiors cannot enact laws in a proper sense.[8] If this is true, and it seems that it is, the reason must be because the

[4] Cf. Suarez, *De religione*, tr. VIII, lib. II, cap. VIII, n. 4.

[5] *Rerum Regularium*, tom. II, pars III, tr. X, qu. 8, n. 14.

[6] Cf. Maroto, *Institutiones*, I, n. 179.

[7] Cf. canons 15, 81.

[8] "Leges in proprio sensu regulariter sola Capitula generalia ferre possunt." —Schaefer, *De Religiosis*, n. 107 (e).

Constitutions of the individual Orders prohibit the local superiors from enacting laws for their subjects, or restrict his power in such a way that his ordinations cannot be said to have the force of law.

In the opinion of the writer, there is nothing in the Code which would prevent the local superior from exercising proper legislative power, or nothing in the very nature of a law, or in the nature of the community over which the local superior presides, or finally in the nature of the jurisdictional power which he exercises, which would prevent him from enacting a true ecclesiastical law. As proof of this thesis the following argumentation is presented.

Of the four elements given by St. Thomas in his definition of law [9] two of them might seem to exclude the possibility of a local superior's being able to pass a law, for a law must be *ad bonum commune,* and *ab eo qui curam communitatis habet.*

If the "common good" is taken to refer to the good of the universal Church as a perfect society, it is evident that neither the local superior nor any other religious superior has power of legislation, for their jurisdiction is confined to members of an imperfect society within the Church itself. In that sense, therefore, the local superior neither has nor can have legislative power. But if the good common to the members of the religious house, taken as an officially recognized part of the Church, is considered, one can see that the ordinations or commands of a local superior can be directed toward such a good. It is in this sense that legislative power is spoken of as applying to religious superiors, that is, as permitting superiors to enact laws for the common good of the community, taken as part of the Church, and not merely as an imperfect society. If the laws are directed to the good of the community, primarily as members of the Church, the superiors will be exercising legislative power proceeding from true ecclesiastical jurisdiction. If such power can be attributed to the supreme superior, there seems to be no reason for saying that the local superior cannot enact law for the common good of his own local community considered primarily as consisting of members of the Church. It might be objected that the ordinations of the supreme superiors are of a more permanent nature than those of a local superior, to which it may be answered, that

[9] *Summa Theologica,* I^a^ II^ae^, qu. XC, art. 4.

there is nothing in the nature of the power of the supreme superior, which would demand that his ordinations should endure beyond his term of office. If they do, it can only be because his power has not been restricted to the duration of his office, as is the local superior's power in most cases. But it may be admitted that if the Constitutions state that the ordinations of the local superior lose their force at the expiration of his office, then he cannot be said to have the power to enact law in the proper sense since every law must be perpetual, at least to the extent that it does not expire when the person who makes it ceases to exercise his office.

Secondly, there is nothing in the nature of the community over which the local superior presides, which would render him incapable of passing a law for them, if they are considered as parts of the perfect society, and not only as an imperfect society. It seems to the writer that no argument against the local superior's possessing legislative power can be drawn solely from the statement that a law is ordained to the common good and the local community does not represent the common good. For if the local community does not in some way represent the common good, how can it be the passive subject of any jurisdictional power, since of its nature all jurisdiction is a public power, and therefore ordained to the *bonum commune?* But because of canon 501, § 1, it is generally admitted, and certainly taken for granted in this study, that a local religious community is the passive subject of its superior's jurisdictional power. Consequently, no argument against its being the passive subject of the same superior's legislative power can be drawn, since legislative power is only a part of jurisdiction. Certainly, if a local community of exempt religious is of such a nature as to be able to be governed by a superior of its own who has jurisdictional authority, because of that same nature it can be the passive subject of that superior's legislative power, if it is evident that he has received such power from the Supreme Ruler of the Church.

Thirdly, there is nothing in the nature of the jurisdictional power which the local superior has received, which would prevent its extension to include legislative power *intra fines sui muneris.* Canon 501, § 1 in giving jurisdiction to clerical exempt superiors gives them also the foundation for true legislative power *ad normam constitutionum et iuris communis.* Since there is nothing in the common law against the use of legislative power by all religious superiors, it remains to consult the Constitutions of each Order. Unless these therefore take away or limit the legislative power of the local superior, it must be said, that he has such power.

To sum up the argumentation so far presented, the writer states that it is not his purpose to prove that in reality local superiors have legislative power. It is his purpose to attempt to show that they *can* have it, inasmuch as they have the fundation for such power in the general grant of jurisdiction given them in canon 501.

Article III. Jurisdictional Precepts

In the previous article the writer has accepted the common teaching that as a matter of actual practice the local superior does not have the power to enact true ecclesiastical law, but he has not accepted the opinion of those who would seem to deny all possibility of such a superior's being granted this power on the ground that his community is not capable of receiving a law. It may now be asked whether or not a local superior can impose jurisdictional precepts, a power closely allied with the power to enact law.

Cicognani writes that a precept differs from a law, in that a law "est pro multitudine et datur stabiliter, praeceptum est pro singulis vel pro multitudine in casu particulari et datur ad tempus, ad mensem, etc., ac quidem ad vitam praecipientis." [10] A precept may be defined as a command given to individuals either binding them for a time or perpetually, or given to a community but in a particular case and binding only temporarily. A precept like a law must always be given by a legitimate superior. Some authors maintain that the precepts referred to in the Code are properly speaking, only those which bind in the external forum, and which proceed from the power of jurisdiction.[11] Others, more correctly, it seems, declare that the precepts referred to in canon 24 can be either juris-

[10] *Commentarium ad Librum I Codicis* (Romae: Ex Schola Typographica "Pio X," 1925), p. 148. Hereafter cited as *Commentarium.*

[11] Cf. Berutti, *Institutiones,* I, n. 70, III; Coronata, *Institutiones,* I, n. 32, 1°.

dictional or dominative in nature.[11a] These precepts may be of two kinds: those given to individuals and those given to an entire community. The latter are sometimes referred to as common precepts or as general precepts. The power of the local superior, with reference to both the particular and to the common precept will be treated separately.

A. "*Praecepta singulis data*"

Canon 24 treats of precepts given to individuals, and of the manner in which they may be imposed. Such precepts bind those affected by them wherever they may be, and are therefore presumed to be personal rather than territorial. However, these precepts cannot be invoked judicially, nor will they remain in effect once the authority of the person giving them ceases, unless they are given in a legitimate document or imposed in the presence of two witnesses.[12]

The local superior can certainly impose the precepts mentioned in canon 24, for he has jurisdictional power over his subjects in the external forum. Pre-Code authors maintained the competence of even local superiors to impose jurisdictional precepts on individuals,[13] and under the present law the same power has its foundation in canon 501, § 1. If the local superior simply gives a precept to any of his subjects but fails to make use of the legal form, his precept will cease once his authority has ceased. If he wishes to issue a precept which will continue to bind even after his authority over a particular subject has ceased, he should either give the precept in writing and have it attested by a notary, or give it in the presence of two witnesses, qualified according to the prescriptions of canon 1757, who will be thus able to testify both as to the existence

[11a] Cf. Schaefer, *De Religiosis*, n. 107 (e); Michiels, *Normae Generales Juris Canonici* (2 vols., Lublin-Polonia; Universitas Catholica, 1929), I, 510. Hereafter cited as *Normae Generales.*

[12] Even though this legal form is not observed, the precept can be invoked extrajudicially in the external forum. Cf. Cicognani, *Commentarium*, pp. 150-151.

[13] Bachofen, *Compendium*, p. 228; Bouix, *De Jure Regularium*, pp. 380, 399.

of the precept, and as to its having been given according to the legal form prescribed in canon 24.

B. *Common Precepts*

Van Hove distinguishes three types of common precept, the first two of which presuppose legislative power in the strict sense in the superior giving them, and the third, a precept which may be given by a superior who has jurisdiction, but who does not have legislative power, or whose community is not capable of receiving a law.[14] An example of the first type of precept is seen in the command of a superior given to a community capable of receiving a law but which in accordance with the wish of the legislator or with the nature of command given is only of a temporary duration. The second type is exemplified in the command given for an individual case by the legislator also to a community capable of receiving a law. The third type may be materially the same as the command in the first two, but it is given either by a legislator to a community incapable of receiving a law, or by a superior who has no strict legislative power, but who can impose jurisdictional commands.

Applying these definitions of the common precept to the local superior's power to command his subjects, one can see that he will be able to give a common precept of either the first or second type, only if he has the power of enacting true laws. Therefore, in most cases he will not be able to impose such a precept. Since the third type of precept does not require legislative power in its strict sense, the local superior can impose it upon his community unless his own Constitutions forbid him to do so.[15] This he can do in virtue of the jurisdictional power which he possesses.

In summary, it may be stated that the local superior can issue

[14] *Commentarium Lovaniense in Codicem Iuris Canonici,* Vol. I, Tom. II, *De Legibus Ecclesiasticis* (Mechliniae-Romae: Dessain, 1930), n. 95.

[15] In the Order of Preachers the conventual prior cannot impose a precept upon the whole community at once without the previous consent of the provincial. Cf. *Constitutiones Fratrum S. Ordinis Praedicatorum* (Romae: Apud Domum Generalitiam, 1932), n. 52, § 1, 2°. Hereafter cited as *Const. S.O.P.,* (1932).

jurisdictional precepts to his subjects, individually and collectively, unless he is prohibited from doing so by his Constitutions. His precepts will continue to bind even after the expiration of his jurisdictional authority if they are given in legal form. Otherwise they cannot be adduced as proof in judicial procedure, and will cease with the authority of the one who imposes them.

Article IV. The Power of Dispensation

One of the functions of legislative power is the right to dispense from ecclesiastical law already enacted. The local superior has been given this power to a limited degree.

A. *Historical Notes*

Pre-Code authors recognized the power of religious superiors to dispense from ecclesiastical law because of the quasi-episcopal jurisdiction which they were held to possess. Even the local superior shared in this power of dispensation, especially in virtue of the constitution *"Romani Pontificis,"* of St. Pius V (1566-1572)[16] Their power was confined to individual cases, and extended principally to laws concerning fast, abstinence, the observance of feasts, and other matters of frequent occurrence.[17]

B. *The Present Law*

The privileges in regard to the power of dispensation in use and not revoked at the time of the promulgation of the Code may still be used by the local superior.[18] The local superior is not given any general power of dispensation in ecclesiastical law such as is conceded to the provincial superior in canons 15, 81, and 2237. He can only dispense therefore from those laws for which he has

[16] 21 iul. 1571—*BRT*, VII, 931. Cf. Piatus Montensis, *Praelectionis Iuris Regularis* (3. ed., 2 vols., Tornaci, 1906), I, qu. 752. Hereafter cited as Piatus, *Praelectiones*. Van Etten, *Compendium Privilegiorum Regularium Praecipue Ordinis Eremitarum S. Augustini* (Romae, 1900), p. 128; Bachofen, *Compendium*, p. 229.

[17] Bachofen, *loc. cit.*

[18] Canon 4.

the faculty. Three such cases are mentioned in the Code, in canons 1245, § 3, 1313, 2° and 1314, and 1320.

The power of dispensation from the law of fast and abstinence or from both, and from the observance of feasts is given to all superiors in clerical exempt institutes to be exercised in individual cases and when a just cause exists for granting the dispensation. The canon uses the word "Superiores" without qualification, and therefore includes local superiors.[19]

In dispensing his subjects, the local superior cannot give a dispensation to the whole community at once[20], but neither is it necessary that he dispense all individually, for his power in this matter is *ad modum parochi* and just as the pastor can dispense individual families so can the local superior collectively dispense individual groups in his community, e. g., all of the novices, all of the students, or all of the priests, if a common cause exists for all.[21]

The cause required for the dispensation need not be a grave one, but only one which in the judgment of the local superior is sufficiently just to merit a dispensation. In doubt concerning the sufficiency of the cause, the dispensation may be granted both licitly and validly.[22]

Since it is necessary at times to dispense subjects from vows, other than the religious vows, the legislator has made provision for such cases. St. Thomas writes that a person who takes a vow makes a law for himself, and binds himself to do something "quod est, secundum se, et in pluribus, bonum." But occasionally it is

[19] Fanfani, *De Iure Religiosorum,* n. 53; Vermeersch-Creusen, *Epitome,* II, n. 556; Schaefer, *De Religiosis,* n. 111; Blat, *Commentarium Textus Codicis Iuris Canonici* (6 vols., lib. III, *De Rebus,* pars II-VI, Romae: Ex Typographia Pontificia in Instituto Pii IX, 1923), III, n. 106. Hereafter cited as *Commentarium.* Coronata, *Institutiones,* I, n. 112.

[20] Augustine (*Commentary,* VI [2. ed., St. Louis: Herder, 1923], 167-168) holds that a religious superior can dispense his whole community in virtue of canon 1245, § 2, but he bases his opinion on the fact that religious superiors are ordinaries. It has already been shown (*supra,* chap. IV, art. III) that the local religious superior is not an ordinary, and consequently cannot enjoy the provision listed in canon 1245, § 2).

[21] Cf. Vermeersch-Creusen, *Epitome,* II, n. 556.

[22] Canon 84, § 2.

necessary to decide that a particular vow is not to be observed, either by dispensing from it entirely or by commuting the obligation to some other good.[23] Canon 1313, 2° gives all clerical exempt superiors the right to dispense their professed subjects, novices and others who reside in the religious house as servants, students, guests, or patients from any vow which is not reserved, provided a just cause exists and the rights of a third party who is unwilling to relinquish them are not involved. It is evident that no religious superior can dispense from public vows taken in a religious institute, for these are reserved and involve also the rights of the whole religious institute.[24] The private vows reserved to the Holy See are listed in canon 1309 as the vows of perfect and perpetual chastity, and the vow of entering a religious Order, provided that these vows have been taken unconditionally and after the completion of the eighteenth year.

In virtue of canon 1314 the local superior may commute a non-reserved vow to an obligation which may be less good than the one originally assumed, if again, a just cause is present, even though not as cogent a cause as that required for a dispensation.

Though a dispensation from an oath is not a dispensation from an ecclesiastical law, it will be treated here as pertaining to the local superior's power of dispensation. Canon 1320 compared with canon 1313, 2° gives the superiors of clerical exempt institutes the power to dispense subjects from the obligations of a promissory oath, or to annul or commute it. An oath is promissory when God is invoked to confirm a promise made by one capable of doing so. The canon includes local superiors also, since, as in the previous canons concerning dispensations, no distinction of superiors is made.

These four canons [25] are the only canons in the Code which give the local superior any power of dispensation. His exercise of this power both in the internal and the external forum is certainly an act of jurisdiction and not of dominative power, which allows a superior only to declare a subject excused from ecclesiastical law and not to dispense therefrom.

[23] *Summa Theologica*, IIa IIae, qu. LXXXVIII, art. 10.

[24] Augustine, *Commentary*, VI, 305.

[25] Canons 1245, § 3; 1313, 2°; 1314; 1320.

C. *Jurisdiction Involved*

A further question may be asked in regard to the jurisdictional power granted by these canons. Is such jurisdiction ordinary, or delegated by the law itself? It appears to the writer that it is annexed to his office *ipso iure* and is therefore ordinary, and not delegated.[26] Ojetti prefers to consider the jurisdiction given in canon 1245 and in similar canons as delegated by the law.[27] He maintains that the jurisdiction given in these canons does not pertain essentially to the office of the superior, and consequently the power given is delegated and not ordinary. In answer one might point out that the Code does not require that the jurisdiction which is annexed in the law to an office be essentially annexed to that office. As long as it is annexed *ipso iure* to an office, whether it be annexed essentially or accidentally, it must be considered ordinary and not delegated.[28] Consequently, the writer believes that the jurisdiction granted the local superior in canons 1245, § 3, 1313, 2°, 1314 and 1320 is not to be considered delegated by the law, but *ipso iure annexa officio superioris localis.*

[26] Cf. canon 197, § 1.

[27] E. g., canons 81, 990, 1043-1045, 2237. Cf. Ojetti, *Commentarium,* II***, 164-170.

[28] Cf. Maroto, *Institutiones,* II, n. 699; Vermeersch-Creusen, *Epitome,* I, n. 272, 2; Coronata, *Institutiones,* I, n. 278; Blat, "De Ordinarii Potestate Delegandi Iuxta Canones 1043 et 1044,"—*Angelicum,* XV (1938), 43; Kearney, *The Principles of Delegation,* p. 68.

CHAPTER VI

JUDICIAL POWER

ARTICLE I. HISTORICAL NOTES

THE quasi-episcopal status of regular superiors in pre-Code legislation was the basis for their exercise of judicial power. Lega notes this as follows: "Ast Romani Pontifices Ordines religiosos donare coeperunt exemptione(m) a potestate Ordinariorum et tunc factum est ut potestas coactiva judicialis transferretur in Praelatos regulares ne homines regulares fierent exleges et poenalium sanctionum expertes. Inde necessario fluit . . . haec conclusio: 'Praelati Ordinum exemptorum potestatem correctivam et judicialem Episcopalem habent'." [1] Local superiors could also exercise this power unless prohibited from doing so by their own Constitutions, since they also shared in this quasi-episcopal power.[2]

The local priors in the Dominican Order were given the privilege of proceeding according to a summary process, as can be learned from a constitution of Boniface VIII (1294-1303) in virtue of which those who exercised judicial power in the Order were able to proceed "rimulis et apicibus postpositis." [3] The traditional interpretation of this constitution is expressed as follows: "In nostro Ordine judices ordinarii, ad quos spectat in delinquentes Fratres compilare processus, sunt Magister Ordinis, Capitulum Generale, et Provinciale, Prior Provincialis, et Conventualis, Vicarii Locorum,

[1] *Praelectiones in Textum Iuris Canonici, De Judiciis Ecclesiasticis* (4 vols., Romae, 1896-1901), IV, n. 500.

[2] "Hanc competentiem obtinent nedum Generales Praelati et Provinciales sed etiam Praelati locales seu conventuales seu Guardiani aut quocumque alio nomine censeantur praepositi aut rectores monasterii, nisi aliud constituant peculiares regulae aut consuetudines."—Lega, *op. cit.*, n. 501.

[3] *"Ad augumentum,"* 10 maii 1296—*Bullarium Ordinis FF. Praedictatorum* (ed. a T. Ripoll, recognitum a A. Bremond, 8 vols., Romae, 1729-1740), II, 47. Hereafter cited as *BOP*. *BRT,* I, 134.

et qui ex officio ordinariam habent jurisdictionem in subitos."[4] Passerinus (+1677) cites a decree of the Sacred Congregation of the Council, without giving its date, in which it was stated that the General of an Order was not to expel anyone except after the securing the consent of six Fathers previously chosen for that purpose, and that the local prior could draw up the process before the case was brought before the General and his council.[5]

One may conclude therefore with other pre-Code authors,[6] that local superiors also exercised judicial power under the former legislation.

Article II. Present Legislation

A. *The Judge of First Instance in the Religious Tribunal*

Under the law of the Code the local superior does not generally act as judge in either contentious or criminal trials involving his own subjects. Canon 1579, § 1 states that in trials involving religious of the same clerical exempt community the judge in first instance is the provincial superior, unless the Constitutions determine otherwise. In the absence of any constitutional prescription, therefore, the local superior has no power to act as judge in first instance, although he may be delegated to act as judge by the provincial. Even then he will not act with ordinary power, as does the *officialis* in diocesan tribunals, but rather with that delegated power similar to the jurisdiction of the synodal or pro-synodal judge.

Canon 1579, § 1 does leave room for the local superior to act as judge in first instance, for he can be designated as such by the Constitutions of the Order.[7] If he is designated, he will act with what-

[4] Fontano-Lo-Cicero, *Constitutiones, Declarationes, et Ordinationes Capitulorum Generalium Sacri Ordinis Fratrum Praedicatorum* (Romae, 1862), s. v. "De Processibus," n. *1, p. 387.

[5] *De Hominum Statibus et Officiis* (ed. nova, 3 vols., Lucae, 1732), qu. CLXXXIX, art. VIII, n. 590. Hereafter cited as *De Statibus*.

[6] Bouix, *De Jure Regularium*, II, 439; Piatus, *Praelectiones*, II, qu. 454.

[7] In the 1940 edition of his work, *De Religiosis*, Schaefer still maintains that "apud Praedicatores Priores locales potestatem judicialem exercere possunt." According to the 1932 edition of the Constitutions of the Order of Preachers (n. 942), this statement is no longer true, since the revised Constitutions reserve this right to the provincial.

ever power is given him in the Constitutions, either ordinary or delegated, and in the absence of any express declaration as to the nature of his power it would seem to be ordinary, similar to the ordinary power given to the provincial superior in the Code. In designating the local superior as judge in the first instance, the Constitutions should also designate to what tribunal an appeal from his judgment may be made, since canon 1594, § 4 does not consider the case of a local superior acting as judge in the first instance, and consequently does not establish the court of appeal.

When the local superior acts as judge in an ecclesiastical trial, he is obliged to follow all the prescriptions laid down in the canons for those who exercise such an office, both the general prescriptions given in the fourth book, and the specific directions governing ecclesiastical judges given in canons 1608-1626, as well as the directions given in the fifth book for the infliction of judicial penalties. He is not to interfere in any way in cases which fall under the exclusive competence of the Holy Office.[8] As often as he undertakes a case he must take the oath "de officio rite et fideliter implendo" in the presence of the notary of the tribunal.[9] Noval bases this obligation on the fact that even though the religious superior acts as judge *ex officio,* nevertheless because he does not belong to the public or general hierarchy, he is not a public magistrate in the Church, and consequently must take the oath before assuming his duties in each case. Coronata quotes Torrubiano as saying that it is sufficient that the oath be taken the first time the judge constitutes the tribunal, and not at the beginning of every new case.[10] It would seem that there is sufficient doubt concerning the interpretation of the wording of the canon to permit one to follow this latter opinion.

The local superior is obliged to make use of a notary in each trial. Since he is not given the power to constitute notaries, he must be

[8] Canon 501, § 2.

[9] Canon 1621, § 2. Noval, *Commentarium Codicis Juris Canonici,* lib. IV, *De Processibus,* pars I, *De Iudiciis* (Augustae Taurinorum—Romae: Marietti, 1920), n. 208. Hereafter cited as *De Processibus.* Vermeersch-Creusen, *Epitome,* III, n. 63.

[10] *Institutiones,* III, *De Processibus* (Taurini [Italia]: Marietti, 1933), n. 1149, note 7.

delegated to do so by the provincial or other major superior, or choose a notary from those designated for that work by the major superior.[11]

As to the place for holding the trial, nothing definite is given in the Code, as is given for the diocesan tribunal.[12] The natural place would seem to be the convent over which the local superior presides, and in which the defendant resides, but since the local superior's jurisdiction is personal and not territorial, any other suitable place could be chosen.

If the local superior has passed the definitive sentence, or has delegated another to act as judge, the same superior also puts the sentence into effect once it has reached the status of a *res judicata* according to the prescriptions of canons 1917-1924. If necessary, he may enforce the sentence with canonical penalties.[13]

B. *Other Rights and Duties Involved in Ecclesiastical Trials*

The local superior has authority to give his subjects permission to act as plaintiff in an ecclesiastical trial,[14] or as procurator and advocate,[15] or as an arbiter.[16] He cannot act in the name of his own community at an ecclesiastical trial without following whatever prescriptions are laid down in the Constitutions.[17] These might possibly demand the consent of his council or even the permission of the provincial superior. If he does not fulfill the prescriptions of the Constitutions, he nevertheless acts validly, if his action can be construed as an act of ordinary administration,[18] but he will not do so licitly.[19]

The local superior is incapable of acting as witness in a case involving his own community in which he is also either the plaintiff or

[11] Cf. canon 503. Blat, "De Potestate Superiorum in Religionibus secundum Codicem I.C.,"—*CpRM,* XVI (1935), 337.

[12] Canon 1636.

[13] Canon 1924.

[14] Canon 1652.

[15] Canons 1657, § 3; 1658, § 4.

[16] Canon 1931.

[17] Canon 1653, § 6.

[18] Canon 532, § 2.

[19] Cf. Noval, *De Processibus,* n. 261.

the defendant,[20] but he can act as witness for the community if one of his subjects is either the plaintiff or defendant in the trial.[21]

C. *The Process of Beatification and Canonization*

In the process prescribed for beatification and canonization the local superior seems to have the right of granting to his subjects permission to be constituted by the proper official as notaries, when the employment of religious in this capacity becomes necessary,[22] but it must be noted that a religious can never act as notary in a case involving a religious of his own institute.[23] Particular legislation might also reserve the granting of such a permission to the major superiors. The local superior is also bound by the obligation common to all superiors to see to it that those of his subjects who ought to testify in these processes do so. He is not permitted either directly or indirectly to induce his subjects to testify favorably or unfavorably.[24]

If the cause for the beatification of any member of his own institute has been instituted, the local superior is bound to see to the publication in his own house of the edict requesting that all the writings of the servant of God in the possession of anyone be sent to the tribunal. At the same time he is obliged to remind his subjects expressly of the necessity of sending, either personally or through a confessor, all the letters which any religious might have received from the person proposed for beatification which in any way might aid in the investigation of his life.[25]

[20] Canon 1757, § 3, 1°.

[21] Cf. Noval, *De Processibus,* n. 467.

[22] Cf. canon 2014.

[23] S.R.C. decr. 16 iul. 1894—*Codicis Iuris Canonici Fontes cura Emi. Petri Card. Gasparri editi* (9 vols. Romae [later Civitate Vaticana]: Typis Polyglottis Vaticanis, 1923-1939. Vols. VII-IX ed. cura et studio Emi. Iustiniani Card. Serédi), n. 6328. Hereafter cited as *Fontes.* Cf. *Codex pro Postulatoribus,* (4. ed., Romae: Apud Libreria del Collegio S. Antonio, 1929), p. 42.

[24] Cf. canon 2026.

[25] Cf. canons 2025, § 2; 2043, § 2.

Part III

Religious Superiors and Their Executive Power

Jurisdictional authority is sometimes divided into its legislative, judicial and coercive functions. A preferable division for the purpose of this study is to employ that division which distinguishes the legislative, judicial, and executive functions of jurisdiction, with a subdivision of executive power into administrative and coercive or penal. By making use of this division, the entire second part of the second book of the Code of Canon Law, "De Religiosis," will logically fall under the section "administrative power." It is with such power that this study will next concern itself. The order to be followed will be the order of the canons as they appear in the Code, with a few exceptions, notably canon 501, which has already been treated as the fundamental canon for this subject in chapter IV, article II.

CHAPTER VII

RIGHTS AND DUTIES UNDER THE LAW *DE RELIGIOSIS*

Article I. Residence

The whole *raison d'être* of the office of the local superior is that he may direct the actions of the members of a religious house, toward the end of the institute, and that they may consult him in their efforts towards this end. This duty of the local superior cannot be properly fulfilled unless he is present in the same house in which his subjects reside. The Church and the legislators within the Orders have at times felt the necessity of impressing this point upon the local superiors. In the *Clementinae* the conventual prior is commanded to reside in the priory, unless he be excused temporarily from such residence because of studies or other reasonable causes.[1]

[1] C. 1, *de statu monachorum vel canonicorum regularium*, III, 10, in Clem.

The present legislation reaffirms the obligation of religious superiors to reside each in his own convent. Unlike the definite legislation regarding absence from duty given in the Code for canons and pastors,[2] the present canon leaves the determination of such times to the Constitutions of the institutes. These may often forbid the absence of the local superior beyond a certain number of days, or during certain times of the year, especially during Advent and Lent. They will also wisely provide for those occasions upon which the local superior may be required to absent himself from the religious house, either in the interests of the community itself, or in his own behalf. At such times he will be careful to place the government of the community in the hands of a vicar, unless the Constitutions determine who will rule in his absence. If he is also the pastor of a church, he must provide a substitute, who in turn must be approved by the local, and perhaps by the religious ordinary, if the Constitutions designate only the latter as the competent superior referred to in canon 465, § 4.

The local superior may be punished by his own ordinary[3] for violations of the law of residence, even with removal from office if higher superiors should see fit to invoke such a penalty, but he would not incur the penalties of canon 2381, which apply only to clerics as such,[4] and not to religious, an interpretation justified by the penalties listed, namely, privation of the fruits of an office, and privation of the office itself *ad normam can.* 2168-2175, canons which do not affect religious.[5]

One might inquire whether or not the obligation of residence pertains to the common life required of all religious in virtue of their profession, and recognized in the Code in canon 594, § 1, the violation of which may be punished according to canon 2389. Usually

[2] Cf. canons 418; 465.

[3] Canons 2220, § 1, and 2222.

[4] Cf. Berutti, *Institutiones,* III, n. 32, II.

[5] Schaefer (*De Religiosis,* n. 143) asserts that the penalty of privation of office could be inflicted as an *ab homine* censure, but seems to imply that the one inflicting the penalty would do so in virtue of canon 2381, 2°. It would seem that this entire canon pertains only to clerics as such, and not to religious. Therefore the superior depriving the local superior of his office would do so in virtue of canon 2220, § 1, or canon 2222.

when reference is made to the "common life" of religious, community of goods is referred to.[6] Taken in a wide sense, the word could certainly include the obligation of residence in common.[7] However, the word should be taken in its strict and less extensive sense when penal laws are involved,[8] and consequently any punishments meted out in violation of the laws of residence will not be regulated according to canon 2389, even though this canon could be employed as a norm for the use of the penal power given in canons 2220, § 1 and 2222. Constitutional law could expressly include the obligation of residence as one of the obligations of common life. If so, it is evident that canon 2389 could be invoked to punish a local superior guilty of gravely culpable non-residence.

Article II. Decrees of the Holy See—Catechetical Instruction

Though the general prescriptions of the Sovereign Pontiffs and Roman Congregations directed to religious are usually promulgated in the *Acta Apostolicae Sedis* and therefore begin to bind according to the norm set down in canon 9, every religious superior is bound to see to it that the documents pertaining to all religious or to those of his community are brought to the attention of his subjects and are observed by them.

The present legislation binds all superiors, major as well as minor, but the application of the first paragraph of this canon would seem to fall more directly upon the local superior since the usual manner of making known such decrees is by reading them publicly, or by posting them in some appropriate place in a religious house.[9]

The decrees mentioned in this first paragraph of canon 509 include all those apostolic pronouncements which pertain to religious

[6] Cf. Smith, *The Penal Law for Religious,* The Catholic University of America Canon Law Studies, n. 98 (Washington, D. C.: The Catholic University of America, 1935), p. 124, note 4.

[7] Augustine (*Commentary,* VIII [St. Louis: Herder, 1922] 481, note 2) considers the law of residence as part of the obligation of common life, and its violation punishable by reason of canon 2389.

[8] Canons 19; 2219, § 1, 3°; Smith, *loc. cit.*

[9] Cf. Berutti, *Institutiones,* III, n. 32, II.

either as religious or as clerics, as missionaries, or as engaged in work among the faithful. At times the Holy See may prescribe the public reading of certain decrees,[10] but frequently it will depend upon the judgment of the local superior to decide what documents should be brought to the attention of his subjects. To accomplish this duty, he will do well to be familiar with the current issues of the *Acta Apostolicae Sedis,* with the official commentary and periodicals of his own Order, and with the periodicals which list the apostolic documents pertaining to religious especially.

The second paragraph of canon 509 specifies certain obligations of the local superior, the first of which is to provide for the public reading of the Constitutions of his institute at least once a year on certain determined days. The same obligation is stated as regards the public reading of any decrees which the Holy See will prescribe.

The day or days upon which the Constitutions are to be read, as well as the manner and place, is left to particular legislation. Usually the Constitutions of each institute will contain such direction, but in the absence of the latter, it will be the duty of the local superior to determine how often during the year the reading is to take place in order to fulfill the prescription of this canon that the entire body of particular legislation be read at least once a year. Vermeersch-Creusen state that where the Constitutions are of great length, approved summaries of these Constitutions which have reference to all the community may be read instead of the entire book of Constitutions.[11] It would not seem to be in the power of the local superior to permit such a practice, aside from a particular indult or particular legislation allowing him to do so.

Formerly the Holy See commanded all religious superiors, especially local superiors,[12] to see to it that various decrees were brought to the attention of their subjects.[13] Four of them are referred to in the footnotes to this canon.[14] The first three of these concerned the

[10] Cf. canon 509, § 2, 1°; S. C. de Religiosis, instr. 1 dec. 1931, § 21—*AAS,* XXIV (1932), 74.

[11] *Epitome,* I, n. 580, 4.

[12] Piatus, *Praelectiones,* I, qu. 795.

[13] S. C. C., decr. 21 iun. 1625, § 15—*Fontes,* n. 2460. Cf. Piatus, *op. cit.,* q. 791; Bachofen, *Compendium,* p. 261.

[14] Canon 509, § 1, note 5.

local superior of clerical exempt religious. These decrees on the necessity of the presentation of testimonial letters before entrance into the novitiate,[15] on the manifestation of conscience,[16] and on cases reserved by the Sacred Congregation of the Holy Office to itself,[17] were to be made known to the religious by their superiors.[18] The obligation to read these or other decrees prescribed before the present Code is no longer binding, and is supplanted by canon 509, § 2, 1°, which commands the public reading of certain decrees which the Holy See may in the future prescribe. The time and manner of reading will depend on the instructions given in the decree. If none are given the local superior will follow the directions of his own superiors, or lacking these, his own judgment, provided always that the decrees are read at least once a year. At the present time there is only one decree so prescribed for all clerical institutes, the instruction of the Sacred Congregation for Religious concerning the training of candidates for the priesthood.[19] It is to be read publicly "sub initio cujuslibet anni." [20]

The local superior is also obliged to see to it that a suitable instruction in christian doctrine is given at least twice a month to the lay-brothers and to the lay servants who reside in the religious house. Moreover he is also to arrange for bi-monthly conferences or sermons to be given to all members of the community, including those already in the priesthood.[21]

The instruction given to the professed lay-brothers and servants ought to be distinct from the weekly instruction given to the lay-brothers who are novices.[22] Though the purpose of canon 509, § 2, 2° would seem to be fulfilled if the professed lay-brothers and servants were allowed to be present twice a month at the special weekly

[15] S. C. super Statu Regularium, decr. *Romani Pontifices,* 25 ian. 1848, § V,—*Fontes,* n. 4375.

[16] S. C. Ep. et Reg., decr. *Quemadmodum,* 17 dec. 1890, § 8—*Fontes,* 2017.

[17] 15 maii 1901—*Fontes,* n. 1254.

[18] The superiors were to see that the first two were read publicly each year, the third made known "quo opportuniori putaverint modo."

[19] *AAS,* XXIV (1932), 74.

[20] *Ibid.,* p. 81, n. 21.

[21] Canon 509, § 2, 2°. Berutti, *Institutiones,* III, n. 32, IV, (2).

[22] Cf. canon 565, § 2.

instruction given to the novices, it would certainly be more in conformity with the law to have two separate instruction groups, one weekly for the novice lay-brothers alone, and another bi-monthly for the professed lay-brothers and servants. If this program is followed out both groups can be better given the special attention called for by these canons.[23] Moreover the Code states that the instruction given to the novices is to be under the direction of the novice master,[24] while the local superior has the duty of seeing to the instruction of the professed lay-brothers and resident servants.[25]

The "*pia exhortatio*" to be given twice a month to the entire community is in addition to any other instructions given to individual parts of the same community. The subject matter may well be taken from that recommended in the documents which formed the basis for this canon [26] and will generally regard matters of regular discipline and the acquiring of virtue. It is to be noted also that the local superior is not obliged to give this conference himself, but may ask other religious to do so.

Authors do not agree on who are included in the term "*familiares*" and in "*omnes de familia*" used in the canon.[27] Michiels considers the "familiares religiosorum" to be "all those who, though not religious, nevertheless are regarded as belonging to the religious family because they live in the convent both during the day and at night, are duly subject to the religious superior of the community, and are supported from the funds of the religious house." [28] Blat [29] includes the "familiares" and all religious as belonging to the "familia" before whom the bi-monthly exhortation is to be delivered, and would therefore require the presence of both groups. There is sufficient weight

[23] " . . . audientium conditioni accomodata" (canon 509, § 2, 2°), " . . . speciali collatione ad eos habita" (canon 565, § 2).

[24] Canon 565, § 1.

[25] Canon 509, § 2.

[26] Cf. Clemens VIII, decr. "*Nullus omnino,*" 25 iul. 1599, § 25—*Fontes*, n. 187; S. C. Ep. et Reg., decr. 22 aug. 1814, no. XI—*Fontes*, n. 1893.

[27] Cf. Michiels, *Principia Generalia de Personis in Ecclesia* (Lublin-Polonia: Universitas Catholica, 1932), pp. 254-257. Hereafter cited as *De Personis.*

[28] *Op. cit.*, p. 255.

[29] *Commentarium Textus Codicis Iuris Canonicis,* Liber II, *De Personis* (2. ed., Romae, 1921), 558.

of opinion to the contrary, however, and it would seem permissible to exclude all but the religious, especially if the "familiares" are able to hear sermons elsewhere.[80]

Article III. The Canonical Visitation

Following the legislation of the Council of Trent,[81] the present Code declares that the major superiors of clerical exempt religious are to conduct a visitation of all the religious houses subject to them, either personally, or if impeded, through a delegate.[82] During the visitation the superiors have an opportunity of inquiring into the manner in which the religious discipline is being carried out in the individual houses and to acquaint themselves personally with the general spiritual and material welfare of each community. For this purpose they will often interrogate all or some of the religious assigned to the house, and these are bound to respond truthfully to the questions asked.

It is evident that the entire purpose of the visitation could be defeated by the interference of the local superior, should he attempt to divert his subjects from their obligation of truthfully responding to the questions of the visitator or otherwise impede the visitation either by sending subjects away from the house on temporary work, or directly or indirectly inducing them not to answer the questions of the visitator, or to dissimulate the truth before him, or finally by penalizing or generally making trouble for a religious because of the answers which he has given to the questions proposed by the visitator.[83] The local superior is forbidden all such action in canon 513. If he nevertheless attempts to impede the visitation in any of the ways referred to, he can be deprived of his office, and declared incapable of exercising any other position involving the government of religious.[84] The penalties which may be inflicted are less rigorous than those of the pre-Code law, which imposed *ipso facto* excommuni-

[80] Cf. Schaefer, *De Religiosis*, n. 144b, 4, (b).

[81] Cf. sess. XXV, *de regularibus*, c. 1, 20.

[82] Canon 511.

[83] Cf. canons 513; 2413, §§ 1, 2.

[84] Cf. canon 2413, §§1, 2. Smith, *The Penal Law for Religious*, pp. 139-143.

cation upon those who impeded the work of the visitator.[35] It is to be noted that the local superior is forbidden only to interfere with the purpose of the visitation. He may of his own accord or if requested advise subjects of their rights and duties as long as his action cannot be interpreted as either directly or indirectly violating the purpose of the visitation. Neither is his general dominative and jurisdictional power over his subjects suspended during the time of visitation, except insofar as its exercise would in any way impede the purpose of the visitation[36] or unless the particular law of the Order limits his authority during such a time.

Article IV. The Council

Very little can be found in pre-Code legislation concerning counsellors of the local superior, as distinct from the local chapter. In 1909 an Instruction of the Sacred Congregation for Religious forbade the local superior to contract any notable debts or notable obligations without the previous consent of his council. Consent of his council and of the Holy See was required for contracting debts over $2,000.[37] Though both the local chapter and council often are called to treat of the same matters,[38] they are distinct entities, and have distinct functions in canonical legislation.[39] Fanfani defines the chapter as the "adunatio plurium religiosorum legitime convocatorum pro negotiis ad religionem ipsorum pertinentibus definiendis"[40] and the council as the "adunatio quorumdam tantum e domo, vel e provincia, vel e religione legitime facta, in qua una cum superiore locali, aut provinciali, aut generali negotia religionis pertractantur."[41] It will be seen therefore that the councillors ("consiliarii") whose consent or counsel is often required before the local superior may validly

[35] C. 2, *de statu monachorum vel canonicorum regularium,* III, 10, in Clem.

[36] Cf. Piatus, *Praelectiones,* I, qu. 873.

[37] S. C. de Religiosis, instr. 30 iul. 1909, n. I—*Fontes,* n. 4394.

[38] Cf. canons 534, § 1; 543; 575, § 2.

[39] Cf. canon 501, § 1.

[40] *De Iure Religiosorum,* n. 62.

[41] *Ibidem,* n. 65.

or licitly act, are principally assistants, aids to the superior, while the local chapter in clerical exempt religious institutes is a collegiate moral person in itself, possessing in its own right dominative and jurisdictional power according to the regulations of common law and of the Constitutions of the institute.

Canon 516 requires the local superior of every religious house in which at least six professed religious reside, to have his council, and to make use of those who constitute it in various negotiations, especially those of greater moment. The superior of a house of less than six professed religious may also have his council, but there is no obligation in common law requiring him to be so assisted.

It is left to constitutional law to prescribe the qualifications of those to be chosen and to determine the superior who will choose them. Generally the provincial superior will designate those who are to form the council of each local superior, but the particular law of each institute must be consulted.

Canon 516 requires the local superior to receive the advice or consent of his council whenever either is required by common or particular law. If the council's consent is required the superior will not act validly until he has secured it; if only the advice of the council is required, in order to proceed validly it will be sufficient for the local superior to seek this advice without necessarily following it.[42] Authors are not agreed as to whether or not the local superior would act validly if he did not seek the advice of the council at all, when it is required either by the Code or by the Constitutions.[43] It appears to the writer that the superior will act invalidly unless he at least convokes the council and listens to its opinion. This seems to be the meaning of the words "satis est ad valide agendum" which if not expressly, at least equivalently, pronounce the invalidity of the opposite procedure.[44] If it is sufficient for validity to act in a

[42] Canon 105, 1°.

[43] Cf. Michiels, *De Personis,* pp. 406-418. He lists the authors and their arguments, and concludes (p. 418) that the more benign opinion is solidly probable, and that until the Holy See authentically solves the doubt, failure on the part of a superior to consult his council when this is required before placing an act will not invalidate such acts.

[44] Cf. canons 11; 18; 105, § 1; 516, § 1.

determined manner, it appears insufficient for validity not to act in that determined manner. However the matter is doubtful, and the opposite opinion which maintains the validity of acts placed in violation of the law requiring the superior to seek the advice of the council is authoritative enough to permit the local superior to feel *post factum* that he has acted validly in spite of his disregard of the law of the canon or Constitution demanding at least consultation with his council.

Difficulty will arise also if the local superior gives his council an opportunity to express the required consent or counsel, but they refuse to do so. If their consent is required and they refuse to give an answer either affirmatively or negatively, it would seem that the superior could not act as though their consent had been secured, but would need to have recourse to the provincial superior. If only their advice is required and it is asked but not given, in practice the superior may proceed to act because of the doubt of law involved as to whether or not he acts invalidly, not having sought the advice of his council at all.[45] It has been proposed that if a councillor is present at the meeting of the council and refuses to respond, his action may be interpreted as not in opposition to the plan of the superior, and that the latter may therefore proceed to act validly, even though the consent of the councillor is required by law.[46] Ojetti believes that, even when the consent of the council is involved nothing more is required of the superior than that he give his councillors an opportunity of expressing their opinions. They are not forced to respond, he states, and if they do not the superior may proceed to act validly.[47] Nothing seems to be stated in common law on the question involved, and if in the Constitutions nothing is prescribed to the contrary concerning the superior's mode of acting, it would seem that the proposals of Michiels and Ojetti just mentioned are of sufficient intrinsic value to merit acceptance. The local superior will act validly, therefore, as long as he gives his councillors an opportunity to express their opinion on the business at hand.

A final question concerns the manner in which the councillors

[45] Cf. *supra*, note 43.

[46] Michiels, *op. cit.*, p. 420. Toso, *Commentaria Minora*, II, tom. I, 54.

[47] *Commentarium*, II, 184-185. Toso, *ibidem*.

are to act. Can the superior ask their consent or counsel verbally, by telephone, or by telegraph, for instance, or by letter, or is it necessary for the councillors to meet and to deliberate as a body? Since the superior's council, unlike the chapter of the house, is not a moral person, it will not necessarily be ruled by the canons governing the deliberation of collegiate moral persons, although these may be used as a norm in fulfilling its obligations. Recourse should therefore be had again to the particular law of the Constitutions to determine the manner in which the council is to act. In its nature as an advisory body, it would seem that the council should meet collectively to carry out its obligations but particular law could require only that its advice be sought in whatever way possible or convenient to the superior or to all involved, e. g., by letter, telephone, etc.[48] If the Constitutions determine that the council is to act as a unit, the local superior is obliged to convoke it in virtue of canon 105, 2°. The obligation seems to be one involving liceity alone, since no invalidating clause appears either explicitly or equivalently in the canon.

All other details involved as to the method of securing the consent or advice of the councillors are left to particular legislation. The norms given in the Instruction of the Sacred Congregation for Religious (1909),[49] which prescribed that the vote of the council was to be secret and in writing, and that the document was to be signed by both the superior and each council member, are no longer of obligation.

Article V. Temporal Goods

A. *Acquisition*

The religious house has the right of acquiring temporal goods as long as the Rule or Constitutions do not legislate to the contrary.[50]

[48] It may be noted that ordinarily it will not be difficult for the local superior to consult his councillors personally, since normally they reside in the same house with him. The question might, however, be raised exceptionally, viz., if consultation should become necessary when some or most of the council members were absent from the convent. Cf. Michiels, *De Personis,* pp. 426-429.

[49] *AAS,* I (1909), 697, VI—*Fontes,* n. 4394.

[50] Canon 531.

Temporal goods may be acquired in whatever manner consonant with either natural or positive law, and the dominion over such acquired goods will ordinarily remain with the moral person acquiring them.[51] For religious, Pejška lists six ways in which temporal goods may be acquired,[52] and in some of these the local superior may play a part. The first involves the acceptance of a pious foundation. The local superior may not accept such a foundation without the written consent of his provincial,[53] to whom it also pertains to dispose of the money or other movable goods so acquired.[54] A copy of the contract entered into is to be retained in the archives of the convent,[55] and the local superior himself is to keep one record listing the obligations to be fulfilled and another of their fulfillment.[56] This record is to be presented at certain intervals for the inspection of the provincial. Temporalities may be acquired also by legacy or by gift. The local superior is competent to accept these in virtue of his powers of ordinary administration, but if the legacy or gift is equivalent to a pious foundation, only the major superior is competent to accept it because of the perpetual obligations it will place upon the community.[57] Another source of income may be the result of the personal labor of members of the convent, for example, Mass stipends and other offerings, or financial returns from the publication of books. These can be administered by the local superior or their administration supervised by him.[58]

Among the ways of acquiring funds may also be listed the solicitation of alms. The Code treats of this subject in canons 621-624. Since only the local superior in religious Orders is being considered in this work, canon 621 will be of special application. Regulars who are mendicants in name and in fact, that is, in the strict sense, and not those who are broadly called such, as for example, religious of

[51] Canon 1499.
[52] *Ius Canonicum Religiosorum,* pp. 63-67.
[53] Cf. canons 1546, § 1, 1550.
[54] Canon 1547.
[55] Canon 1548.
[56] Canon 1549, §§ 1, 2.
[57] Canon 1546, § 1.
[58] Canons 516, § 2; 532, § 2.

the Order of Preachers,[59] may seek alms in those dioceses in which their house is established, provided they have the written permission of their own superior. This would seem to mean the local superior unless the Constitutions should demand the permission of the major superior.[60] No special permission of the bishop of the diocese is required since in permitting mendicants to enter the diocese, he is presumed also to have given them permission to seek alms.[61] The mendicant local superior could not permit his religious to seek alms in another diocese without the added permission in writing of the ordinary of that diocese. Neither does it seem licit for a mendicant belonging to a house situated in one diocese to seek alms in another, solely with the permission of his own local superior, even though there exists a house of his Order in this second diocese. A local mendicant superior could, however, permit a visiting religious of his own Order to solicit alms in the diocese, even though the visitor is habitually resident in another diocese.

Religious of those Orders formerly incapable of possessing temporal goods, but now in possession of that faculty and even though still called mendicants, e. g., religious of the Order of Preachers, require both the permission of their own local superior, and that of the bishop of the diocese even when they have a house in the diocese.[62]

In giving his subjects permission to solicit alms, the local superior should be guided by the prescriptions of canon 623 which allow him to send only the professed and the more mature, never those who are still engaged in studies. He should be guided also by the rules given by the Sacred Congregation for Religious in the decree, "De *eleemosynis colligendis.*" [63] These regulations are still in force in those matters which pertain to the manner and discipline concerning the seeking of alms, for it would seem that the Code has at least implicitly confirmed these prescriptions in canon 621.[64] By a faithful observance of such regulations the local superior will safeguard the

[59] *PCI,* 16 oct. 1919, n. 10—*AAS,* XI (1919), 478.

[60] Blat, *Commentarium,* II, 689.

[61] S. C. de Religiosis, decr. 21 nov. 1908, n. I, 1°—*Fontes,* n. 4391; Vermeersch-Creusen, *Epitome,* I, n. 472; Schaefer, *De Religiosis,* n. 433.

[62] *PCI,* 16 oct. 1919—*AAS,* XI (1919), 478, n. 10.

[63] 21 nov. 1908—*Fontes,* n. 4391.

[64] Cf. Schaefer, *De Religiosis,* n. 431, 6.

Church and his Order from the criticism and ridicule of even the faithful, who have often suffered from violations of similar regulations in the past.[65]

B. *Administration*

1. The Procurator of the Convent

In its twenty-fifth session the Council of Trent prescribed that "the administration of the property of monasteries or convents shall belong to the officials thereof only, who are removable at the will of their superiors." [66] These officials have been known under various titles, such as Econome, Procurator, Syndic, or Bursar.

Clement VIII in the decree *"Nullus omnino"* [67] declared that the local superior was not to administer the goods of the convent, but that such a duty belonged to three minor officials. Thus, Fagnanus (+1678) writes,[68] was confirmed the opinion of Hostiensis (+1271) and Joannes Andreae (+1348), both of whom held that the direction of temporal affairs did not belong to the office of the prior, since his office had to do with spiritual matters.

The Code of Canon Law prescribes that each religious house shall have its own procurator, who is to exercise his office under the direction of the superior. It will be the duty of the local superior therefore to supervise his administration in such ways as he shall deem prudent and to the advantage of the community. Supervision implies the right to receive a report of the quantity and value of the

[65] Cf. S. C. de Religiosis, decr. 21 nov. 1908,—Preamble—*Fontes*, n. 4391; *Concilii Plenarii Baltimorensis II., in Ecclesia Metropolitana Baltimorensi, a Die VII. ad Diem XXI. Octobris, A. D., MDCCCLXVI., Habiti, et a Sede Apostolica Recogniti, Decreta* (Baltimorae, 1880), n. 119; *Acta et Decreta Concilii Plenarii Baltimorensis Tertii* (Baltimorae, 1886), n. 295.

[66] *Conc. Trident.*, sess. XXV, *de regularibus*, c. 2; Schroeder, *Canons and Decrees*, p. 218.

[67] 25 iul. 1599, § 12—*BRT*, X, 664. Cf. Vermeersch, *De Religiosis, Institutis et Personis* (2 vols., Vol. I, Brugis, 1902; Vol. II, 3. ed., Brugis, 1904), II, 309. Hereafter cited as *De Religiosis*. (This paragraph of the decree is not in the *Fontes*.)

[68] *Commentaria in Quinque Libros Decretalium* (5 vols. in 3, Coloniae Allobrogum, 1759), ad c. 2, X, *de statu monachorum et canonicorum regularium*, III, 35, n. 74.

property; to demand an account as to the safe investment and the faithful application of donations; to apply remedies for negligent and incompetent administration. At the same time it seems to have been the mind of the legislator in instituting the office of procurator to relieve the local superior of much of the material labor and duties involved in the administration of temporalities. Even though he may incur debts in the name of the community according to canon 532, § 2, he should leave these duties to the procurator and not exercise that office personally, unless in his own judgment or in the judgment of the higher superior, necessity should demand his control of both offices. Even then this would ordinarily be only a temporary expedient, and should be remedied by the appointment of a local procurator. It is evident that the local superior can administer the procurator's duties while the latter is temporarily impeded, though at such times it would seem that another should be charged with the office, rather than that the local superior be burdened with the administration of temporal affairs, often to the detriment of both the spiritual and temporal welfare of the community.

Vermeersch-Creusen say [69] that it may be tolerated that a local superior be also procurator of the province or of the Order, and Larraona would go further, stating that it is not only tolerated "sed et *admitti* potest cumulatio utriusque muneris, ut saepe fit. . . ." [70] Such a procedure, except in the case of a local superior of a very small community, would seem to be contrary to the end of the law, which in the opinion of the writer, considers the good of the local community as well as the welfare of the province or Order. Even though the province or Order would profit by the capable administrative ability of a procurator who was also a local superior, as a rule the two offices would seem incompatible.[71] Larraona [72] argues for the licitness of such a practice from the use of the word "ipse" in canon 516, § 3, as referring respectively to the general and provin-

[69] *Epitome,* I, n. 368.

[70] "Commentarium Codicis,"—*CpR,* X (1929), 36, note 709.

[71] Cf. Vromant, *De Bonis Ecclesiae temporalibus ad usum praesertim Missionariorum et Religiosorum* (Louvain: Editions du Muséum Lessianum, 1927), n. 229. Hereafter cited as *De Bonis Ecclesiae Temporalibus.*

[72] *Art. cit.*

cial superior, and therefore not inclusive of a local superior. Such an argument may be admitted and therefore one cannot say that the words of this canon explicitly exclude the local superior from exercising the office of either provincial or general procurator.[73]

2. Acts of Ordinary Administration

Presupposing the right of an individual religious house to acquire and possess temporal goods, one is naturally led to a consideration of the administration of these goods, and of the rights and duties of the local superior in that regard. It has already been seen that since the administration of temporalities ordinarily involves a great deal of time and personal supervision, the Code in canon 516, § 2 wisely commands the appointment of a procurator for each house, thus relieving the local superior of this burden and allowing him greater opportunity to care for the spiritual welfare of his subjects. Yet the same canon prescribes that the procurator is to exercise his office under the direction of the local superior, and in canon 532 the fundamental right of the local superior to incur expenses and to carry out juridical acts of ordinary administration at all times is recognized, even though subordinate officials including the procurator himself may have been appointed for such acts.

Administration involves the exercise of acts directed toward the conservation, and where the nature of the property permits, the fructification of the temporal goods of the institute. Vermeersch-Creusen define it as the "gubernatio rerum temporalium secundum naturam suam et fines suos." [74]

Evidently therefore it will be the personal duty of the local superior at certain times and in the manner designated both in common law and in the Constitutions to see to it that the "res frugiferos fructus suos afferant" . . . and "consumptibilia recte impendantur prout ius vel officium suadet seu exiget." [75]

[73] It goes without saying that the Constitutions of an Order could declare such offices incompatible. (Cf. *Const. S. O. P.* [1932], n. 295, § II, where it is provided that the same religious cannot be prior and either provincial or conventual procurator.)

[74] *Epitome,* I, n. 601. Cf. Wernz, *Ius Decretalium,* III, n. 147.

[75] Vermeersch-Creusen, *loc. cit.*

Even though the administration of temporalities is entrusted to a procurator, canon 532, § 2 recognizes the validity of the local superior's acts of ordinary administration, i. e., of those acts which are "regularly necessary for the upkeep of property and for supplying current needs." [76] These may be determined specifically in the Constitutions or in the general or provincial chapters, and will usually include the collection of debts paid in installments, the buying of those things necessary for daily use, and the banking of sums of money, unless any of these acts be excluded from his competence by particular legislation. He cannot validly place acts of extraordinary administration which will involve future obligations upon the community or other superiors, such as the acceptance of legacies, the purchase of property, or the making of very notable repairs on the property already possessed.[77]

It cannot be overemphasized that as a juridically recognized administrator, the local superior will also be bound by the general ecclesiastical laws governing administration of church property when he undertakes such work ordinarily left to the procurator. Therefore he is obliged to conserve the goods of the house, keeping in mind the regulations of both canon and civil law, to collect whatever rents or other returns are due for the use of the community's goods, to keep a well-ordered account of the income and expenses which he lawfully reserves to himself, to safeguard the documents, papers and titles, etc., concerning the property of the house, and to forward copies of these to the provincial archives, if the Constitutions so demand.[78]

Worthy of special note are the prescriptions of canon 1524 regarding the "just and adequate wage" to be paid by ecclesiastical administrators to those who are employed in the service of the

[76] Cf. Larraona, "Commentarium Codicis,"—*CpR,* XII (1931), 358; McManus, *The Administration of Temporal Goods in Religious Institutes,* The Catholic University of America Canon Law Studies, n. 109 (Washington, D. C.: The Catholic University of America, 1937), p. 80.

[77] Cf. Vromant, *De Bonis Ecclesiae Temporalibus,* n. 173. The list of acts of extraordinary administration usually given by authors follows that drawn up by the S. C. de Prop. Fide (C. G.), 21 july 1856—*Collectanea S. Cong. de Prop. Fide* (2 vols. Romae, 1907), n. 1127, art. 20 (*Fontes,* n. 4841). Hereafter cited as *Collectanea.*

[78] Cf. canon 1523.

Church. The local superior who assumes this duty should not forget that he and not his employee has taken the vow of poverty. If the superior will observe the prescriptions of Pope Leo XIII's encyclical, "*Rerum Novarum,*" partly summarized in canon 1524, he will make sure that those employed in the service of the religious house will always be examples of the Church's constant solicitude for both the spiritual and the temporal welfare of the working class.

Finally, in his administration the local superior will be directed especially by the prescriptions of his own Constitutions, and the regulations of the provincial chapter, for the Code generally leaves the details of the manner in which ecclesiastical property held by religious is to be administered to the Constitutions and other particular regulations of the institute. Particular law may often demand that the local superior seek either the advice or consent of his council before carrying out some of the more important acts of even ordinary administration, and before proceeding with any acts of an extraordinary nature.

C. *Alienation*

1. Historical Notes

Civil and ecclesiastical law at various times in the history of the Church have forbidden the alienation of Church property without a just cause. The local superior as the administrator of the community property entrusted to his care was bound by law to protect and to conserve these temporal goods, and forbidden to dispose of them without the necessary permission of the proper ecclesiastical authority.

Clement V (1305-1314) in the Council of Vienne (1311-1312) forbade the alienation of any of the temporal goods of the monastery, priory, or church, except when necessity or utility demanded, and then only with the consent of the conventual council, or of the proper superior ("*praelati proprii*").[79] Paul II (1464-1471) forbade the local religious superior among others to alienate ecclesiastical property, except in the cases permitted *a iure,* under penalty of

[79] C. 1, *de rebus Ecclesiae non alienandis,* III, 4, in Clem.

deprivation of office.[80] Paul IV confirmed and renewed these prescriptions in 1555.[81]

Particular laws of the various Orders also forbade alienation without the necessary permission.[82] The superior competent to give permission for alienation was not as a rule the local superior; but the consent of the master general or the provincial was required in all Orders.[83] The reason for this lack of competence in the local superior may be ascribed partly to the desire of the Church to reserve this "negotium gravissimum" to those prelates in the Church who were expected to have a wider and more inclusive vision in regard to the welfare of the entire Church and Order than was perhaps expected of the local superior governing a single monastery or convent.

In an Instruction issued on the 30th of July, 1909, the Sacred Congregation for Religious promulgated definite norms to be observed even by local superiors when they assumed notable debts or obligations. The local superior was obliged to secure the previous consent of his council and of the master general and his council before contracting any such debts or obligations.[84]

2. Present Legislation

In canon 534 the Code gives special legislation for the alienation of the property of religious. This is in addition to the general regulations given in canons 1530-1534 for the alienation of all ecclesiastical property. It will occasionally be the duty of the local superior to transact such business, and consequently he should be familiar with these canons.

The local superior ought to have a clear notion of what is meant by alienation as referred to in the Code. The definition given in a letter of the Apostolic Delegate to the United States, addressed to all religious superiors, may be pointed out: "The term *alienation* in-

[80] Const. *"Ambitiosae,"* 1 mart. 1467—c. un., *de rebus Ecclesiae non alienandis,* III, 4, in Extravag. com.; *BRT,* V, 194.

[81] Const. *"Iniunctum nobis,"* 14 iul. 1555—*Fontes,* n. 88; *BRT,* VI, 496.

[82] The Dominican Constitutions adopted the constitution of Paul II (*supra,* p. 73). Cf. *BOP,* VIII, "Tractatus de Consensu Bullarum," Tit. I, Q. XIV, Sec. IV.

[83] Cf. Tamburini, *De Jure Abbatum,* Tom. III, Disp. XIII, qu. 8, n. 4.

[84] *Fontes,* n. 4394, I, c.

cludes not only purchases or transfers of property, but includes as well any contract, debt, or obligation. The Canon Law regards all transactions which may render the financial condition of the Institute, Province, or religious house less secure, as alienations."[85] Alienation, according to Augustine, may take place by sale, exchange, payment, donation, mortgage, lease, bailment, security, or the voluntary giving up of a right acquired.[86] The matter concerned is that which has a material value or price. In the understanding of the true nature of alienation, it must be remembered that only expenditures involving the use of *stable capital* are properly speaking alienations. By stable, invested, or fixed capital is meant, "that money which is not being used primarily as a medium of barter or exchange, but which has been invested in property or holdings of some kind, whether these be in the form of corporeal or incorporeal property, either movable or immovable."[87] Money in circulation, used for ordinary administration, is known as unstable, free, or fluctuating capital, and is changed into stable capital "only when so designated by an externally manifested act of a competent ecclesiastical authority."[88]

When confronted with problems involving alienation, including the incurring of debts and obligations, the local superior should naturally be well acquainted with the particular law of his own Order which will usually give definite norms as to his competency in such matters. It may be noted that he must have the consent of his own council or chapter for any alienation at all,[89] and at all times he will be bound by the general laws of the Code governing the alienation of ecclesiastical goods.[90]

[85] Letter of the Most Reverend Apostolic Delegate to the United States, 13 nov. 1936—Bouscaren, *The Canon Law Digest*, 2 vols. and Supplement—1941 (Milwaukee: Bruce, 1934-1941), Supplement (1941), p. 78.

[86] *Commentary*, VI, 593.

[87] Doheny, *Practical Problems in Church Finance* (Milwaukee: Bruce, 1941), p. 43.

[88] Doheny, *op. cit.*, p. 43.

[89] Canon 534, § 1.

[90] Cf. Letter of the Most Reverend Apostolic Delegate to the United States, 13 nov. 1936, Preamble—Bouscaren, *The Canon Law Digest*, Supplement (1941), p. 78.

Of particular application to the religious superiors in the United States are the special norms governing the alienation of temporalities, issued by the Sacred Congregation for Religious and communicated to religious superiors in the letter of the Apostolic Delegate just referred to. Two systems of collecting money are mentioned, "(1) the issuance of bonds or debentures upon ecclesiastical property and the sale of such bonds and debentures in the public market or to private investors, and (2) the system of soliciting or accepting funds under the so-called annuity agreement providing for the payment of an annuity to the donor for life. *Both of these systems of obtaining money fall within the provisions of canon 534.*"[91]

For the validity of acts involving the alienation of the goods of a religious house, or the assumption of obligations, the local superior must always have the permission of competent authority. This authority is designated in canon 534, § 1 as the Holy See if the amount involved exceeds $6,000 (Gold). For amounts less than that sum, the permission of the superior designated in the Constitutions is required, which superior is obliged also to obtain the consent of his council or chapter.

In order that the act of alienation be licit as well as valid, it will be the duty of the local superior to see to it that the ecclesiastical goods involved in the transaction be appraised in writing by trustworthy experts, and that there exist a just cause such as urgent necessity, obvious advantage to the religious house, or the performance of some "genuinely Christian work of religion, charity, or of mercy."[92] Moreover, where the alienation of goods is involved, these should not be sold for less than they were appraised, the sale should take place by auction unless some other method is more advisable, and the sum realized from the act of alienation should be invested safely and profitably.[93]

Local superiors, especially those in charge of churches attached to a religious house, must remember that any precious objects of notable value, important relics, or images of great value, or relics or images which are held in great honor by the people, or votive

[91] Cf. Bouscaren, *The Canon Law Digest,* Supplement (1941), p. 79.

[92] Canon 1530. Cf. Doheny, *Practical Problems in Church Finance,* p. 30.

[93] Canon 1531.

offerings cannot be alienated or transferred to another church without the permission of the Holy See.[94]

D. *Investments*

Pre-Code legislation regarding the investment of money may be seen in a letter of the Sacred Congregation of the Propagation of the Faith to the Bishop of Roermond in which it was stated that ecclesiastical persons are not to be disturbed if they wish to buy "actiones seu titulos mensae nummulariae," provided that they abide by the regulations of the Holy See in these matters, and that no species of negotiation is involved.[95]

Leo XIII in a letter to the bishops of England gave norms for deciding when a gift may be considered as given to the religious themselves, and when to the mission to which they were attached.[96] These norms will be helpful even now when it becomes the duty of the local superior to decide whether money which is to be invested has been given to the religious house absolutely, or "intuitu paroeciae vel missionis," and consequently to be regulated by canon 533, § 1, 4°. Since the investment of the money of a religious house is *per se* not an act of alienation [97] unless the money to be invested is taken from the stable capital of the religious house or is of such an amount as to render the financial condition of the religious house less secure, the canons regulating alienation will not apply. Consequently the legislator devotes a separate canon to the investment of the money of religious institutes.[98] This canon will apply to the local superior in religious Orders only when he is investing funds which have been received "intuitu paroeciae vel missionis."[99] For their investment he needs the permission of the local ordinary. This permission is necessary for the liceity of the investment, but without it the act would be valid.

[94] Canons 534, § 1; 1281, § 1.

[95] 7 iul. 1893—*Collectanea*, n. 1841; *Fontes*, n. 4925. Cf. S. C. S. Off., 15 apr. 1885—*Fontes*, n. 1091.

[96] Const. *"Romanos Pontifices,"* 8 maii 1881, § 26—*Fontes*, n. 582.

[97] Pistocchi, *De Bonis Ecclesiae Temporalibus* (Taurini [Italia]: Marietti, 1932), p. 402. Vermeersch-Creusen, *Epitome*, I, n. 602.

[98] Canon 533.

[99] Canon 533, 4°.

In investing all funds other than those received "intuitu paroeciae vel missionis," the local superior is obliged to follow the regulations given in his own Constitutions.[100] These will very often require him to secure the permission of his council or of the provincial or general superior.

E. *Responsibility for Debts and Obligations*

From canon 536 it may be determined to what extent the local superior is responsible for the debts and obligations contracted by his subjects. He himself has no personal obligation of answering for any contracted by himself in the name of the religious house, provided that he has contracted them legitimately and with the permission of the competent higher superiors, where such permission is required. In all legitimate temporal transactions the local superior acts as administrator for the religious house, and not for himself. If it should happen, however, that particular law would declare the religious house incapable of responsibility in temporal affairs, the moral person represented by the superior will be accountable.[101] It may be noted also that if the superior exceeds the power given him, he then becomes personally responsible for the debts or obligations contracted illegitimately.[102] The religious house is likewise responsible for any debts contracted by its members who have the permission of the local superior, since in giving such a permission he acts in virtue of his ordinary administration, not in his own name but in the name of the house. Berutti notes that a local superior cannot validly give a religious with solemn vows permission to contract debts for which the subject will be personally responsible.[103]

It is not necessary that the religious superior give explicit permission to his subjects before the religious house will become accountable for their debts and obligations. Tacit and even presumed permission suffices. Lacking any permission at all, the re-

[100] Canon 533, § 1.

[101] McManus, *The Administration of Temporal Goods in Religious Institutes*, pp. 165-166.

[102] Fanfani, *De Iure Religiosorum*, n. 157.

[103] *Institutiones*, III, n. 61, II, A.

ligious himself, and not his superior, becomes responsible, even though he be bound by solemn vows.[104]

F. *Donations*

The sources given in the Code for canon 537, which treats of donations and gifts made from the common goods of the institute, show that the pre-Code legislation was very strict in this matter. Alexander III (1159-1181) seems to recognize the capacity of an abbot to make donations, but declares that the quantity of the gift and the custom of the place must be considered when the validity of these gifts is questioned by the community.[105] Clement VIII (1592-1605) forbade all superiors to make donations of any kind, except with the permission of the general chapter,[106] although with the consent of the superior the religious might exchange small gifts among themselves.[107] Urban VIII (1623-1644) modified the latter part of this regulation, and permitted the religious to make gifts to externs but always with the permission of the local superior.[108] In 1909 the Sacred Congregation for Religious declared that gifts and donations were to be made only after fulfilling the conditions laid down by the Holy See, by particular Constitutions, by chapters, and by general superiors.[109] Thus it may be seen that in the later legislation previous to the Code religious generally were permitted to make donations provided that they had the permission of their local superior.[110] Under the present legislation gifts or donations made by the local superior from the goods of the house are permitted as long as they are made "ratione eleemosynae vel alia justa causa," and according to the prescriptions of his Constitu-

[104] Berutti, *Institutiones*, III, n. 61, II, C.

[105] C. 3, X, *de donationibus*, III, 24.

[106] Const. *"Religiosae congregationes,"* 19 iun. 1594, §§ 1, 2—*Fontes*, n. 178; decr. *"Nullus omnino,"* 25 iul. 1599, § 21—*Fontes*, n. 187.

[107] Const. *"Religiosae congregationes,"* § 4—*Fontes*, n. 178.

[108] Const. *"Nuper,"* 16 oct. 1640, § 1—*Fontes*, n. 220; apparently the local superior was still required to obtain the permission of the general chapter, if he wished to make donations himself.

[109] Instr. 30 iul. 1909, n. XIII—*Fontes*, n. 4394.

[110] Cf. Piatus, *Praelectiones*, I qu. 283, 2°.

tions.[111] If the gift or donation were to assume large proportions, particular legislation would probably demand the consent of his council, or even the consent of the provincial. Gifts made from the stable capital of the house would constitute alienation, and consequently would require the observance of the canonical regulations therein involved.[112]

It will also be the right of the local superior to grant his subjects permission to bestow gifts upon others when charity or any other just cause presents itself. The canon refers only to superiors and does not specify further which superior is competent but ordinarily the local superior will be competent unless the value of the contemplated gift exceeds the amount for which particular law recognizes him as competent.[113]

Article VI. The Postulancy

Since lay-brothers who wish to enter the novitiate of a religious Order are obliged to make a postulancy of six months in a religious house of the Order, the question of their relationship to the local superior naturally arises.

The Code says nothing concerning the superior who is competent to admit candidates to the postulancy. It would seem to be entirely in conformity with the nature of the candidate's request for admission into the Order that the major superiors, who represent the Order more directly than the superior of an individual house, be competent to admit the candidates, and such is the general practice.[114] However, the particular law of an institute could declare the local superior competent [115] to receive the aspirant, and to assign him to the special direction of the master of postulants.[116]

[111] Canon 537.

[112] *Supra,* chap. VII, art. V, C.

[113] Canon 537.

[114] Cf. Beste, *Introductio in Codicem* (Collegeville, Minn.: St. John's Abbey Press, 1938), p. 358. Hereafter cited as *Introductio.*

[115] Cf. Berutti, *Institutiones,* III, n. 66, I. It does not seem probable that the local superior of clerical exempt religious in centralized Orders would *ex officio* have the right of admitting postulants to the Order.

[116] Canon 540.

During the period of postulancy the local superior exercises dominative power over the postulant, and jurisdictional power in the cases mentioned in common law. Thus, in virtue of his jurisdictional power, he has the right to dispense postulants from the common law of fast and abstinence and from the observance of feasts or of both,[117] and to dispense them according to canons 1313, 2° and 1320 from private non-reserved vows and from promissory oaths. He can also administer Viaticum and Extreme Unction to a sick postulant, in virtue of canon 514, § 1, since a postulant is understood to dwell in the religious house day and night *causa educationis*.[118] It is likewise the right of the local superior to confer delegated power upon other priests who hear the confessions of the postulants.[119] On the other hand, postulants who die either in the religious house or elsewhere are buried according to the rules governing the burial of all the faithful, that is, they are buried from their own parish church, unless they may have chosen another church during life.[120] Therefore, the local superior, even of clerical exempt religious, has not the same rights over postulants who die in the religious house as he has over the novices and the professed,[121] and over those engaged in actual service of the community.[122]

In virtue of his dominative power, the local superior may grant a postulant permission to be absent from the religious house, but he should take care that the absence is not prolonged so long as to break the integrity of the period of postulancy. Authors define such a period variously.[123]

[117] Canon 1245, § 3.

[118] If the postulant is ill outside the house, the local superior does not have this right. Cf. *PCI*, 16 iun. 1931—*AAS*, XXIII (1931), 353. Cf. *infra*, pp. 140-142.

[119] Canon 875, § 1.

[120] Canon 1222.

[121] Canon 1221, §§ 1 and 2. Cf. *PCI*, July 20, 1929, IV—*AAS*, XXI (1929), 573.

[122] Canon 1221, § 3.

[123] Berutti says an absence of beyond thirty continuous days would destroy the moral unity necessary for the integrity of the postulancy (*Institutiones*, III, n. 65, C). Beste (*Introductio*, p. 358) would allow a postulant

The local superior is not competent to prolong the period of postulancy, since the Code reserves this faculty to the competent major superior.[124] Neither does he seem competent to shorten it, even though Schaefer holds that for a just cause the superior could shorten the period by a few days.[125] This would seem to be reserved to the major superior, since he is the superior charged with the duty of seeing to it that candidates for entrance into the novitiate are endowed with the requisite qualifications.[126]

Article VII. The Novitiate

The Code divides the law concerning the novitiate of religious into two articles, the first treating of admission to the novitiate, and the second dealing with the training or formation of the novices received. Generally it is not the *ex officio* duty of the local superior to be concerned in either of these aspects of the novitiate, but since the novice spends his period of training in a religious house, the local superior has certain rights and obligations in respect to him.

A. *Admission*

In reference to the admission of a candiate, whether he be a lay-brother postulant who has already spent his six month period of experimentation in the postulancy, or an aspirant to the clerical state, canon 543 vindicates the right of admission [127] to the novitiate to the major superiors who act in conjunction with the council or chapter designated for this duty in the Constitutions of each insti-

to be absent fifteen days (even though he left the house with the intention of not returning), without being forced to repeat the period of postulancy; *e contra,* Schaefer, *De Religiosis,* n. 216.

[124] Canon 539, § 2.

[125] De Religiosis, n. 216.

[126] Canon 543.

[127] The right to *admit* a candidate to the novitiate must be clearly distinguished from the right to bestow the habit of the Order upon the candidate. This latter action is sometimes spoken of as admission to the Order, but is an admission only in the wide sense, and follows upon the formal acceptance of the candidate into the Order by the provincial or other major superior. The right to bestow the habit of the Order is very often within the competency of the local superior of the novitiate house.

tute. Therefore, the local superior, as a minor superior, is not competent to admit a candidate to the novitiate.[128] A candidate, though otherwise fully qualified, admitted by a local superior would not make a valid novitiate, or valid profession following such an invalid novitiate.[129]

Since it is the right of the major superior to admit candidates to the novitiate, the consequent duties of inquiring into the qualifications necessary for valid and licit admittance also belong to the major superior. He will often be obliged to depend on others for information concerning a particular candidate's qualifications. Therefore, it will often devolve upon the local superior of the novitiate house to examine the candidate, and, especially at the major superior's request,[130] to seek the testimonials required by canon 544.[131] If the local superior is delegated to seek the testimonials, his request constitutes a juridicial petition, to which those obliged to give testimonials must respond according to the prescriptions of canon 545, § 1. After securing the testimonials, he is bound to the secrecy demanded of all who receive such testimonials, as provided for in canon 546. The local superior of the novitiate house is not competent to give the testimonials required of a former novice who now seeks entrance into another community. This is the duty of the major superior.[132]

B. *Training of the Novices*

Canon 555, § 1, nn. 2-3 prescribe that the period of the novitiate is to continue for an interval of a continuous year in the novitiate house. Occasion for a novice's leaving the novitiate temporarily

[128] Berutti, *Institutiones,* III, n. 70, II.

[129] Canon 572, § 1, 3°. Cf. Schaefer, *De Religiosis,* n. 225, 5, note 255.

[130] Cf. Schaefer, *loc. cit.*

[131] If a candidate has left a seminary for any cause at all, the religious superior must have recourse to the Sacred Congregation for Religious before the candidate can be admitted.—*AAS,* XXIII (1941), 371. Cf. *The Jurist,* II (1942), 61; Hannan, "Ex-Seminarian and Novice," *The Jurist,* II (1942), 380-382.

[132] Canon 544, § 3. In pre-Code law the local superior of the novitiate house could give such a testimonial if his Order was not divided into provinces. Cf. S. C. super Statu Regularium, declar. 29 maii 1857—*Fontes,* n. 4382.

will sometimes present itself. At such times the local superior will usually be competent to grant permission, for an unlimited number of days, less than thirty, or for a part of these, according to the particular law of the institute.[133]

For absences of fifteen days or less the Code states that the superiors may prescribe that these be supplied.[134] Again recourse must be had to particular law, to decide what superior is meant. In the absence of an express right given to the local superior, it would seem that he does not enjoy this power, but that it is reserved to the major superiors, who also have the exclusive right of prolonging the novitiate.[135]

Attention is called in canon 556, § 3 to the necessity for a just and grave cause being present before any superior may give permission for a novice to remain not only outside the novitiate house but even outside the bounds of the novitiate enclosure.[136] Such a cause would be the serious illness or death of parents, or the necessity of seeking hospital care.[137]

C. *The Novice Master*

On the 19th of March, 1603, Clement VIII (1592-1605) issued a decree, *"Cum ad regularem,"*[138] on the admission and training

[133] Cf. canon 564. For the ordinary permissions the Constitutions will usually designate the novice master as the competent superior. Ordinarily, the local superior can not grant any of his subjects, novices included, permission to remain away from the religious house beyond a few days. Permission for longer absence is usually reserved to the major superior.

[134] Authors list various examples of the interruption of the novitiate. Though the local superior might be involved in granting the necessary permissions, the writer feels that this matter belongs rather to an *ex professo* treatment of the novitiate, rather than to this study. Cf. Coronata, *Institutiones,* I, nn. 582-583, Schaefer, *De Religiosis,* nn. 238-242.

[135] Canon 571, § 2, and canon 634.

[136] The S. C. for Religious issued a decree on May 3, 1914, in which it was stated that the novitiate was interrupted if the novice, even with permission of the superiors, remained *extra novitiatus septa* beyond thirty days.—*AAS,* VI (1914), 229—*Fontes,* n. 4419.

[137] Cf. Schaefer, *De Religiosis,* n. 240.

[138] *Fontes,* n. 189. This decree was renewed and its observance commanded to all superiors by Urban VIII (1623-1644) in a decree issued by the S. C. C., September 21, 1624.—*Fontes,* n. 2454.

of novices which has remained as the basis for a large part of the common law [139] governing the novitiate, and for an even greater part of the particular law of individual institutes. In this decree the novice master's rights and duties are clearly defined, both in relation to the novices and to the local superior. The present Code has adopted much of this decree in the legislation on the training of the novices in religious institutes. The entire decree will frequently serve as a directive norm for the guidance of both novice master and local superior. If a novice, even with the local superior's permission, remains outside the novitiate house more than thirty days, whether these be continuous or not, the superior of the house can not allow him to continue his novitiate, but must demand that the novitiate year be begun over. The novitiate is also interrupted if the novice is dismissed by a competent local superior, or higher superior if the Constitutions do not give this power to the local superior, and if he leaves the house without the superior's permission, with the intention of not returning.[140]

On the other hand, absences of beyond fifteen days but not beyond thirty, do not affect the validity of the novitiate, provided these are supplied after what would normally be the end of the novitiate year, had the absence not been necessary.

The Code has provided for the institution of a novice master, has defined his duties, and stated his relationship to the superiors of the institute in canons 559 and 561. While the local superior is not explicitly excluded in common law from exercising the office of novice master, in the majority of institutes his own duties as superior of the novitiate house will practically always exclude him

[139] This decree is quoted thirteen times as a source of legislation in canons 542 to 571.

[140] Cf. canon 571, § 1. Usually the Constitutions will designate the provincial or other major superior as competent to dismiss a novice, but the Constitutions could also declare the local superior of a novitiate house competent, especially in urgent cases. Cf. *Const. S. O. P.* (1932), n. 111; Schaefer (*De Religiosis*), n. 238. Schaefer states that if the Constitutions are silent as to which superior can dismiss a novice, the major superior alone would seem to be the competent superior, since the right of admission is reserved to him in virtue of canon 543.

from undertaking both offices, especially since the novice master is not to engage in any office or duty which can impede his care and direction of the novices.[141] Moreover, particular law generally declares the office of local superior incompatible with that of novice master.[142]

Renewing the legislation of Clement VIII (1592-1605), as expressed in the decree, *"Cum ad regularem,"* the legislator reserves to the novice master the right and duty of providing for the training of the novices. To him alone is entrusted the government of the novitiate, so that it is not permitted to anyone, except to those superiors designated in the Constitutions and to visitators, to interfere under any pretext in novitiate affairs.[143] In this study the question naturally arises as to the authority of the local superior over the novices and novice master. In whatever pertains to the discipline of the entire house, both professed and novices are subject to the jurisdictional and dominative power of the local superior.[144] Thus he can regulate the hours of Mass and office, and of the other spiritual exercises which the novices and professed undertake in common, as well as the hours for meals. His jurisdictional authority over the novices in certain matters is unquestioned, viz., canon 514, § 1, in regard to the administration of Extreme Unction and Viaticum; of canon 875, § 1, in regard to delegating jurisdiction to hear their confessions; of canon 1245, § 3, with reference to dispensations from the observance of feasts and of fast and abstinence; and of canon 1313, 2° and 1320 in regard to dispensations from vows and oaths. In general, whatever duties the novices have as members of the religious house are regulated by the local superior of the novitiate house, and whatever duties they have strictly as novices are regulated by their own novice master.

As is usual in cases of divided authority, it will be difficult at times to decide what constitutes the internal government of the novitiate, and therefore it will be equally difficult for the local

141 Canon 555, § 3.

142 Cf. *Const. S. O. P.* (1932), n. 295, § II.

143 Canon 561, § 1.

144 Canon 561, § 1.

superior to determine the extent of his authority over the members of the novitiate. The Code gives the general principles but allows the Constitutions of the individual institutes to be more specific in defining both the limits of what constitutes the internal government of the novitiate and how far the local superior may enter into this government.[145]

In the *"Cum ad regularem"* of Clement VII (1592-1605) the local superior was explicitly mentioned as one of those who could enter into the government of the novitiate,[146] but the present Code leaves the determination of what superiors other than the novice master will have power over the novices to the Constitutions. Therefore, if these do not mention the local superior in this connection, he has no power whatsoever in regard to the internal affairs of the novitiate, or to the training and government of the novices, since no such power would then be given him either in the Code or in the particular law of the institute.

As a practical rule, therefore, it must be asserted again that the competency of the local superior to enter into the internal government of the novitiate must be ascertained from the particular law and custom of each institute.

Article VIII. Admission to and Reception of Religious Profession

The Code reserves the right of *admission* to religious profession, whether simple or solemn, to the major superiors.[147] The local

[145] Cf. Larraona, "Consultationes,"—*CpR,* II (1921), 297.

[146] "Habeat etiam Magister plenam, et absolutam potestatem circa Novitiorum institutionem, ac Novitiatus regimen, ita ut in illis nemini (Visitatoribus, ac Superioribus majoribus, vel etiam localibus exceptis) quovis colore se ingerere liceat," § 9—*Fontes,* n. 189. Larraona (*art. cit.,* p. 296) states that in the 1912 schema of the Code, this passage of the *"Cum ad regularem"* was reproduced in these words: "exceptis Visitatoribus, Superioribus maioribus ac localibus (c. 434, § 1)," but that influenced by the growing tendency to subtract all power of the government of the novitiate from the office of the local superior and to reserve it to the novice master and major superiors, the legislators changed the wording to what is now presented in canon 561.

[147] Canon 572, § 1, 2°, and canon 543.

superior can *receive* the profession of his subjects, if he is designated as competent by the Constitutions of the institute.[148] When referring to the prolongation of temporary profession, the Code gives this right to the "legitimate superior," not distinguishing whether he be local or major, but the superior who has the right to admit a religious to profession is undoubtedly meant. Consequently, in view of the legislation in canon 539, as regards the prolongation of the postulancy, and of canon 571, § 2, as regards the prolongation of the novitiate, both of which are reserved to the major superiors, it must be concluded that the prolongation of temporary profession is likewise reserved to the major superiors, and not to the minor local superior.[149] The same may be said as regards the superior competent to permit that temporary profession be anticipated according to canon 577, § 2.[150]

Since particular Constitutions will frequently render the local superior competent to receive the temporary or solemn profession of his subjects, or since he may be delegated by the major superior in individual cases to do so, on him therefore will fall the obligation of seeing to it that the profession is made according to the rite prescribed in the Constitutions,[151] and that the professed sign a document signifying that they have made profession in the Order. The local superior who has received the profession is also obliged to sign the document, which is then kept in the archives of the religious house or province.[152] If the local superior has received the solemn

[148] Cf. canon 572, § 1, 6°; Coronata, *Institutiones*, I, n. 591, 6°, note 2; Beste, *Introductio*, p. 385; Blat, *Commentarium*, II, n. 634; *Const. S. O. P.* (1932), n. 152, § I, 159, § I.

[149] In pre-Code law the local superior of the novitiate house had the faculty of delaying the solemn profession of a subject in those Orders or institutes which were not governed by provincial superiors. Cf. S. C. super Statu Regularium, litt. encycl. *"Neminem latet,"* 19 mart. 1857—*Fontes*, n. 4381.

[150] This would be practical in the renewal of temporary profession to be made by the lay-brothers, if this renewal is prescribed in particular law. Cf. *Const. S. O. P.* (1932), n. 158, § II.

[151] Canon 576, § 1.

[152] Canon 576, § 2. The constitution of Clement VIII, *"Cum ad regularem"* (19 mart. 1603, § 24—*Fontes*, n. 189), required the superior of the novitiate house to keep a special book in which the profession of each novice

profession of a religious, he is obliged personally or through a delegate to send a notification of the fact to the pastor of the church in which the professed was baptized.[153]

In accordance with an Instruction of the Sacred Congregation for Religious, issued on December 1, 1931,[154] moderators of all clerical institutes are obliged to require a written petition before temporary profession from each novice, in which the candidate bears witness to the fact that he has a vocation to the religious and clerical state and that he wishes to embrace the clerical state as a regular.[155] A similar petition is to be demanded by the religious superiors before the religious receives the subdiaconate.[156] In religious Orders of solemn vows, before he makes solemn profession, the religious is obliged to present to his superiors a declaration signed and sworn to concerning his freedom and willingness to receive the order of subdiaconate.[157] The superior in clerical exempt religious Orders is bound to require this same declaration, and oath signed and sworn to a second time, that is, before the religious receives the subdiaconate.[158]

would be registered and the notice signed by the professed and two witnesses. Canon 576, § 2 has revised this legislation so that now only a "document" is referred to, and this is to be signed at least by the professed and the one receiving the profession, and is to be kept in the archives of the institute. Particular law has retained much of the Clementine directions in the various Orders. (The "*Cum ad regularem*" as given in the *Fontes*, n. 109, contains only §§ 1-16 and §§ 20-22. The entire constitution may be found in Vermeersch, *De Religiosis*, II, 137-142.)

153 Canon 576, § 2.

154 *AAS*, XXIV (1932), 74.

155 Instr. n. 14.

156 Instr. n. 16.

157 Instr. n. 18.

158 Instr. n. 17. The Instruction does not make explicit mention of the necessity of taking the oath "again" when the religious of solemn vows is about to receive the subdiaconate, but this is the interpretation which seems correct to the present writer. Some confusion is due to the fact that the Instruction mentions the oath as necessary before the subdiaconate in number 17, and then speaks of the necessity of taking the oath before solemn profession in number 18, whereas in reality the religious makes his solemn pro-

Throughout the entire Instruction, the Sacred Congregation makes mention of "Superiores" without qualifying the term in any way. The question might be asked whether or not the local superior of the house in which the religious is located is referred to in the Instruction.

Though the Instruction was addressed to the supreme moderators of religious institutes, its prescriptions do not bind them alone. No doubt it was the wish of the Sacred Congregation that the supreme moderator in each institute should communicate the Instruction at least to those major superiors in each institute to whom the Constitutions assign the duty of admitting candidates to religious profession and to Sacred Orders, for to these belongs the *ex officio* duty of ascertaining the qualifications of their subjects before admitting them to profession,[159] and in clerical exempt institutes, of issuing dismissorial letters.[160] Since the major superiors frequently delegate the local superior of the house in which the religious resides to undertake these duties, the local superiors also will be obliged to follow the requirements of the Instruction. Therefore, it can be said that though the local superior is not expressly referred to, he is to be included under the general term "Superiores" whenever in virtue of the particular law of the institute,[161] or of the delegation of the major superior, he undertakes the duty of examining his subjects before their admission to profession or Sacred Orders.

fession before receiving the subdiaconate. Practically the same oath is required of the secular clergy before each of the major Orders. Thus, there is no incongruity in requiring the repetition of the oath for religious.

[159] Cf. canon 543.

[160] Cf. canon 964, 2°.

[161] In the Order of Preachers it is prescribed that the testimony, signed and sworn to, demanded by the Instruction, is to be required of each candidate for solemn profession by the superior of the convent (*Const. S. O. P.* [1932], n. 166). Thus the local superior has this duty before solemn profession in the Dominican Order. The same Constitutions do not state what particular superior is to receive the declaration before temporary profession, and again before the subdiaconate (cf. n. 147, n. 733, § I), nor is it determined before what particular superior the candidate for subdiaconate is to give the signed and sworn testimony required in n. 17 of the Instruction (cf. n. 733, § II). The practice seems to be to have the local superior exercise this duty in all cases.

Article IX. The *Studium*

While the direction of the *studium* in all that pertains to the disposition of studies and the hours of class is generally reserved to officials [162] other than the local superior of a house of studies, he is obliged especially to take care that a thorough and most perfect spirit of regular observance exists in the entire religious house, lest otherwise the program of clerical studies should suffer in any way.[163]

His first duty will be to see that in the house of studies the common life may flourish in perfection, for otherwise the students can not be licitly promoted to tonsure or any of the Orders. Moreover, he should see to it that the students and masters make the annual retreat, and, unless lawfully impeded, assist at meditation and other community exercises, and that they have an opportunity to receive the Sacrament of Penance weekly and the Holy Eucharist daily.[164]

The Holy See has ever been solicitous for the welfare of her clerical students, and in canon 590 she seeks to free the clerical student from all occupations which might impede him in his studies or interfere with the curriculum as followed out in the *studium*. The canon as applied to the local superior prohibits him from assigning any duties to the professors or clerical students which would call them away from their studies or from class.

To further the progress of study, the local superior may prudently dispense his subjects from some of the community exercises and even from the choral obligation, as often as this might seem

[162] The spiritual care of the students is reserved in a special way to the *magister spiritus* (canon 588). His duties in regard to the students and his relation to the local superior can be compared to the duties of the master of novices towards the novices, and to the relationship of the novice master to the local superior. The professed as students are subject to the *magister spiritus* and to the officials of the *studium*; as members of the local community they are subject to the local superior. The local superior and the *magister spiritus*, according to the mind of the legislator, should be distinct persons. (Cf. Canuto, "De regimine domus studiorum in religione clericali exempta ad normam can. 588"—*Apollinaris*, IX (1936), 35-39.)

[163] Cf. canon 587, § 2; 588, § 3. Canuto, *art. cit.*, pp. 27-29.

[164] Canon 588, § 3, compared with canon 595.

necessary for the advancement of study.[165] This power of dispensation in the local superior is to be exercised in particular cases. The Constitutions will usually provide for dispensations and exemptions of a permanent nature.

The prohibition of canon 589, § 2, while it would not forbid the local superior to allow student priests and professors the occasional exercise of ministerial work, as long as such duty does not interfere with studies or with the class schedule, does nevertheless forbid the habitual use of student priests and professors in preaching, or in hearing confessions or in other exterior works of the institute. In regard to the student priests, this can be seen more clearly by a comparison of this canon and the declaration of the Sacred Congregation for Religious forbidding any exercise of the care of souls to student priests who have been ordained before the middle of their fourth year of theology.[166] The same Sacred Congregation makes this a grave obligation in conscience for all superiors.[167]

Prummer writes that the "ministerium animarum, dummodo sit

[165] Cf. canon 589, § 2. Clement VIII (1592-1605) recognized the power of superiors to dispense from the choral obligation students, lectors and preachers, but restricted the use of such dispensation in the case of the lectors and preachers to "iis tantum diebus, quibus eos legere aut praedicare contigerit."—decr. *"Nullus omnino,"* 25 iul. 1599, § 1—*Fontes,* n. 187. Since the Code uses the word "tempore studiorum" in canon 589, § 2, authors agree that in the present law such dispensations are not necessarily to be restricted to the days upon which class is held, but can be extended also to the time of vacation, if such a practice fosters a spirit of study, even during the vacation time. Prümmer, *Manuale I. C.,* qu. 220, r. 5; Coronata, *Institutiones,* I, n. 596; Berutti, *Institutiones,* III, n. 103. Passerinus (1594-1677) (*De Statibus,* Q. CLXXXVII, art. I) and other authors interpret the decree of Clement VIII to include authority to dispense even during the time of vacation if the lectors use this time to prepare future classes and methods of teaching.

[166] October 27, 1923—*AAS,* XV (1923), 549. The words of the declaration "vetito interim quocumque animarum ministerio" seem at first to prohibit every exercise of the ministry, but the following words "ne *destinetur* concionibus habendis . . ." etc., would seem to allow the local superior the occasional use of student priests for these duties. Cf. Vermeersch, "Annotations,"—*Periodica,* XII (1923), 156.

[167] S. C. de Religiosis, declar. 27 oct. 1923—*AAS,* XV (1923), 549.

breve et valde moderatum, videtur potius prodesse quam obesse studio theologico. . . ."[168] Such an opinion would seem to aid the local superior in judging whether or not he will feel justified in assigning professors in the *studium* to ministerial work, provided always that the work assigned is truly "breve et valde moderatum," and would seem also to be reconcilable with the declaration of the Sacred Congregation for Religious to which reference has just been made.

Another excellent means for the promotion of study, especially among those who have already completed the ordinary philosophical and theological course as given in the houses of study before the ordination of a religious, is provided for in the monthly discussion and solution of moral and liturgical cases, in those houses of clerical religious where there are at least six members, four of whom are priests.[169] It will be the duty of the local superior to preside at these conferences or to delegate some other capable subject to do so. If he should so desire, he may provide for a discussion, disputation or exposition of some dogmatic, scriptural, canonical, philosophical or historical point.[170]

Canon 591 prescribes attendance for all the professed clerics, whether they are still engaged in study or have completed their course, but allows the particular law of the Constitutions to make exception to this rule. Therefore, the local superior will be guided by these prescriptions, especially in regard to determining whether separate conferences are to be held for the younger students, or whether they are obliged to attend the general conference held for all.

Article X. Obligations of Religious

Almost from the beginning of monasticism the Popes constantly exhorted religious and religious superiors to greater fervor in carry-

168 *Manuale, I. C.*, qu. 220, r. 5.

169 Canon 591. The canon seems to presuppose an oral discussion and solution of the cases proposed, but particular law may demand that those who are absent or impeded at the time the conference is held present the solution in writing, either to the local or provincial superior. Cf. *Const. S. O. P.* (1932), n. 191.

170 Cf. Berutti, *Institutiones*, III, n. 106, III, b.

ing out the Rule and Constitutions through which they strove to attain perfection. But only a few of the later papal enactments are referred to in the sources for canon 595. Clement VIII (1592-1605), writing to the Servites, admonished all their superiors to the exact observance of all that the Rule and Constitutions prescribed concerning mental prayer, silence, the fast, and the chapter of faults.[171] The same decree was renewed by Urban VIII (1623-1644) in 1624,[172] and in 1814 the Sacred Congregation of Bishops and Regulars urged again the observance of all the spiritual exercises previously prescribed by the sacred canons, by apostolic decrees, or by individual Rules and Constitutions. It was the work of the local superior particularly to see to it that all these regulations were put into effect in the convent.[173]

As regards the reception of Penance and the Holy Eucharist, the religious were urged to partake of these sacraments more frequently than the laity, who were usually content with the yearly confession and communion prescribed in the IV General Council of the Lateran (1215).[174] Clement V (1305-1314) prescribed that all religious should confess once a month and receive Holy Communion on the first Sunday of every month,[175] but the Council of Trent recommended that all the faithful receive Communion each time they assisted at Mass.[176] On December 17, 1890, the Sacred Congregation of Bishops and Regulars decreed that superiors were to permit all to approach the Holy Eucharist who had the permission of their confessor[177] and commanded all local superiors to put the prescriptions of the decree into effect.[178] The proximate source for all the legislation urging the superior's promotion of frequent Communion is the decree of the Sacred Congregation of the Council,

[171] Decr. *"Nullus omnino,"* 25 iul. 1599, § 25—*Fontes*, n. 187.

[172] S. C. C. decr. 21 sept. 1624, § 1—*Fontes*, n. 2454.

[173] S. C. Ep. et Reg., decr. 22 aug. 1814, n. XI—*Fontes*, n. 1893.

[174] C. 12, X, *de poenitentiis et remissionibus*, V, 38.

[175] C. 1, *de statu monachorum vel canonicorum regularium*, III, 10, in Clem.

[176] Sess. XXII, *de sacrificio missae*, c. 6.

[177] Decr. *"Quemadmodum,"* § 5—*Fontes*, n. 2017.

[178] *Ibidem*, § 7.

"Sacra Tridentina Synodus" of December 20, 1905.[179] This decree commanded the promotion of frequent and even daily Communion, and ruled that the superiors of each house see to it that the decree be read in common each year.

A. *The Retreat, Daily Spiritual Exercises, Weekly Confession, Frequent Holy Communion*

Canon 595 obliges all superiors to see to it that those under their care fulfill the daily, weekly and annual obligations generally associated with the life of a professed religious. Specifically mentioned are the annual retreat, attendance at Mass, mental prayer and other spiritual obligations required of the religious by their Rule and Constitutions, weekly confession and frequent Holy Communion.

Both the major and minor superiors are obliged to see to the fulfillment of this duty, but the obligation will more directly regard the local superior "intra fines sui muneris," for upon him especially devolves the ordinary and daily direction of the religious to the end of the institute. Therefore while the major superior will be concerned in a general way with these obligations for all the religious of his Order or province, especially at the time of visitation, the local superior must consider such obligations a part of his daily solicitude and care for the religious of his own house.[180] Moreover the local superior [181] of a house of studies is obliged to see that all these obligations are carried out in a most perfect manner, even more so than in any other house.[182]

The first obligation mentioned has reference to the annual retreat

[179] *Fontes,* n. 4326.

[180] Beste, *Introductio,* p. 405, without denying the power of a superior even by precept to oblige his subjects to fulfill their obligations, urges that he do so rather by instruction and exhortation. Clement VIII urged superiors to provide for a weekly instruction on religious discipline and regular observance, that the observance of the Rule and Constitutions might bear greater fruit.—Decr. *"Nullus omnino,"* 25 iul. 1599, § 25—*Fontes,* n. 187.

[181] Cf. Blat, *Commentarium,* II, 651.

[182] Canon 588, § 3.

required of all religious. Ordinarily the Constitutions of each institute will prescribe the manner, and the length of time for the annual retreat, and the local superior will be required only to see that such regulations are carried out. Whatever details of time or of place or of other circumstances are not prescribed in the Constitutions would seem to be left to the discretion of the local superior, unless the provincial or general superior should prescribe otherwise. In the event that the determination of the length of the retreat is left to the local superior, he would seem to have a wide latitude of from a few days to a month.[183]

The local superior is obliged also to see that all his subjects who are not lawfully impeded assist at daily Mass[184] and assiduously apply themselves to mental prayer and to the performance of any other exercises of piety prescribed by the Rule and Constitutions. Again particular law and custom must be primarily considered as to what constitutes a lawful impediment, but the local superior would certainly feel safe in requiring less evidence of a lawful impediment to the daily assistance at the community Mass for a priest-religious who daily celebrates his own Mass, than he would require of a religious who is not also a priest, and would not be able to assist at Mass at any other time. In regard to the practice of mental prayer the superior will see to it that it is made in the manner prescribed by the particular law of the institute; in the absence of any such law, he himself will be the judge of the manner in which this prescript of the Code is to be carried out. The Code likewise urges the superior to look after the performance of whatever other spiritual exercises may be prescribed in the Rule and Constitutions. Under this heading, would often be included the daily recitation of the Rosary, and possibly visits to the Blessed

[183] Cf. Pius XI, Ency. Litt., *"Mens nostra,"* 20 dec. 1929—*AAS,* XXI (1930), 689; Fanfani thinks the time ought not to be less than one week—*De Iure Religiosorum,* n. 255. This opinion is at variance with the minimum of a "few days" referred to (but not therefore commended) by Pius XI in the above-mentioned encyclical.

[184] This canon does not require or permit the local superior to demand the *daily* celebration of Mass by his priest-religious. The frequency of the celebration of Mass is prescribed by canon 805. Cf. *infra,* chap. VIII, art. II, pp. 133-134.

Sacrament, and examination of conscience, all of which would be carried out according to the direction of the local superior if specific determinations are not given in the particular law of the institute. Berutti notes that no religious should be required to undertake duties of such a nature as often (*saepius*) to prevent him from fulfilling these obligations in a suitable, worthy, and complete manner.[185]

Religious are indirectly bound to approach the Sacrament of Penance at least weekly, in virtue of the direct obligation placed on the religious superior of taking care that his subjects do so. The obligation is expressed by the word "curent" and as used here seems to involve more than mere encouragement even though the Code Commission interpreted the word "curent" of canon 1451, § 1 to mean "suadendum est." [185a] It may be the duty of the local superior to provide his subjects with the confessors required by canon 518, § 1. [186] According to a private Instruction issued by the Sacred Congregation of the Sacraments on the 8th of December, 1938, the superior is obliged to see that his subjects "have the opportunity" to make a confession also shortly before the time of Communion.[187]

In order to determine whether or not his subjects are fulfilling the obligation of weekly confession, the local superior has the right to ask his subjects whether they are fulfilling the law of weekly confession, and where, and when. He may even go so far as to require some proof of the subject's having approached the tribunal "si forte prudenter exigi videatur." [188]

With reference to the promotion and reception of frequent and even daily Holy Communion, canon 595, §§ 2 and 3 adopt many of the norms established by Pius X in the decree *"Sacra Tridentina Synodus"* of December 20, 1905.[189] The local superior is obliged first of all to promote the frequent and even daily reception

[185] *Institutiones*, III, n. 110.

[185a] 12 nov. 1922, VI—*AAS*, XIV (1922), 663.

[186] Cf. *infra*, p. 158.

[187] No. II, 2. Cf. Bouscaren, *The Canon Law Digest*, Supplement (1941), p. 99.

[188] Cf. Schaefer, *De Religiosis*, n. 339, 1, (c).

[189] *Fontes*, n. 4326.

of Holy Communion, and secondly, to permit his subjects who are properly disposed, frequent and even daily access to the Sacrament.

The Instruction issued by the Sacred Congregation of the Sacraments in 1938 endeavored "to prevent as far as possible all abuse," in this matter.[190] Even though the Instruction was issued privately and addressed only to the local ordinaries and major superiors of religious Orders, its prescriptions will ordinarily be carried out in religious institutes by the local superior, and will certainly serve as a directive norm in fulfilling the obligation imposed upon him by canon 595, § 3. In accordance with this Instruction the local superior in exhorting his subjects to frequent and daily Holy Communion, must at the same time inform them that daily Communion is not of obligation, and that those who wish to receive the Holy Eucharist daily must be in the state of grace, and must do so with a right or pious intention.[191]

The Sacred Congregation seems also to insist upon the continued observance of the necessity of the penitent's obtaining the advice of the confessor before receiving daily, as prescribed by the decree of Pius X, *"Sacra Tridentina Synodus,"* n. 5.[192] Therefore it would seem that the local superior is still obliged to insist upon this condition, even though some authors [193] teach otherwise in view of the present common practice of all religious of receiving Holy Communion daily. The superior is likewise instructed to tell his subjects that "he is in general much pleased with their frequent approach to the Holy Table, but that he has no word of reproach for those who do not receive." [194] Finally, though the local superior

[190] 8 dec. 1938, n. II—Bouscaren, *The Canon Law Digest,* Supplement (1941), pp. 97-104.

[191] Instr., n. II, 1.

[192] Instr., n. II, 1, (b).

[193] Schaefer, *De Religiosis,* n. 340. Vermeersch-Creusen (*Epitome,* I, n. 638) say that the religious is not bound to a positive interrogation of the confessor, but that daily Communion is considered to be tacitly approved. Perhaps this opinion may still be maintained, if the religious has at least the tacit approval of his confessor, which in practically all cases would seem to be true.

[194] Instr. II, 3, (a). Cf. Bouscaren, *The Canon Law Digest,* Supplement (1941), p. 102.

will always be most solicitous that the sick members of the community also have an opportunity to receive Holy Communion frequently and even daily, "he should see to it that Holy Communion be not brought to the sick who do not expressly ask for it."[195] The local superior can certainly establish some method by which the sick can signify their intention of receiving Holy Communion without making it necessary for them to ask the superior himself each day, but it seems to be the intention of the Sacred Congregation that they make this request (not necessarily to the superior) explicitly each time they wish to receive Holy Communion.

While canon 595 demands that each religious be permitted access to frequent and even daily Communion, the same canon gives the local superior authority to prohibit the approach of a religious who has, since his last sacramental confession, given grave scandal to the community, or committed a serious external fault, until he shall have again approached the Sacrament of Penance.[196] The purpose of this canon appears to be principally disciplinary, i. e., the faculty given is prescribed in the interests of the community, rather than as a penalty imposed upon the offending religious. Therefore a religious who has given grave scandal or committed an external fault which is serious only in that it has interfered very notably with the discipline of the religious house, even though he be not subjectively guilty of grave sin, may be required by the superior to go to Confession before receiving Holy Communion.[197]

Once the subject has presented himself at the confessional, the superior cannot prohibit his reception of Holy Communion, in virtue

[195] Instr., II, 3, (d).

[196] The canon repeats the words of the decree of the S. C. Ep. and Reg., "*Quemadmodum,*" 17 dec. 1890, n. 5—*Fontes,* n. 2017.

[197] Beste, *Introductio,* p. 405. Cf. Vermeersch-Creusen, *Epitome,* I, n. 698, § 3. Schaefer (*De Religiosis,* n. 341) disagrees with this interpretation and states that the scandal or fault must be theologically grave, "cum simus in odiosis, et canone 901 perspecto rectiore videtur sententia, quae dicit: requiri peccata theologice gravia et externa." Such a conclusion in the opinion of the writer would be justified only if the end of the law were essentially penal, rather than disciplinary.

of this canon, since the superior is not given the right to ascertain whether or not the penitent asked for or received absolution.[198]

B. The Religious Habit

The seriousness with which former writers insisted upon the constant wearing of the religious habit may be noted from a study of the sources given for canon 596. Boniface VIII (1294-1303) decreed *ipso facto* excommunication against a religious who deliberately laid aside his habit, whether in school or any other place, unless he had the permission of his own proper superior acting on the advice of his council.[199] Clement V (1305-1314) prohibited religious from wearing any other clothing except their religious habit, without reasonable cause. Violators were to be punished by their superiors.[200] The Council of Trent prohibited superiors from granting permission to any regular to wear the habit of his Order secretly.[201]

Piatus writes that the faculty of dispensing directly from this common law obligation was never given to the religious superiors, but that they could dispense indirectly when, e. g., for just cause, they commanded or permitted some work to be done which required the laying aside of the habit. In case of doubt about the necessity of putting aside the habit, recourse was to be had to the superior.[202]

In the present legislation the penalty for laying aside the religious habit is no longer attended by *ipso facto* excommunication. Religious are to wear the habit both inside and outside the convent. Boniface VIII (1294-1303) asked only that there be a just cause,[203] and pre-Code authors [204] held that a reasonable cause was

[198] Cf. Blat, *Commentarium,* II, 662. The religious is of course bound not to receive Holy Communion sacrilegiously (cf. canon 856).

[199] C. 2, *ne clericis vel monachi saecularibus negotiis se immisceant,* III, 24, in VI°.

[200] C. 2, *de vita et honestate clericorum,* III, 1, in Clem.

[201] Sess. XXV, *de regularibus,* c. 19.

[202] *Praelectiones,* I, qu. 344. Cf. Suarez, *De religione,* tr. VIII, lib. I, cap. V, n. 16.

[203] C. 2, *de vita et honestate clericorum,* III, 1, in Clem.

[204] Suarez, *De religione,* tr. VIII, lib. I, cap. V, n. 13. Bouix, *De Jure Regularium,* II, 558. Piatus, *Praelectiones,* I, qu. 344.

sufficient to permit a religious not to wear the habit. The present Code requires a grave cause, leaving the judgment of its gravity to the major superior, and in case of urgent necessity, to the local superior. Certainly convenience or the desire of getting around more freely in public would not in themselves constitute a grave cause.[205] Certainly travel through cities or countries hostile to the faith would be sufficient reason for judging that a grave cause exists.[206] Between the two extremes the local superior may be guided by the customs of his Order and province, as well as by the regulations which may have been enacted for the good of the Church in particular localities. Ordinarily however the local superior would seem to have little occasion to make use of his right in this matter, since usually the reasons sufficiently grave to permit habitual use of other clothing can be foreseen in time to consult the provincial or other major superior, while often local custom will have long previously established a manner of action in this regard.[207]

C. The Cloister

Monks were often prohibited from going out of their monasteries without the permission of the Abbot,[208] and were not permitted to go out at all to preach to the people.[209] The mendicants, because of the nature of their work, were much more lenient in giving the superiors power to send the friars away from the cloister on apostolic work. Nevertheless the permission of the superior was always needed. The Council of Trent renewed the previous legislation on this point, and forbade the regulars to leave the cloister without permission of their superior.[210] Clement VII (1592-1605) decreed that

[205] Cf. Schaefer, *De Religiosis,* n. 344, 4. The Sacred Congregation for Religious forbade religious who have permission to go to certain health resorts to leave aside their habit for any cause whatsoever—15 iul. 1926; cf. *CpR,* VII (1927), 295. (Not published in *AAS.*)

[206] Vermeersch-Creusen, *Epitome,* I, n. 699.

[207] No permission of any superior is required for what pre-Code writers termed the "material" deposition of the religious habit, that is, in cases of ordinary necessity.

[208] C. 35, C. XVI, q. 1.

[209] C. 11, C. XVI, q. 1.

[210] Sess. XXV, *de regularibus,* c. 4.

each superior was to appoint a "janitor" who would guard the door of the religious house, allowing no religious egress unless he was accompanied by a companion and had the permission of the superiors.[211]

The "passive cloister" was observed also in the exclusion of women from the monasteries of men. St. Pius V (1566-1572) commanded that all women be kept out of the monasteries, and that the superiors who introduced or admitted them were to be deprived of their office and rendered ineligible for other offices, and besides were *ipso facto* suspended.[212] Pius IX (1846-1878) in the list of excommunications reserved to the Holy Father, included that against superiors who admitted women to the cloister of men religious.[213]

The Code contains the following legislation affecting the local superior in regard to the cloister:

In every canonically constituted religious house of regulars, even though not a formal house, the papal enclosure must be observed.[214] It belongs to the provincial or other major superior or even to the general chapter, according as the Constitutions of the institute decide, and not to the local superior, to prescribe accurately those parts of the house which are to be considered as cloistered, and also to change the original limits of the enclosure.[215] Ordinarily the duty of seeing to the actual observance of the cloister will fall to the local superior [216]

The first duty of the local superior therefore will be to acquaint himself with the confines of the cloister as previously constituted by the major superior.

As regards the entrance of others into the cloister, under no condition whatsoever may the local superior allow women, other than the wives of those who are the supreme rulers of the state, entrance

211 Decr. "*Nullus omnino,*" 25 iul. 1599, § 11—*Fontes,* n. 187.

212 Const. "*Regularium,*" 24 oct. 1566—*Fontes,* n. 115.

213 Const. "*Apostolicae Sedis,*" 12 oct. 1869, § II, 7—*Fontes,* n. 552.

214 Canon 597, § 1. Since this study is concerned only with the local superior in religious Orders, only the papal cloister is referred to in this section.

215 Canons 597, § 3; 599, § 1.

216 Cf. canons 598, 599, § 2; 606, § 1.

into the cloister, not even, as Vermeersch-Creusen point out,[216a] when there might be a question of allowing the mother of one of the religious to visit her son who is very seriously ill. Men are not forbidden entrance to the cloistered sections of the house by any prohibition of the Code, but the particular regulations of the Order or province might forbid the superior to allow them access to the enclosure, except perhaps in an individual case, but not habitually.

For a good reason the local superior may permit women to enter places which are outside the cloister but which are reserved for pupils of the institute or other students.[217] Schaaf writes that all schools maintained by the religious for day-students as well as for boarders, fall under the prescriptions of this canon, and notes also that it will depend upon the prudence and good judgment of the superior to decide who shall be admitted and at what time and under what circumstances.[218] It is to be remembered also, as stated in the canon, that permission is given to enter only such places as are outside the cloister. The local superior could not grant such a permission to women, if the classes for the pupils were held within the cloister.

No permission of the local superior is needed for women to enter other parts of the house outside the enclosure set aside expressly for the purpose of providing a place for the instruction of women, or for the making or mending of vestments, clothing, etc. On the other hand, permission of the superior is required for the religious themselves to go out of the cloister into such places.[219]

It may also be noted that even where permission has been granted for the entrance of men into the cloister, or of women to the places set aside for visitors, the local superior will always be obliged to see

[216a] *Epitome*, I, n. 704.

[217] Canon 599, § 2; cf. Schaefer, *De Religiosis*, n. 349.

[218] *The Cloister*, The Catholic University of America Canon Law Studies, n. 13 (Washington, D. C.: The Catholic University of America, 1921), pp. 102-103.

[219] Berutti (*Institutiones*, III, n. 114, II) gives as an example places in the houses of regulars reserved for religious women who prepare the food or mend the clothing of the members of the convent.

that the discipline of the house and its religious atmosphere be always preserved in spite of the admission of visitors.[220]

A local superior who introduces or admits women into the cloister incurs *ipso facto* excommunication, and can be deprived of his office and of his right to vote and to be elected.[221] Much has been written concerning the meaning of the words "introduces" and "admits," but the conclusion of authors [222] who have studied the matter thoroughly, is that the problem of whether or not the penalties have been incurred is to be solved in accordance with the degree of cooperation involved, as determined in canons 2231 and 2309. Therefore if the local superior cooperates to the extent of physically helping the woman to enter, or opens a door leading into the cloister or even without physically cooperating, gives advice as to entrance without which the woman would not have entered, and does not retract before she enters, he incurs the excommunication, and may be deprived of his office and of active and passive voice. The local superior is charged with the duty of seeing to the observance of the cloister, and therefore if his neglect in this matter amounts to consent in the offense of the woman violating the law, he also will incur the penalties; if the neglect is not considered formal coöperation he would not incur the penalties of canon 2342, but could be punished in some other way by his superiors for neglect of duty.

The observance of the cloister also involves duties on the part of the local superior in regard to permitting religious to leave the enclosure.[223] The legislation in this canon as it affects the local superior may be divided into two parts: his duties with relation to permission for the ordinary temporary egress from the cloister, and his relation to the permission necessary for absence of some duration.

The canon charges all superiors with the duty of accurately observing the prescriptions of their own Constitutions on either the egress of their own religious, or on the receiving of visiting externs. The Code thus leaves the matter of the ordinary going out from

[220] Canon 605.

[221] Canon 2342, 2°.

[222] Cf. Schaaf, *The Cloister*, pp. 92 ff. Smith, *The Penal Law for Religious*, pp. 66 ff.

[223] Canons 606; 644, §§ 1, 3.

the cloister to particular legislation. Usually the individual Constitutions will permit the local superior to grant permission for his subjects to leave the enclosure for the space of at most a few days, reserving any further prolongation to the provincial or higher superior. Nevertheless the local superior's permission need not always be explicit or express. Implicit and tacit or presumed permission may within legitimate bounds (to be determined by the particular law of the institute) be considered as sufficient to prevent a religious from actively violating the cloister, or from becoming an apostate or fugitive.[224] Generally the Constitutions will give explicit instructions as to the conditions to be fulfilled by those who with permission leave the cloister, and it will be the duty of the local superior more than of any other superior to see to their observance, lest, as Berutti points out, "the end toward which the law of the cloister is ordained be frustrated." [225]

It is not permitted to any superior in giving these permissions to allow his subjects to dwell outside a house of his own institute, except for a grave and just cause, and for as brief a time as possible. This canon does not forbid the religious to dwell outside his own religious house, but outside a house of his own religious institute. The distinction is of some importance, but is generally understood. While permission is always required for a religious to go to another house of the institute, such a permission is not governed by the prescriptions of the second paragraph of canon 606, which prohibits a superior from giving permission to a religious to remain outside any house of the institute. The gravity and justice of a cause will be judged by the local superior, if permission necessary for the absence be within the limits of his competence; otherwise it will be the province of the major superior to decide whether the cause is sufficiently grave or not. Generally admitted as grave and just causes are: the serious illness or death of a parent or member of the family, the necessity of hospitalization on the part of the religious himself, and the necessity of recovering one's strength and energy after periods of strenuous labor. If the absence is to exceed six

224 Cf. canon 644.

225 *Institutiones*, III, n. 120, I.

months, except in the case of the absence of those who are engaged in study, the permission of the Holy See is required. Generally the local superior would not be able to grant permissions for a period of time relatively long but even much shorter than six months. Particular law must be consulted in this matter.

Closely allied in nature to the permission which a local superior gives to a subject to leave the cloister, is the permission which particular law may require before religious subjects are permitted to correspond with others in writing. The Code does not legislate specifically in this matter, but refers to the practice indirectly when it states in canon 611 that all religious may send letters to the Holy See, to the representative of the Pope in each nation, to the Cardinal Protector of the institute, to their own major superiors, and even to the local superior if he is absent from the religious house. The local superior therefore must respect this concession of the Code, and may demand its observance by others in regard to correspondence addressed to him while he is outside the house.

D. Parochial and Diocesan Work

Canon 608, § 1 exhorts superiors to furnish help to the local ordinaries whenever the needs of the faithful require it. The canon is based on pre-Code legislation as contained in the Papal constitution, *"Super cathedram,"* [226] of Boniface VIII (1294-1303), and the constitution, *"Dudum,"* [227] of Clement V (1305-1314). These constitutions regulated the extent of diocesan and parochial work which religious were permitted to perform. Since the history of the parochial and diocesan work of religious parallels the history of their relation to the Sacrament of Penance and to preaching, a thorough treatment of it will be reserved to the historical section of the local superior's jurisdiction in regard to the Sacrament of Penance and to preaching.[228] It will be sufficient to note here that the religious

[226] 18 febr. 1300—c. 2, *de sepulturis*, III, 6, in Extravag. com.—Potthast, *Regesta Pontificum Romanorum inde ab A. post Christum natum MCXCVIII ad A. MCCCIV* (2 vols., Berolini, 1874-1875), n. 24913. Hereafter cited as Potthast, *Regesta*.

[227] 6 maii 1312—c. 2, *de sepulturis*, III, 7, in Clem.

[228] Cf. *infra*, chap. VIII, art. 3, and chap. IX, art. 5.

superior's permission was always required before religious could engage in any parochial or diocesan work. It is not clear that the local superior was always competent to give the permission required for preaching and the hearing of the confessions of the faithful at least before the V General Council of the Lateran (1512-1517). At that time reference was made to the "*Superiores*" without qualification. It seems therefore that the local superior could give his subjects the necessary permission to engage in all parochial and diocesan work, at least after the V General Council of the Lateran, unless particular law reserved the granting of such permission to the higher superiors.[229]

Canon 608, § 1 presupposes that the religious will be designated by their superiors to aid in parochial work, and then urges the superiors to take care that those designated should willingly stand ready to assist the bishop and pastors in the work of the diocese. Reserving for a later chapter the discussion of the superior competent to present the religious to the bishop for faculties to preach and to hear the confessions of the faithful, the writer wishes to assert here only that the local superior will be included in the prescriptions of this canon unless the particular law of the institute declares him incompetent to act in these matters. Authors consulted do not treat the question of what superiors are referred to, but in view of the principle adopted earlier in this study of including the local superior under any general reference to superiors used in the Code, it is again maintained that if the Constitutions do not reserve the supervision of this work to the major superiors, even the local superior has this duty. It would even seem to be he rather than any other who would be charged with designating those already approved for hearing confessions or for preaching to exercise these faculties in particular cases, especially in the ordinary parochial work undertaken by his particular house.

In the supposition that it is frequently the duty of the local superior to supply religious for such work, it will be his duty to supply priests to aid in whatever parochial work is compatible with the

[229] Cf. Leo X, const. "*Dum intra,*" 19 dec. 1516—Mansi, XXII, 970; *BRT*, V, 685; *Fontes*, n. 72.

work of the Order, and with the observance of religious discipline in the house. Obviously he would not be compelled to accede to the request of a bishop or pastor to send all his subjects out on parochial work, with the result that the choral obligation, for instance, could not be fulfilled. If certain subjects are engaged in teaching or in study, naturally this work should not be seriously interfered with in order to supply parochial needs. However all such assignments are left to the prudent judgment of the local superior, who mindful both of the needs of the faithful, and of the obligations of his own subjects, will attempt to serve both.

The local superior will also be obliged to see that the carrying out of the religious functions in his church does not interfere with the catechetical instruction or with the explanation of the Gospel given in the parochial church.[280] If the pastor of a neighboring parish felt that these functions were being interfered with he could have recourse to the local ordinary, who in turn could request the local superior to remedy the situation.

E. The Religious Pastor

Closely allied to the local superior's duty of seeing that his subjects assist actively in parochial and diocesan work are the obligations arising from the fact that the church which his religious community uses is often a parochial church.[281] According to canon 452, § 1 a parish cannot, without an apostolic indult, be united "pleno iure" to a moral person in such a way that the moral person is the pastor. Therefore permission of both the Sacred Congregation of the Council and of the Sacred Congregation of Religious is required if the superiors of an Order should desire to hold the parish in the name of the religious house, appointing the superior of the house or another religious as vicar. If the local superior is appointed to be pastor, an additional indult would seem to be required since the two offices are apparently incompatible.[282] Immemorial

[280] Canon 609, § 3.

[281] Cf. canon 609, § 1.

[282] Blat (*Commentarium,* II, n. 500) bases this incompatibility on a decision of the Sacred Congregation of Regular Discipline, which he dates as of May 28, 1845. This decree is not listed in the *Fontes,* but a similar decree of

custom or privilege might be adduced as permitting the cumulation of the offices, but either would have to be proved.

Often the local superior may be designated in the Constitutions as competent to present one of his subjects to the local ordinary as a candidate for the office of pastor.[233] If the local superior is given authority in the Constitutions to present the religious who is to exercise the office of pastor or parochial vicar,[234] he may also remove such a pastor or vicar after advising the local ordinary of his intention, and even without the latter's consent. The local ordinary has the same right without being obliged to seek the consent of the local superior.[235]

If the pastorate attached to a conventual church becomes vacant, the local superior may have the right of consent to the ordinary's choice of a vicar econome, if the Constitutions give him such a right.[236] Whether he has this right or not, he is explicitly desig-

the same Sacred Congregation, dated May 28, 1715, may be found in Ferraris, *Prompta Bibliotheca Canonica, Iuridica, Moralis, Theologica, necnon Ascetica, Polemica, Rubricistica, Historica* (11 vols., Venetiis, 1782-1794), s. v. "Parochus," Art. II, n. 85. (Hereafter cited as *Prompta Bibliotheca.*) Blat also believes that the local superior is forbidden to hold both offices in virtue of canon 452, § 1, which permits a moral person to retain only the habitual care of a parish. Since the local superior takes the place of the moral person (the religious house in this case) in its relation with the actual pastor (cf. canon 609, § 1, compared with canon 415, § 3), it is not difficult to see the incongruity of having the same person exercise both offices, especially in the event of a conflict of rights as between the pastor and the religious house. Consequently, apart from any argument as to the advisability of a superior of a religious house, charged with the spiritual care of his subjects, becoming implicated in parochial business, the two offices may be said to be incompatible. Particular law might possibly declare them so. (Cf. *Const. S. O. P.* [1932], n. 295, § 2.)

233 Canons 456, 1425, § 2. Augustine (*Commentary,* II, 526) writes that generally speaking only the major superiors are intended. This conclusion has the added value of being true in practice, but even Augustine admits that "the competent superior is he whom the Constitutions of the respective Order clothe with the right of presentation" (*loc. cit.*).

234 Canons 456, 471, § 3.

235 Canons 454, § 5; 471, § 3.

236 Canon 472, 1°. Ordinarily it would seem that the local superior would enjoy this right only if he were also competent to present a candidate for the parochial office in accordance with canon 456.

nated in canon 472, 2° as the ruler of the parish in the interim between the vacancy of the parish and the appointment of the vicar econome, and it becomes his duty to notify the local ordinary as soon as the vacancy occurs.

Canon 474 refers to the vicar substitute of a parish, and in the appointment of such a vicar in the absence of a religious pastor the Code gives definite regulations. In addition to the permission of the local ordinary, the religious pastor needs the consent of his own superior if he wishes to absent himself from the parish.[237] His substitute must be approved both by the local ordinary and by the competent religious superior who may be the local superior, since the canon again employs the word "Superior" without restriction.[238]

The approval of the substitute by the local superior while certainly necessary as a matter of religious obedience on the part of the religious who will act as substitute, is nevertheless not necessary for the validity or liceity of his assistance at any marriage which might be performed in the parish during the time that he acts as substitute, as long as he has the permission of the local ordinary.[239] A similar answer was given by the Pontifical Commission to the question as to whether the vicar substitute could give another priest permission to assist at a marriage in the parish, after the approval of the ordinary but before the approval of the substitute by the religious superior.[240] Coronata notes that the reply of the Pontifical Commission of July 14, 1922, was given in reference to assistance at marriage, but believes that the principle can be extended to other acts of jurisdiction.[241] If so, the local superior's permission seems to be necessary only as a matter of religious discipline, since according to this opinion, all of the parochial acts of the religious vicar would be valid and licit without the superior's permission, as long as the vicar had the permission of the local ordinary. Nevertheless the failure of the vicar to secure the permission of his religious superior before accepting the position as vicar substitute would cer-

[237] Canon 465, § 4.
[238] Canon 465, § 4.
[239] *PCI*, 14 iul. 1922—*AAS*, XIV (1922), 527, V.
[240] 20 maii 1923—*AAS*, XVI (1924), 114. V.
[241] *Institutiones*, I, n. 483, I, 2°, (b), note 3.

tainly be a violation of canon 465, § 4, which demands the approval of both the religious superior and the ordinary before the vicar substitute can licitly assume the position.

In regard to the appointment of the vicar adjutant (*vicarius adjutor*) to the pastor of a church entrusted to religious, the local superior may present a subject to the bishop, if the Constitutions generally admit his competence in these matters.[242] The same superior may also present his subjects for appointment as assistants (*vicarii cooperatores*) if they are needed in the parish entrusted to religious, but he is obliged to consult the pastor of the parish before doing so.[243] If the local superior fails to consult the pastor, he will act illicitly at least, and in the opinion of the writer invalidly.[244]

Any of the four vicars just considered (*oeconomus, substitutus, adjutor*, or *cooperator*) is removable at the will of his religious superior, who must, however, inform the local ordinary of his action.[245]

If a church is attached to a religious house, but is one which is not parochial and one which the community to which it is attached does not use to carry out its religious exercises, its rector, it would seem, is to be appointed by the local superior.[246] According to canon 486 the rector of such a church is removable in the same way as are religious pastors and vicars. Consequently the local

[242] Canon 475, § 1. The canon does not distinguish what superior is competent.

[243] Canon 476, § 4. Augustine (*Commentary*, II, 574) states that the religious superior is to consult the pastor only "as to the necessity, not the person, of the assistant." It seems to be more in conformity with the end of the law that the consultation concern also the person to be supplied, although according to the strict letter of the law, Augustine's conclusion is warranted. Beste (*Introductio*, p. 301) believes that the consultation should include both matters.

[244] Cf. the reasons given for this conclusion, *supra*, chap. VII, art. IV, p. 64, with reference to the prescription of canon 105, 1°.

[245] Canons 477, § 1; 454, § 5. Whether the local superior can remove any of these vicars will depend again on whether or not he is declared competent in the Constitutions or other particular law of his Order. If he is permitted to appoint these vicars, he in all probability will be given the power to remove them.

[246] Cf. canon 480, § 2.

superior is competent to remove him in the same measure as he is capable of removing a pastor or vicar appointed by himself.[247]

This section may be concluded with an enumeration of the rights of both the religious pastor and of the religious house, represented by the local superior,[248] in the case where a parish is united to a religious house.[249] If the local superior is recognized in the particular law of the Order as the competent superior in such a case, he has the following obligations:

(1) the custody of the Blessed Sacrament, another key remaining in the possession of the pastor.

(2) the obligation of seeing to it that the liturgical laws are observed in the functions performed by the pastor.

(3) the care of the church and the administration of its goods and pious legacies, but always observing the prescriptions of canons 631, § 3, 533, § 1, n. 4°, and 535, § 3, n. 2°, which provide for the administration of goods and legacies given to a parish *"intuitu paroeciae."*

The rights of the religious pastor are the same as those of the pastor of a capitular church, and may be found in canon 415, § 2.

F. The Religious Subject as Pastor or Vicar

The religious [250] who has been permitted by his superiors to assume the government of a parish remains always a religious, subject to the observance of his vows, and to the Constitutions of his institute.[251] Particular legislation will usually exempt him from many of the observances carried out in the religious house to which he is assigned, such as attendance at the choral recitation of the office, at least in part. Since the care of souls, to which he is bound, should not suffer because of its being exercised by a religious pastor rather than a secular pastor, it is recommended that the religious pastor be regarded as legitimately impeded or excused from attendance at

[247] Cf. canons 454, § 5; 477, § 1.

[248] Cf. Berutti, *Institutiones,* III, n. 122, I, (A).

[249] Cf. canon 609, § 1, compared with canon 415.

[250] The religious pastor referred to in this section is one who dwells in a religious house, subject to a local superior.

[251] Canon 630.

those community exercises which interfere with the opportune carrying out of his parochial functions.[252] Nevertheless, in all matters pertaining to his own personal religious life, the religious pastor is subject to his local superior.

The Code also gives the pastor's religious superior the right of vigilance over the reception, collection, administration, and expenditure of alms destined for the general welfare of the parishioners, or for Catholic schools, or other places connected with the parish.[253] A question might be asked as to what superior is competent, and in what does his "vigilance" consist. Since the Code uses the singular "Superioris" it would seem to refer to some definite superior rather than to more than one. This conclusion seems to be substantiated by the use of the plural number "Superiorum" in the same section of this canon, when the legislator speaks of the parochial church. In the absence of any definite legislation in the Constitutions, the writer believes that the superior referred to is the superior who is competent to act in conjunction with the local ordinary in the appointment of the pastor or vicar.[254] If such initial action was only proper to the provincial or other major superior, only such a superior has the right of vigilance referred to in this canon. If the local superior presented the religious to the bishop, or consented to his appointment in the case of certain vicars, he would seem to have the right of vigilance. When the local superior has the right of vigilance over the alms referred to, he can request an account of the funds received, and of the manner in which they are being administered, but he cannot administer them

[252] Cf. Berutti, *Institutiones,* III, n. 143.

[253] Canon 630, § 4.

[254] In the case where in virtue of some private agreement between the local ordinary and the religious community, made at the time that the local ordinary entrusted the parish to the religious (cf. canon 471, § 2), whereby he reserved to himself the appointment of the religious pastor without any presentation on the part of any religious superior, the right of vigilance would seem to pertain to that superior whose duty it was to permit the religious chosen by the local ordinary to accept the appointment. This, in the case of a parish given to a religious house, could very well be the local superior of that house.

himself.[255] It will be his duty to see that the pastor is acting in these matters in accordance with the prescriptions of the common law, especially in regard to investments[256] and alienation[257] and in accordance with whatever particular law of the institute or diocese may apply in these matters.

Canon 630, 4°, allows the competent superiors more than the right of vigilance over funds which are destined for the *church edifice* belonging to the religious community, whether such funds are to be used in building, maintaining, restoring, or ornamenting the parochial church.[258] The same right which the pastor has of collecting and administering alms destined for the parochial school or other parish institutions, is reserved to the religious superior in the case of funds destined for the parochial church itself.[259] Again the question presents itself as to what superior or superiors are meant. The solution seems to be found in the manner in which the parish is held by the religious. If it is united or entrusted to the religious house, in contradistinction to the province or whole Order, the local superior would appear competent. As in all these cases, however, the particular law of the Order must be consulted, for this law may determine that even where the parish is united or entrusted to the religious house, nevertheless only the major superior or superiors are competent to act wherever the common law refers to "Superiores" without any further qualification of the term. Even if the local superior is competent to administer the funds of the parochial church, it would seem to be the mind of the legislator in using the plural "Superiorum" that more than one superior may have a hand in the administration, thus admitting the provincial superior even where the church is united or entrusted to a particular religious house.

[255] Cf. Fanfani, *De Iure Parochorum ad Normam Codicis Iuris Canonici* (Taurini-Romae: Marietti, 1924), n. 408, A.

[256] Canon 533, § 1, n. 4, and § 2.

[257] Canon 534.

[258] Cf. canons 609, § 1; 415, § 3, 3°.

[259] The religious superior is always bound to render an account of the parochial goods to the local ordinary. Cf. *PCI*, 25 iul. 1926—*AAS*, XVIII (1926), 393, ad IV.

Augustine believes that this prescription of the Code places "an unbearable burden on religious superiors who have many parochial churches." [260] In accord with his teaching that, generally speaking, "parishes are incorporated only with such houses as have a major superior, or in other words, with a provincial house. . . " [261] he was apparently considering major superiors in referring to "this last clause of § 4. . . ." [262] Certainly the burden placed by canon 630, § 4 on a competent minor local superior in religious Orders would not seem to be an "unbearable" one, because ordinarily no more than one parish would be attached to a religious house. Moreover, if the parish is united *"pleno iure"* to a religious house, any notable transaction whereby the parochial *church* is involved would of its very nature be the concern chiefly of the moral person to whom the habitual care of souls is entrusted,[263] rather than of the actual vicar. Consequently the local superior as the general representative of the moral person in all other matters assumes a role which in this case, in virtue of the specific provision of law in canon 631, § 3, becomes more of an actual than of an habitual nature. In the case of a competent local superior, canon 631, § 3 would therefore seem to be both a necessary, advisable, and not too burdensome prescription of common law.

Though the Code in canon 630 recognizes the rights of the religious superior over a religious pastor in regard to those things affecting religious discipline, it also repeats the teaching of Benedict XIV (1740-1758), recognizing the rights of the local ordinary to supervise the parochial action of the pastor, and, if necessary, to impose penalties upon the religious pastor, *qua* pastor.[264] But even

[260] *Commentary,* III, 361. *Idem, The Canonical and Civil Status of Catholic Parishes in the United States* (St. Louis: Herder, 1926), p. 361. Hereafter cited as *Canonical Status of Pastors.*

[261] *Canonical Status of Pastors,* p. 190.

[262] *Commentary,* III, 361.

[263] Cf. canon 452.

[264] Cf. Benedict XIV, const. *"Firmandis,"* 6 nov. 1744, §§ 8-10—*Fontes,* n. 349. The following instances among others are listed: whether the religious pastor exercises the care of souls by legitimate title, whether he observes the law of residence, goes to the diocesan synod when invited, fulfills Mass obliga-

in this latter case the local ordinary is not empowered to act independently of the religious superior, but in conjunction with him,[265] as long as their punitive measures do not conflict.[266] If the religious pastor is subject to a local superior, and the latter is recognized by the Constitutions as competent to deal with the appointment and removal of religious pastors from among his subjects, the local superior will also be the superior referred to in this canon, though the local ordinary would always be free to refer to the major religious superior, if he felt the breach of discipline demanded this higher recourse. Such a competent local superior should enforce the penalties of the local ordinary, if necessary even by penalties of his own.[267] Needless to say, he would also be obliged to defend the conduct of his subject-pastor, if he felt that the local ordinary was not justified in penalizing the pastor. In such a controversy the local superior would be obliged to carry out the local ordinary's decrees, but could have recourse to higher authority.[268]

G. *Choral Obligation and Conventual Mass*

The practice of reciting divine office publicly in choir has been commanded by many Popes, and its obligation imposed on many religious institutes. Clement V (1305-1314) in the Council of Vienne (1311) commanded all regular superiors to see to the proper carrying out of the choral obligation,[269] and the Sacred Congregation

tions, instructs the faithful, keeps parochial registers, etc. Cf. also canons 358; 465-468; 1330, 1°; 1332-33; 1344-45; 1550.

[265] Cf. canon 631, § 2.

[266] "Superior religionis jus cumulativum habet parochum subditum, monendi, visitandi, ac dirigendi, simul cum Ordinario loci. . . . Superior religionis, in explendo praesenti jure et officio utilem directionem hauriet ex dispositionibus can. 442 [canon 447 is probably the canon meant], Vicario foraneo praescriptis."—Vromant, "De Regimine Paroeciarum et Quasi-Paroeciarum Religiosis Sodalibus Concreditarum"—*JP*, XIII (1933), 281.

[267] For the relationship between the local superior and the ordinary in this regard, consult the norms given in an Instruction of the S. Cong. de Prop. Fide, 8 dec. 1929—*AAS*, XXII (1930), 260.

[268] Canon 631.

[269] C. 1, *de celebratione missarum et aliis divinis officiis*, III, 14 in Clem. Cf. Clement VIII, decr. *"Nullus omnino,"* 25 iul. 1599, § 1—*Fontes*, n. 187; S. C. C., decr. 21 sept. 1624, § 1—*Fontes*, n. 2454.

of Bishops and Regulars insisted upon its observance in the houses of strict observance which it had commanded to be established in Rome.[270] The obligation of seeing to the proper fulfillment of the choral obligation in each house was primarily incumbent upon the local superior. Benedict XII (1334-1342) pointed this out when he ordered the *"Custodes et Guardiani"* to see that the prescribed manner of saying the office was observed.[271] Donatus (+1661) writes that the obligation falls especially on the prelates of the convents, "Quia quoties obligatio aliqua cadit in aliquod corpus misticum (*sic*), seu fictum . . . magis afficit caput, quam membra dicti corporis. . . ."[272] Because of the penalty imposed by Clement V (1305-1314) in the Council of Vienne against superiors who were negligent in carrying out their duties in regard to the choral recitation, pre-Code authors concluded that the superior was bound *sub gravi* to see to it that the obligation was fulfilled.[273]

The obligation of a daily conventual Mass is so closely connected with the obligation of reciting the office in choir that legislation affecting the one often affects the other also.[274] Specific directions for the conventual Mass, however, can be found particularly in various decrees of the Sacred Congregation of Rites.[275]

The divine office must be recited chorally each day in those institutes which have the obligation whenever there are present in the house at least four religious, bound to choir and not actually impeded.[276] The same religious are likewise bound to the celebration

[270] S. C. Ep. et Reg., decr. 22 aug. 1814, n. XI—*Fontes*, n. 1893.

[271] Const. *"Redemptor noster,"* 28 nov. 1336, § 4—*BRT*, IV, 392.

[272] *Rerum Regularium*, tom. III, tr. XVIII, qu. 23, n. 2.

[273] C. 1, *de celebratione missarum et aliis divinis officiis*, III, 14 in Clem.; Donatus, *op. cit.*, tom. III, tr. XVIII, qu. 23, n. 1.

[274] Cf. canon 413, § 2.

[275] Local superiors are not permitted without the permission of the bishop to prescribe collects to be said in the Mass by their subjects, either for the necessities of the Order or for a common necessity.—S. R. C., decr. *"Ordinis Minorum Observantium Reformatorum S. Francisci*, 27 mart. 1779—*Decreta Authentica Congregationis Sacrorum Rituum* (6 vols., Romae, 1898-1927), n. 2514, ad 6. Hereafter cited as *Decreta Authentica.*

[276] Cf. canon 610, § 1.

of the daily conventual Mass,[277] but not to the celebration of two conventual Masses on those days on which they are prescribed in the General Rubrics of the Missal, unless particular law determines otherwise.[278]

With reference to the local superior's obligations in regard to the choral recitation of the office and to the daily celebration of the conventual Mass, two questions may be proposed. Is it his duty to institute the choral recitation and community Mass in the religious house of which he is the head, and secondly what are his obligations as to the actual fulfillment of the already constituted obligations?

To the first question one might reply that the local superior, or even the major superior, does not impose the choral obligation upon any community, for in every house whether *formata* or *non formata*, where there are at least four religious obliged to choir and not actually and lawfully impeded, the obligation arises directly from the ecclesiastical law of the Church without any declaration on the part of any religious superior. However, the decision as to whether the members of a particular community are lawfully impeded or not must rest primarily with the local superior, though his decision, in this as in all other matters, is always subject to correction by the major superiors, especially at the time of visitation. In deciding whether or not subjects are lawfully impeded, the local superior will be guided by the Constitutions of the institute. These will usually determine who are to be regarded as impeded either physically or morally,[279] or whether individuals are dispensed from the obligation of choir or of the conventual Mass. Once the status of the individual members has been determined, the local superior will know

[277] Canon 610, § 2.

[278] *PCI*, 16 oct. 1919, n. 10—*AAS*, II (1919), 478.. Cf. Pauwels, "Annotationes," *Periodica*, XIII (1925), 119; *idem*, "De missa religiosis praescripta,"—*Periodica*, XIII (1925), (20).

[279] "Ad actu impeditos (physice vel moraliter) pertinent (a) infirmi, (b) legitime occupati, (c) legitime dispensati. Legitimi occupati sunt imprimis ii, qui ratione exercitii sacri ministerii impediuntur, ex. gr. si agitur de Domo religiosa, quae paroeciam ita habet unitam, ut omnes sacerdotes vel ii saltem, qui necessarii sunt ad complendum numerum necessarium, ut de facto urgeat chori obligatio, ipsius paroeciae servitio addicti sunt."—Schaefer, *De Religiosis*, n. 366, 2.

whether or not and at what times his community is bound to the choral observance. If the subjects cannot lawfully be present for every part of the office, it does not follow that the community has no obligation of choral observance at those times during the day or week when they are not actually and lawfully impeded.[280]

As regards the fulfillment of the obligation once it is recognized to exist, the following observations may be made: just as authors before the Code maintained that the duty of seeing to the fulfillment of the choral obligation rested primarily on the superior of the house, so also after the Code authors unanimously agree that the superior has the primary obligation gravely binding in conscience to see to the choral recitation of the office. But of the many authors consulted no one makes explicit mention of the local superior.[281] However the very nature of the obligation in question seems to refer without doubt to the local superior, for the canon imposes the obligation "in singulis domibus," and therefore primarily upon the local superior of each house. It will be his duty, therefore, to see to the proper fulfillment of the obligation. He is bound to take care not only that the divine office be said in choir, but that it be said properly, both according to the rite prescribed by the Church, and according to the particular law of each institute. Generally one may say that the local superior has the obligation of seeing that the divine office is said "digne, attente ac devote," at the proper time and in the proper place. His attention to the rubrics prescribed by general and particular law will insure its devout recitation.

In regard to the time of the recitation, the superior is bound to take care that it is said within the time assigned or permitted by the rubrics.[282] If he foresees that at a time ordinarily assigned for

[280] Cf. Schaefer, *De Religiosis*, n. 367, 3.

[281] Beste, *Introductio*, p. 413. Berutti, *Institutiones*, III, n. 123, I. Schaefer, *De Religiosis*, n. 367. Prümmer, *Manuale I. C.*, qu. 235. Creusen-Ellis-Gareschê have: "the superior who represents the community . . ."—*Religious Men and Women in the Code* (3. ed., Milwaukee: Bruce, 1940), n. 298, 1.

[282] Beste (*Introductio*, p. 414) writes that matins and lauds cannot be habitually anticipated unless the institute enjoys a papal indult. He would also allow the superior (presumably the local superior) to permit this anticipation but only in a particular case.

the recitation of a particular hour a sufficient number cannot be present in choir, he has the duty of transferring the time of the office to a more convenient hour within the time prescribed by the rubrics, if this can be done without serious inconvenience to the community.[283] If such a procedure cannot be followed, either because the rubrics forbid the transfer (e. g. the recitation of vespers and compline in the early morning), or because the same condition exists at other times during the day, or because the transfer would seriously inconvenience the community, the obligation to recite that particular part of the office chorally ceases.[284]

The local superior must likewise take care that the office is recited in that part of the house set aside for the choral recitation of the office and known as the choir. This is the ordinary place for the recitation of the office, though it may be said also in the church attached to the religious house, or even in the sacristy, private oratory, or other room contiguous to the church.[285] A private oratory or sacristy which does not open out into the church cannot be used as a place for the fulfillment of the choral obligation, but a local superior can permit the celebration of the office outside the church in an oratory of the house or in the sacristy for a few months during the year when because of the heat or cold such a procedure would seem to him to be advisable, provided that the oratory or sacristy is joined to the church, "aperto muro vel accessu." [286]

The local superior has no faculty in common law to dispense his

[283] Cf. Goyeneche, "Consultationes," *CpR,* VI (1925), 360.

[284] The statement of Augustine (*Commentary,* III, 325) that the superior is not allowed to dispense from the choral obligation "except in case that there be not sufficient members present to perform it" is not strictly correct if reference is made to the local superior. The local superior has no power to dispense the entire community at any time, at least from common law. However, in the example given no dispensation is needed, since the obligation ceases when it becomes impossible of fulfillment.

[285] S. R. C. *Ordinis Minorum Conventualium S. Francisci,* 12 dec. 1879, ad II—*Decreta Authentica,* n. 3506.

[286] S. R. C. *decr. cit.,* ad III. Cf. Coronata, *Institutiones,* I, n. 616, VI, 3°, (a). Prümmer (*Manuale I. C.,* qu. 235, 3) and Schaefer (*De Religiosis,* n. 369, f) in reproducing this decree of the Sacred Congregation of Rites reprint the reply to the third *dubium* incorrectly. Both authors have: "Ad III. Pro-

entire community from the choral obligation, but he may in particular cases dispense both professors and students from choir as often as such a dispensation may seem necessary for the advancement of study.[287] Power to dispense his subjects other than students or teachers is not granted in the Code, but the local superior may have such power from a privilege conceded to his Order, or from a privilege in which his Order communicates.

In the institutes which have the choral obligation, solemnly professed members who have been absent from choir must, the lay-brothers excepted, recite the canonical hours in private.[288]

With regard to the private recitation of the office, at least the following privileges may be used by the local superior:

(1) Clement VIII (1523-1534) permitted regular superiors to dispense their subjects who were occupied in preaching, hearing confessions, studying or teaching theology or canon law, or who were temporarily impeded by sickness, or by the work of the ministry, or in the service of the sick, from the recitation of the office, and to assign instead the recitation of a certain number of psalms (not less than seven), together with seven Our Fathers and the Apostles' Creed twice.[289]

(2) If in the judgment of the local superior there exists a reasonable cause, clerical religious who are not as yet *in sacris* may say the prayers prescribed for the lay-brothers instead of the divine office.[290]

visum in primo," a reading which contradicts the true sense of the reply, the correct rendition of which is: "Ad III. Provisum in secundo." Cf. *Decreta Authentica*, n. 3506.

287 Canon 589, § 2. This power of dispensation is an act of ecclesiastical jurisdiction, and as such is not to be confounded with acts of dominative power by which a superior who has no jurisdiction declares a subject excused from the observance of some particular ecclesiastical law. Cf. Donatus, *Rerum Regularium*, tom. III, tr. XVIII, qu. 64, n. 1.

288 Cf. canon 610, § 3.

289 Const. *"Dudum,"* 7 mart. 1533, § 2—*BRT*, VI, 161.

290 Cf. Coronata, *Institutiones*, I, n. 617. (The author does not give the date of this privilege, granted by Innocent IV [1243-1254], or the source from which it is taken, except to quote Ferrari, *De Statu Religioso* [2. ed.], n. 74, pp. 183-184.)

Article XI. Egress and Dismissal of Subjects

A. *Historical Notes*

Under the law of the Decretals, provision was made for the expulsion of religious.[291] Innocent III (1198-1216) approved a sentence of excommunication and dismissal passed by a prior of a community of Canons Regular.[292] It was not until after the Council of Trent (1545-1563), however, that the process for dismissal was required to be conducted by the superior general and six of the senior Fathers.[293] Innocent XII (1691-1700) in 1694 allowed the provincial and six other religious appointed in the provincial chapter to dismiss a religious, provided the sentence of dismissal was approved by the general.[294] In the decree "*Auctis admodum*" of November 4, 1892,[295] the Sacred Congregation of Bishops and Regulars renewed the previous decrees of Urban VIII and Innocent XII, and gave rules of procedure for the trial. If the formal trial could not be carried out the same Sacred Congregation was to be petitioned for the faculty of proceeding "summario modo." Explicit mention of the local superior in regard to the process of dismissal was made in a decree of the Sacred Congregation for Religious, May 16th, 1911.[296] There it was stated that the general and not less than four assistants were to constitute the tribunal, but before the religious could be tried he was to be canonically warned, three times, "a legitimo superiore etiam locali, de mandato tamen vel licentia superioris provincialis seu quasi-provincialis." [297] Thus from common law the local superior had little, if any, ordinary jurisdiction in the process which was generally instituted for the dismissal of a religious.

[291] Cf. Michalicka, *Judicial Procedure in Dismissal of Clerical Exempt Religious,* The Catholic University of America Canon Law Studies, n. 19 (Washington, D. C.: The Catholic University of America, 1923), pp. 6-9.

[292] C. 10, X, *de maioritate et obedientia,* I, 33.

[293] S. C. C. decr., 21 sept. 1624—*Fontes,* n. 2454.

[294] S. C. C. decr., 24 iul. 1694—*Fontes,* n. 2942.

[295] *Fontes,* n. 2020.

[296] *Fontes,* n. 4409; *AAS,* III (1911), 235-239.

[297] *Idem,* § 5.

B. *Present Legislation*

In treating of the present legislation, separate consideration will be given to the dismissal of novices and of the professed. It has already been shown that either the religious superior or the chapter may dismiss a novice during the period of his novitiate, according as individual Constitutions may determine.[298] It would therefore follow that the local superior may be competent to dismiss a novice if the Constitutions of his institute give him that power. Since the major superiors are the only superiors who can admit a novice to the novitiate, it is not likely that the local superior would be given the power to dismiss a novice without the consent of the higher superior, but again particular law must determine this matter.[299]

When a novice after the period of novitiate is found to be certainly unfitted for the life of the Order to which he has aspired, he is not to be allowed to make temporary profession, but must be dismissed.[300] Canon 571, § 2 does not mention what superior is competent, but it would seem to be the same superior who is competent to dismiss a novice even before his period of training is over. However, since the major superiors and not the local superiors, have the right to admit a novice to profession[301] it will be more likely that the Constitutions will give the major superior power also to dismiss those who have not the qualifications necessary for profession. Particular law could, however, give that right to the local superior either with or without the consent of his council, or of the provincial or other major superior.

Once a novice has made profession he is not free to leave the institute until the expiration of the time for which he made his vows, but when that time has expired he needs no further permission of the local superior or of any other superior to leave the religious life.[302]

[298] *Supra,* chap. VII, art. VII, p. 85.

[299] Canon 571, § 1. The local prior with his council and with the consent of the provincial is competent to dismiss novices in the Order of Preachers, and in urgent cases the local prior and his council may do so without the provincial's consent. (*Const. S. O. P.* [1932], n. 111, § 1.)

[300] Canon 571, § 2.

[301] Canon 543.

[302] Canon 637.

A novice lay-brother may be excluded from the renewal of temporary vows, and a cleric may be excluded from solemn profession.[303] The superior competent to act in both of these cases is not determined in the Code, but the Constitutions will usually designate the major, rather than the local superior. Schaefer believes that this dismissal at the expiration of temporary profession is not necessarily reserved to the major superior, but says that if the Constitutions are silent in the matter, the exclusion pertains to the major superior, just as does the admission to profession.[304]

Before the expiration of vows, a religious may have obtained an indult of secularization or of exclaustration. In both cases the local superior has no authority over his former subject.[305] If a subject is elected to any office in the Church by any collegiate body having such a right, he needs to obtain the permission of his religious superior before accepting it, more probably the permission of the major superior,[306] since the local superior cannot usually give a subject permission to dwell outside the house of his assignment for any prolonged period of time, as would often be necessary if an ecclesiastical office were conferred upon a religious. Subjects chosen by the Holy See as bishops or cardinals would seem to need no permission of the local or major superior before accepting the dignity, since all religious are subject to the Holy See by their vow of obedience.[307] The local superior has no power over his subjects when they are chosen cardinals or bishops.[308] If, however, the Holy See allows the religious to accept or to reject the episcopal dignity, particular law may demand the permission of the major superior

[303] Canon 637.

[304] *De Religiosis*, n. 539.

[305] Canon 639. Even if the religious obtains an indult or faculty permitting him to remain away from the religious house for longer than six months, he is still subject to his local superior and to other superiors. Such an indult is not to be confused with an indult of exclaustration (Cf. Schaefer, *De Religiosis*, n. 544). But even when a religious has obtained an indult of exclaustration, he is still bound to obey the local superior's command to return to the religious house "etiam perdurante indulto." (Cf. Schaefer, *op. cit.*, n. 546, 3, a.)

[306] Canon 626, § 2; this canon would seem to refer to the major superior.

[307] Canon 499, § 1.

[308] Canon 627, § 2.

before acceptance.[309] His authority over apostate and fugitive religious remains intact.[310] He is bound to effect their return to the religious house if possible, and to receive them back if they are penitent. These latter obligations, based on the law of charity, are to be found in Gratian, in the Decretals of Gregory IX, in the legislation of the Council of Trent, and in the decrees of the Sacred Congregations.

As for the dismissal of professed religious, the local superior's authority is very much restricted, though he will often be called upon to furnish the major superiors with information and help in determining the innocence or guilt of religious alleged to have committed actions which might call for their dismissal.

In cases of *ipso facto* dismissal incurred by religious who commit the offenses listed in canon 646, § 1, the local superior will have little more to do than to inform the major superior of the fact, if this be necessary; any further action is reserved to the major superior (canon 646, § 2).

The dismissal of religious who have taken temporary vows in clerical exempt religious institutes is reserved to the highest superior in the Order.[311] The local superior, however, may be compelled to call the attention of the major superior to a subject's grave lack of religious spirit, which has become a scandal to others and which the subject has refused to correct, even after having been warned repeatedly[312] and after having been subjected frequently to the performance of penances. He may likewise be requested by the highest superior to transmit to him the rebuttal which is guaranteed every accused religious in such cases by canon 647, § 2, 3°, or even to

[309] Cf. *Const. S. O. P.* (1932), n. 216.

[310] Canon 645.

[311] Canon 647, § 1.

[312] Cf. canon 647, § 2, 2°. The "monitio" referred to in this canon is not the canonical warning given by the major superior or his delegate before he can initiate the process of dismissal for religious of solemn vows (cf. canons 656, 658, 659). Reference is made in canon 647, § 2, 2° to the ordinary warnings which the local superior even more than the other superiors can give subjects who are delinquent. Cf. Goyeneche, "Consultationes," *CpR,* XIII (1932), 100; Berutti, *Institutiones,* III, n. 160, I.

transmit a copy of the entire charges made against the religious, since such action in the cases of religious with temporary vows is not reserved to the immediate major superior, as it is in cases involving religious of solemn vows.[313]

The dismissal of religious in solemn vows is also reserved to the highest superior in the Order, except where a subject has caused or is about to cause grave exterior scandal or very grave injury to the community. In these two cases the religious can be dismissed immediately by the provincial or other major superior, or even by the local superior with the consent of his council, if there is danger in delay, and if there is no time available to have recourse to the major superior,[314] but even in these cases the ordinary process is to be instituted and carried out later.

The local superior has no part *ex officio* in the judicial process for the dismissal of one of his subjects who has taken solemn vows, but he may be delegated to perform various duties in the course of the process, such as collecting the documents which prove the offense of the subject to be notorious,[315] making the investigation required by canon 658 into the notoriety of the alleged offenses, or giving the canonical admonition demanded in such cases. This he could do, after being delegated by the immediate major superior of the accused religious [316] but the duty of adding opportune exhortations, corrections, penances and penal remedies,[317] and certainly the duty of transferring the religious to another house [318] belongs to the major superior *ex officio.*

Canon 672, § 1 will apply to the local superior if a dismissed religious, still bound by his vows, should choose to return to the religious house, for then he would again come under the supervision of the superior of the house, but the decision as to whether the

[313] Canon 663.

[314] Canon 668.

[315] Cf. Berutti, *Institutiones,* III, n. 171, II, (B).

[316] Canon 659; Augustine, *Commentary,* III, 403. If the local superior gives the admonition he must take care to do so before a notary, or before two witnesses, or by mail with a request for a return receipt.

[317] Canon 661, § 1.

[318] Canon 661, § 2.

religious had given signs of perfect reform would probably rest with both the local and the major superiors. However, the local superior would not be bound to receive back into the community a religious *ipso facto* dismissed for any of the offenses listed in canon 646.[319]

[319] Cf. *PCI,* 20 iul. 1934—*AAS,* XXVI (1934), 494.

CHAPTER VIII

THE SACRAMENTS

THE rights and duties of the local superior as expressed in the law "De Religiosis" have naturally occupied the greatest part of this study up to this point. Of both historical and current interest is the question of the local superior's jurisdiction in regard to the administration of the Sacraments. The rights and duties of the local superior in regard to the administration of the Sacraments of Baptism and Confirmation are confined to permitting his subjects to act as sponsors, while those in regard to the Sacrament of Extreme Unction will be treated in conjunction with the legislation on the administration of Holy Viaticum. Scarcely any of the numerous canons of the Code concerning the Sacrament of Matrimony will directly apply to the local superior as superior of a religious community. Numerous rights and duties, however, will be involved in the administration of the Sacraments of Penance and of the Holy Eucharist.

ARTICLE I. BAPTISM AND CONFIRMATION

Of all the canons dealing with the Sacraments of Baptism and Confirmation, only two refer explicitly to rights of a local superior. According to canons 766, 4° and 796, 3° compared with 766, 4°, a religious may not licitly be permitted to act as sponsor either at Baptism or at Confirmation except in cases of necessity, and then only with the express permission of at least the local superior. Formerly a monk was forbidden to leave his monastery to act as a sponsor at Baptism.[1] Pope St. Gregory the Great (590-604) forbade the Abbot Valentine to permit his monks to act as sponsors for women.[2] This prohibition against regulars acting as sponsors remained even until the Code.[3]

[1] C. 8, C. XVI, q. 1.

[2] C. 20, C. XVIII, q. 2.

[3] Cf. Vermeersch-Creusen, *De Religiosis*, n. 504, 4; *Idem, Epitome*, II, n. 48;

According to the present legislation the local superior may grant permission to both novices and professed to act as sponsors both at Baptism and at Confirmation, if in his judgment there is some necessity for so doing.[4] Such an occasion might arise especially in parishes entrusted to religious, if the sponsor or sponsors designated by the person to be baptized, or by parents or tutors, or by the minister of the Sacrament are at the last moment found to be unqualified to act as sponsors, either validly or licitly, and there is no other available, except a religious attached to the parish. In such a case the local superior could permit one of his subjects to act as sponsor.[4a] The mere wish of the person to be baptized, or of his parents, that a religious (related, perhaps, to the one to be baptized) assume the sponsorship would not seem to be sufficient reason for a local superior to permit a religious so to act, unless the superior would be able to judge that, in such a case, there is a moral necessity of complying with the request, lest he or the community incur the great displeasure of the baptized or of those who request the religious to assume the duty.[5]

Since the local ordinary could permit the placing of a baptismal font in a non-parochial church or public oratory attached to a religious house,[6] the question might be asked whether or not the local superior could baptize or assist there at the marriage of convert *familiares* or others who might reside in the religious house after the manner of those mentioned in canon 514, § 1. The response must necessarily be in the negative, for the *familiares* are subject to the local superior of the religious house only in regard to those things which are expressly mentioned in the Code. The jurisdiction of the pastor of the territory in which the religious house is located is not taken away in regard to the baptism or marriage of *familiares*.[7]

Wernz, *Ius Decretalium,* III, n. 730, III; Prümmer, *Manuale Iuris Ecclesiastici,* tom. II, *Ius Regularium Speciale* (Friburgi Brisgoviae, 1907), Q. 142. Hereafter cited as *Manuale I. E.*

[4] Canon 765, 4°.

[4a] However, a religious who is *in sacris* needs the express permission of his proper ordinary (provincial superior). Canon 766, 5°.

[5] Cf. Blat, *Commentarium,* lib. III, pars I, p. 60.

[6] Canon 774, § 2.

[7] Cf. canons 462, 464; Blat, *Commentarium,* II, 562.

Article II. The Holy Eucharist and Extreme Unction

A. *The Sacrifice of the Mass*

1. The *Celebret*

As early as the Council of Chalcedon (451), clerics had been forbidden to exercise the ministry outside their own city without testimonial letters from their own bishop.[8] The Council of Trent (1545-1563) commanded local ordinaries to forbid any wandering or unknown priest to celebrate Mass.[9] The same Council ruled that "no cleric who is a stranger shall, without commendatory letters from his ordinary, be admitted by any bishop to celebrate the divine mysteries and to administer the Sacraments." [10] This decree was of a general nature and applied also to regulars.[11] Benedict XIV (1740-1758) commanded religious about to assume missionary duties to present testimonial letters from their own superiors to the vicars apostolic before they attempted to say Mass.[12] The Sacred Congregation of the Holy Office likewise made reference to the testimonials which religious had obtained from their superiors.[13] It will be noted that the Council of Trent demanded the testimony of each one's ordinary,[14] but Pope St. Pius V (1566-1572) gave the local superior the same authority over his subjects as the bishop had over seculars.[15] Consequently, it would seem that the local superior, as a prelate exercising quasi-episcopal jurisdiction, could issue the testimonial letter required by the Council of Trent. Two encyclical letters of Benedict XIV (1740-1758) seem to confirm the right of the local superior, for they refer to the testimony *"superiorum*

[8] C. 7, D. LXXI—Hefele, II, 518.

[9] Sess. XXII, *de observandis et evitandis in celebratione Missae*; Schroeder, *Canons and Decrees*, pp. 151, 423.

[10] Sess. XXIII, *de ref.*, c. 16; Schroeder, *op. cit.*, pp. 174, 445.

[11] Gasparri, *Tractatus Canonicus de Sanctissima Eucharistia* (2 vols., Parisiis, 1897), I, n. 372.

[12] Ep. encycl. *"Apostolicum ministerium,"* 30 maii 1753, § 6—*Fontes*, n. 425.

[13] 11 aug. 1649—*Fontes*, n. 729.

[14] Sess. XXIII, *de ref.*, c. 16; Schroeder, *Canons and Decrees*, pp. 174, 445.

[15] Const. *"Romani Pontificis,"* 21 iul. 1571, § 3—*BRT*, VII, 931.

suorum," making no distinction.[16] The same terminology is used by the Sacred Congregation of the Holy Office [17] and by the Sacred Congregation of Bishops and Regulars.[18] The pre-Code authors do not seem to treat the matter of what superior was competent.[19]

The present Code renews the previous legislation in canon 804. It is stated that a religious is to present commendatory letters from his own superior if he asks to be allowed to celebrate Mass. The Code does not distinguish whether this superior is the local superior or otherwise. A careful search among the commentaries has failed to reveal a common opinion among the authors, since only three of the authors consulted attempt to determine the particular superior referred to in this canon. Blat [20] and Pejška [21] declare that even the local superior can issue the *celebret,* while Cappello [22] reserves this right to the major superior. None of these three states any reasons for his conclusion; to the present writer, it seems that the local superior is competent to issue the testimonial letter, commonly known as the *celebret,* for the following reasons:

1. From an examination of the text of the canon, one can see that the legislator has made an evident distinction between the secular priest and the religious; the former needs the testimonial of his own *ordinary,* the latter that of his own *superior.* If the legislator wished only the religious ordinary to be the competent superior, it would appear that he would have retained the use of the words "sui Ordinarii" instead of "sui Superioris," as did the Council of Trent when treating of this matter,[23] or that he would have used the words "Ordi-

[16] Ep. encycl. "*Apostolicum ministerium,*" 30 maii 1753, § 6—*Fontes,* n. 425; Ep. encycl. "*Quam grave,*" 2 aug. 1757, § 12—*Fontes,* n. 443.

[17] 11 aug. 1649—*Fontes,* n. 729.

[18] *Comen.,* 27 oct. 1593—*Fontes,* n. 1496; *Feltren.,* 15 febr. 1595—*Fontes,* n. 1532.

[19] Cf. Piatus, *Praelectiones,* II, qu. 278; Bouix, *De Jure Regularium,* II, 198; Wernz, *Ius Decretalium,* II, n. 532.

[20] *Commentarium,* III, n. 105.

[21] *Ius Canonicum Religiosorum,* p. 264.

[22] *Tractatus Canonico—Moralis de Sacramentis* (3 vols. in 6, Vol. I, 2. ed., 1928; Vol. II, pars I, 2. ed., 1929, Taurinorum Augustae: Marietti), I, n. 737, 1. Hereafter cited as *De Sacramentis.*

[23] Sess. XXIII, *de ref.,* c. 16; Schroeder, *Canons and Decrees,* pp. 174, 445.

narii proprii," as referring to the ordinary of either the secular or the religious priest.

2. The legislator did not distinguish between superiors, though such a distinction is very often made in the Code, and could easily be made here by the simple addition of the qualifying word "maioris," as inserted, unwarrantedly in the opinion of the writer, by Cappello in his paraphrase of this canon.[24]
3. There is nothing in the nature of the *celebret* which would require that it be issued only by a religious ordinary rather than by the local superior. The *celebret* is the testimony of a legitimate superior that the priest who bears it is worthy of the privileges of the clerical state, and that he is free from censure and irregularity. The local ordinary gives this testimony in the case of a secular priest because he is the secular priest's immediate superior, but the religious priest is immediately subject to his local superior who is, therefore, according to the wording of the canon, the superior competent to issue testimonial letters.[25]
4. The legislator appears to be incorporating as common law a right which the conventual prior seems to have enjoyed by privilege under the pre-Code legislation in virtue of the quasi-episcopal power given him in the constitution of St. Pius V, *"Romani Pontificis."*[26]

The local superior will also be obliged to examine the credentials of visiting priests who present themselves at the church or oratory of the religious house seeking an opportunity to say Mass.[27] This obligation on the part of a local superior was stressed by the Sacred Congregation of the Holy Office in a letter to the superiors of religious institutes, urging them to command the local superiors to examine diligently the testimonial letters of unknown visitors, either of their own or of another institute. In the case of the secular clergy, the local superior was required to look for the signature of the vicar

[24] *Loc. cit.*

[25] The Constitutions of an Order may define the circumstances under which the local superior may issue such a letter, and may determine the period of time during which his testimony will be valid. Needless to say, the Constitutions may also restrict the right to issue this testimonial to the provincial superior.

[26] 21 iul. 1571—*BRT,* VII, 931, § 3.

[27] Canon 804, § 2.

general or the vicar forane of the diocese in which the religious church or oratory was located, as proof of the fact that the visiting priest had presented himself before the diocesan authorities.[28] The present legislation would allow the local superior to admit a visiting secular priest who is not known to him to celebrate Mass provided he has a testimonial letter of his own ordinary, without its being necessary for the priest to present himself at the diocesan chancery or before the vicar forane.[29] If the visitor is known to the superior, he may be permitted to say Mass even though he lacks the testimonial letter. Even if he is not known to the local superior and has no testimonial letter he may be permitted to say Mass once or twice, provided that the prescriptions of canon 804, § 2 are verified. It must be noted, also, that the local superior will be obliged to request a testimonial even of a member of his own Order if the latter is unknown to him, and in such a case, as in all others in which the priest is unknown, the local superior has the grave obligation of examining the *celebret* diligently.

2. *The Obligation of Celebrating Mass*

Canon 595, § 1, 2° commands religious superiors to see to it that all their subjects who are not lawfully impeded attend Mass daily. The second paragraph of the same canon 595 obliges the superior to promote the frequent and even the daily reception of the Holy Eucharist and to allow those who are rightly disposed the opportunity of going to Holy Communion daily. In regard to the celebration of Mass, the legislation states that priests have an obligation of saying Mass "pluries per annum,[30] a phrase generally interpreted to mean three or four times a year,[31] but at the same time the bishops and religious superiors are urged to take care that their priest-subjects celebrate Mass at least on Sundays and other feasts of precept.[32]

[28] 11 aug. 1649—*Fontes*, n. 729; *Acta Sanctae Sedis* (41 vols., Romae, 1865-1908), XXIV (1891), 701. Hereafter cited *ASS*.

[29] Canon 804, 1°. Cf. Cappello, *De Sacramentis*, I, n. 737, 3.

[30] Canon 805.

[31] Cf. Blat, *Commentarium*, lib. III, pars I, 507.

[32] Canon 805. Innocent III refers to certain prelates who scarcely cele-

Since it is the duty of the local superior to see to the observance of this canon, it will not be irrelevant to this study to point out that the canon refers to the minimum number of times that a priest is obliged to say Mass, and to those days at least on which the superior is to take care that Mass is said. However it will certainly be the duty of the local superior, as a superior guiding his subjects along the way of perfection, to exhort his priests to a more frequent and even daily celebration of Mass, even though the canon does not impose any canonical obligation upon him to do so, or upon the subject to carry out such exhortations.

In 1298 Boniface VIII (1294-1303) declared that a bishop ought to say or attend Mass daily. Now, in virtue of canon 805 and of the duty imposed in the Code[33] upon superiors to see that their subjects attend Mass daily, it can also be said that the local superior is obliged by the common law of the Church to take care that his priest-subjects who are not lawfully impeded are present at the daily community Mass and celebrate Mass themselves at least on Sundays and other feasts of precept. The particular law of the Constitutions will very likely urge also a daily celebration of Mass by religious priests unless they are lawfully impeded[34] and in such a case the local superior will be obliged to see to the observance of this constitutional obligation.

Finally, reference may also be made to the power of the local superior to command his subjects even in virtue of obedience to celebrate Mass according to any intention which the Constitutions or the superior himself may prescribe.[35]

Though charity and the particular law of the institute may

brated four times a year and attempts to eradicate such an abuse "sub poena suspensionis,"—c. 9, X, *de celebratione missarum et sacramento Eucharistiae et divinis officiis,* III, 41. The Council of Trent when it ordered bishops to see to the observance of the same obligation made no reference to religious superiors (Sess. XXIII, *de ref.,* c. 14). Schroeder, *Canons and Decrees,* pp. 173, 444.

[33] Canon 595, § 1, 2°; cf. Boniface VIII's decree in c. 12, *de privilegiis,* V, 7, in VI°.

[34] Cf. *Const. S. O. P.* (1932), n. 581, § 1.

[35] S. C. de Religiosis, *Suessonien. et Aliarum,* 3 maii 1914—*AAS,* VI (1914), 231. Cf. "Annotationes," *Periodica,* VIII (1919), 40.

demand that religious superiors celebrate Mass occasionally for the welfare of their subjects, there is no canonical obligation requiring that they do so, for the Code is silent on this matter. Under the pre-Code legislation some authors [36] held that regular prelates, including conventual priors, were bound to offer Mass on Sundays and feast days for their subjects, basing this obligation on the prescription of the Council of Trent, concerning the Mass *pro populo,* but it was never commonly held that to do so was of obligation.

A dubium was proposed to the Sacred Congregation of the Council on March 15th, 1710, asking whether or not the superiors (including the "superiores locales et conventuales") of the Augustinian Order were bound to offer and to apply Mass for their subjects, but the Congregation never replied to the question.[37]

Authors now commonly teach that there is no obligation incumbent upon religious superiors to do so, but lest the religious be in a less favorable condition than the rest of the faithful who share in the *pro populo* Mass of their bishop and pastors, the local superior ought in charity to offer and apply Mass, occasionally at least, for his subjects. The Constitutions of individual Orders will often determine certain days upon which Mass is to be offered for the community.

3. *Mass Stipends*

Canon 842 declares that the right and duty of seeing to the fulfillment of Mass obligations pertains in the churches of religious to the superiors of the institute. Again, it may be said that the local superior as the immediate superior in each house will be obliged to carry out the prescriptions of this canon.[38] He may entrust the recording of the Masses received, as to the intentions for which they are to be said, the amount of the offering, and the date of the cele-

[36] Tamburini (*De Jure Abbatum,* tom. II, disp. 5, qu. 5, a. 5) thought that a regular prelate ought to celebrate Mass daily or at least very frequently for his subjects.

[37] Verhoeven, *De Praxi a Parochis Observanda in Celebratione Missae pro Populo* (Hasseleti, 1849), pp. 90-93; Wernz, *Ius Decretalium,* III, n. 694.

[38] Cf. Blat, *Commentarium,* lib. III, pars I, p. 169.

bration,[39] to a religious appointed for this work, but the obligation of seeing to the fulfillment of all the obligations will always rest primarily on the local superior, who in turn is subject to the annual vigilance of the provincial superior in regard to the manner in which the recording of the obligations assumed and fulfilled is carried out.[40] In exercising his right and carrying out his duties in regard to the fulfillment of obligations assumed, the local superior will naturally be guided by the general provisions of the Code recorded in canons 824-841 regarding the acceptance, custody, and distribution of the stipends.

B. *Holy Communion and Extreme Unction*

1. Administration *devotionis causa*

At the time of the foundation of the first mendicant Orders in the 13th century, religious priests in general, and consequently the local superior also, were greatly restricted in regard to the administration of the Holy Eucharist to the faithful. The decree *"Omnis utriusque sexus"* of the IV General Council of the Lateran had prescribed annual confession "proprio sacerdoti," [40a] and ruled also that the faithful should receive the Holy Eucharist at least annually at Easter. According to the common interpretation given to this decree, the Easter Communion was also to be received from one's parish priest, and even at other times during the year Communion was not to be received from another priest without the permission of the pastor.[41] Regulars, however, received many privileges allowing them to administer Holy Communion to all who sought it,[42] and among these was the privilege of administering Holy Communion to those who without reasonable cause had been denied the Sacrament by their own parish

[39] Cf. canon 843, § 1.

[40] Canon 843, § 2.

[40a] C. 12, X, *de poenitentiis et remissionibus*, V, 38.

[41] Cf. c. 1, *de privilegiis et excessibus privilegiatorum*, V, 7, in Clem.

[42] Cf. Benedict XIV, *De Synodo Diocesana* (2. ed., 4 vols., Mechliniae, 1842), lib. IX, cap. xvi, n. III; Engel, *Collegium Universi Juris Canonici* (Salisburgi, 1726), lib. III, tit. XLI, n. 21.

priest.[43] All these privileges were given to individual religious "semper tamen licentia praelati supponitur," thus giving the local superior the right of permitting or denying his subjects the use of the privileges. Gradually, however, these restrictions were removed, and even before the Code religious could administer Holy Communion to all the faithful, even on Easter Sunday.[44]

According to the present legislation, the local superior like every priest, may administer the Sacrament of Holy Eucharist to his subjects and to any of the faithful who present themselves before him during and even outside the celebration of Mass, observing the prescriptions of canon 846. He may therefore administer Holy Communion immediately before or after Mass, if he celebrates privately, but he may not do so clothed in the vestments proper to the Mass, before or after the conventual Mass.[45] He may bring Holy Communion, even "per modum devotionis," to those who are sick within the religious house, but if they are confined to a hospital outside the religious house, i. e., "extra septa monasterii," the right to bring Holy Communion *publicly* even to religious, belongs to the pastor of the territory in which the hospital is located. In case of necessity, however, the local superior or any other priest, may bring Holy Communion, even publicly, to the sick religious, as long as he has at least the presumed permission of the territorial pastor or of the Ordinary of the diocese.[46] He may bring Holy Communion *privately* without any further permission if he carries the Blessed Sacrament from his own religious church or oratory,[47] but to bring Holy Com-

[43] Cf. Passerinus, *De Statibus*, Q. CLXXXVII, art. I, n. 938.

[44] S. C. C., 28 nov. 1912—*Fontes*, n. 4363; *AAS*, IV (1912), 726; cf. "Annotationes," *Periodica*, VII (1914), 70.

[45] S. R. C., *Ordinis Fratrum Minorum Provinciae Apuliae*, 19 jan. 1906—*Decreta Authentica*, n. 4177.

[46] Canon 848. Cf. *PCI*, 16 iun. 1931—*AAS*, XXIII (1931), 353.

[47] Cf. canon 849, § 1. The local superior himself is the custodian of the Blessed Sacrament reserved in the oratory or church of the religious community. In virtue of canon 609, § 1, compared with canon 415, § 3, 1°, he is also the custodian of the Blessed Sacrament reserved in a parochial church which is united *pleno iure* to the religious house, because he as superior repre-

munion privately to a sick religious the local superior, like all other priests, needs the presumed permission of the priest to whom the custody of the Blessed Sacrament is entrusted, if he takes the Blessed Sacrament from any church or oratory other than his own.

2. *Administration of Viaticum and Extreme Unction*

In regard to the administration of the Holy Eucharist as Viaticum, the Church has ever been solicitous that the proper pastor attend the sick person. From a natural point of view this attitude would seem only right, for it is certainly fitting that the one to whom principally the spiritual life of a soul has been entrusted should also prepare that soul for eternity. Before the present Code all religious, and consequently superiors as well as subjects, were prohibited from administering Viaticum or Extreme Unction to the general faithful except in case of necessity,[48] but in virtue of the privilege of exemption religious superiors were always given jurisdiction in sacramental matters over their own subjects. As regards these subjects the local superior was, in fact, regarded as the proper pastor referred to in the IV General Council of the Lateran (1215) when the fulfillment of this decree concerned religious. Both Gregory IX (1227-1241) and Clement V (1305-1314) reaffirmed the generally admitted right of religious to administer the Holy Eucharist to their own subjects.[49] Clement V expressly included the *familiares*. The Council of Trent (1545-1563) reaffirmed the exemption of the *familiares*,[50] provided they were engaged in the actual service of the religious house, resided within it, and were under obedience to the religious superior.[51]

sents the community to which the rights listed in canon 415, § 3 belong. Therefore he would not need the permission of anyone to take the Blessed Sacrament from these oratories to a sick religious.

[48] C. 1, *de privilegiis et excessibus privilegiatorum,* V, 7, in Clem. Leo X (in Conc. Lateranen V), const. *"Dum intra,"* 19 febr. 1516, § 7—*Fontes,* n. 72. Pius IX, const. *"Apostolicae Sedis,"* 12 oct. 1869, § II, n. 14—*Fontes,* n. 552.

[49] C. 16, X, *de excessibus praelatorum et subditorum,* V, 31. C. 1, *de privilegiis et excessibus privilegiatorum,* V, 7, in Clem.

[50] Sess. XXV, *de regularibus,* c. 11. Schroeder, *Canons and Decrees,* pp. 224, 492.

[51] Cf. *Conc. Trident.,* sess. XXIV, *de ref.,* c. 11. Gregory XIII, const.

As regards the "hospitii" or those who dwelt as guests in the religious house, the local superior had no jurisdiction over them in the administration of Viaticum or of Extreme Unction, nor had he any right to bury them from the church of the religious.[52] The same may be said of the "alumni," or those who lived in the religious house *causa educationis,* for if they were not also *familiares* the local superior had no sacramental jurisdiction over them,[53] at least in virtue of common law, though some institutes had secured privileges in this matter, and such privileges were often communicated to other Orders.[54]

The present legislation of the Code incorporates much of the previous law in canon 514, and settles many of the previous disputes as to what classes of those who live in the religious house come under the jurisdiction of the religious superior. In reference to the administration of Viaticum and Extreme Unction the Code recognizes the rights and duties that superiors have to administer, either personally or by delegate, those Sacraments in case of sickness to the professed members, to the novices, and to other persons dwelling day and night in the religious house by reason of service, education, hospitality, or for the purpose of recovering health.[55]

It is immediately evident that the legislation in canon 514, § 1 is a change from that of the previous law. According to the present Code all clerical exempt superiors have the jurisdiction referred to.

"Circumspecta," 25 nov. 1580—*BRT,* VIII, 361, § 2. The S. C. Ep. et Reg. *Zagrabien,* 14 dec. 1674—*Fontes,* n. 1809, refers explicitly to the local prior and the *familiares.* Cf. *Collectanea in usum Secretariae Sacrae Congregationis Episcoporum et Regularium,* cura A. Bizzarri, (Romae, 1885), p. 564, note (1). Hereafter cited as *Collectanea. Fontes,* 1954, n. 1. Reiffenstuel, *Jus Canonicum Universum,* VII, 208, Animad. XI, § I.

[52] S. C. C. *Astensi, Iurium Parochialium,* 27 nov. 1717. Cf. Bizzarri, *Collectanea, loc cit.*; Reiffenstuel, *loc. cit.*

[53] S. C. Ep. et Reg. *Zagrabien,* 14 dec. 1674—*Fontes,* n. 1809.

[54] Cf. Piatus, *Praelectiones,* II, qu. 287, 4°, 5°. S. C. Ep. et Reg. *Parmen.,* 21 iul. 1648—*Fontes,* n. 1954.

[55] Cf. canons 514, § 1, 850. Canon 514, § 1 includes also the right to administer whatever rites or blessings are usually associated with the administration of the Last Sacraments, e. g., the imparting of the Apostolic Benediction, the recitation of the prayers for the dying, etc.

They have this right and duty not only in regard to their own subjects, and to the *familiares,* but also in regard to the students and guests who reside in the religious house. This right is given to all religious superiors, since the canon makes no distinction, but it is evident that the local superior is referred to particularly, since he, in virtue of his office, will have charge of the religious house.[56]

The local superior's jurisdiction in reference to the administration of Viaticum and Extreme Unction to his own professed subjects and to the novices presents no difficulties as long as they are ill within the religious house, or *intra septa monasterii.*[57] When they are confined to a hospital outside of the precincts of the religious house, he still has the right of administering Viaticum and Extreme Unction to his professed subjects and to the novices,[58] but if he wishes to carry Viaticum to them publicly he is obliged to have at least the presumed permission of the pastor of the territory.[59] As has already been noted in regard to the private administration of the Holy Eucharist to his subjects outside the religious house, even *devotionis causa,* it may be repeated here that the local superior needs only the permission of the priest in charge of the custody of the Blessed Sacrament reserved in the church or oratory from which the superior wishes to take It.[60] If he carries the Blessed Sacrament as Viaticum from the church or oratory attached to his own house, he needs no permission to do so, since he himself as the local superior is the custodian of the Blessed Sacrament reserved in the church or oratory of his own religious house.

With regard to the jurisdiction of the local superior in religious Orders over the lay-brother postulants, and over those postulants who are aspiring to the clerical state, such as students in an apostolic school *intra septa monasterii,* or aspirants making the prescribed retreat before admission to the novitiate, one may ask

[56] Cf. Cappello, *De Sacramentis,* I, n. 323, 3, (c). Larraona, "Commentarium Codicis,"—*CpR,* IX (1928), 104, (c).

[57] Augustine, *Commentary,* III, 142.

[58] Cf. *PCI,* 16 iun. 1931—*AAS,* XXIII (1931), 353. Cf. Vermeersch, "Annotationes," *Periodica,* XXI (1932), 38.

[59] Cf. canon 848, § 1.

[60] Cf. canon 848, § 2, and *supra,* pp. 137-138.

whether or not they are included among those mentioned in canon 514, § 1, in view of the fact that they are not expressly mentioned in that canon. Assuredly they are to be included, if they can be classed in some one or other of the four categories of those mentioned in the canon.

Pejška considers postulants as equivalent to servants,[61] and Toso to guests.[62] Other authors [63] who wrote before 1929 considered postulants as sharing at least in part in the privileges and favors granted to the religious institute, thus extending to them the privilege granted to novices in canon 567, §1. This opinion has lost most of its value in view of an official interpretation of the Pontifical Commission, in which it was stated that canon 1221, in which reference is made to the burial of the professed religious, novices, and servants, is not to be extended to postulants.[64] From this response it is certain only that postulants are not subject to the jurisdiction of the local superior as regards burial rights. The Commission was not asked to decide the question as to whether postulants share generally in the favors and privileges granted to religious, but the response given in reference to canon 1221 might possibly, but certainly not necessarily, serve as an indication of the mind of the Commission in regard to the participation of postulants in other privileges and favors granted to the professed religious and novices. From such an interpretation of the Commission's response, it might be concluded that postulants do not share in these privileges and favors unless they, too, are expressly mentioned.

In the opinion of the writer, apostolic students and postulants are certainly subject to the jurisdiction given the local superior in canon 514, § 1, if they can be included under those who reside in the religious house *causa educationis*.[65] Certainly postulants can be

[61] *Ius Canonicum Religiosorum*, p. 87.

[62] *Commentaria Minora*, II, P. II, 56.

[63] Vermeersch-Creusen, *Epitome*, II, n. 530. Coronata, *Institutiones*, I, n. 587.

[64] *PCI*, 20 iul. 1929, IV—*AAS*, XXI (1929), 573.

[65] This is also the classification chosen by Berutti, though he would also consider postulants as equivalent to novices, for the application of canon 514, § 1. (*Institutiones*, III, n. 27.)

so regarded, as can apostolic students if they are not merely attending classes during the day but dwell also within the precincts of the religious house during the night.

It is preferable to include postulants under those classed as students rather than as servants or guests, inasmuch as those who reside in the religious house *causa famulatus aut hospitii* are a class entirely separate from those aspiring to admission into the institute. While not all students are also postulants, all postulants are certainly students of the religious life which they seek to follow later as novices and as professed lay-brothers or clerics.

It is not necessary, therefore, or even advisable, to consider the postulant as included in the term *novitiis*, or as a guest or servant, but rather as a student subject to the jurisdiction of the local superior, and included among those who dwell habitually in the religious house *causa educationis*.

The local superior's jurisdiction over servants includes those who work for the religious and dwell within the precincts of the religious house under the habitual, though not the religious, obedience of the superior of the house.[66] Even though the servants receive a fixed salary, as long as they are resident day and night in the religious house, they are subject to the jurisdiction of the local superior. The local superior can claim no jurisdiction over day students, since they do not dwell in the religious house *diu noctuque*.

Some authors insist that before the sick (excluding the sick religious) become subject to the superior's jurisdiction they must be within the religious house for a space of time beyond, but generally longer than, twenty-four hours.[67] Such an opinion is probably correct, unless the sick person should manifest his desire of staying in

[66] The term *familiares* is a wider one than *famuli*—"Familiares sunt qui in religiosa domo diu noctuque degunt causa famulatus aut educationis aut hospitii aut infirmae valetudinis, ut famuli, postulantes, alumni, convictores exceptis feriis, hospites vel infirmi saltem per aliquot dies in ipsa religiosa domo, quamvis extra clausuram diu noctuque degentes."—Genicot-Salsmans, *Institutiones Theologiae Moralis* (ed. 10, 2 vols., Bruxellis, 1922), II, n. 338. Cf. Ramos, "De Conditione Saecularium in Domibus Religiosorum,"—*CpR*, VII (1925), 136-140.

[67] Cf. Genicot-Salsmans, *loc. cit.* Augustine, *Commentary*, III, 142.

the religious house for at least a day and a night before he has actually spent a full day and night in a religious house. The intention of remaining for at least one day and night would be sufficient to place one under the jurisdiction of the local superior from the time such an intention was manifested, and even before the passage of one day and night.[68]

What has been written up to this point regarding the administration of Viaticum and Extreme Unction by the local superior to postulants and *familiares* has treated principally of the administration of these Sacraments in the religious house. As was pointed out above in regard to the administration of Viaticum to the professed religious and novices,[69] the Pontifical Commission declared that the jurisdiction given the religious superior in canon 514, § 1 applied to the professed religious and novices also when they are ill outside the religious house. The Commission had been asked whether the superior in such circumstances had the right to administer to all the persons mentioned in canon 514, § 1, when they are ill outside the religious house.[70] In its reply, however, the Commission affirmed such jurisdiction in regard to the professed and to the novices only, and declared that it did not extend to those who resided in the religious house *diu noctuque . . . causa famulatus aut educationis aut hospitii aut infirmae valetudinis* when these latter were ill outside the religious house. Wherefore, all servants, students, guests, and the infirm, when outside the religious house are subject to the jurisdiction of the pastor of the place where the house in which they reside is located,[71] and not to the local superior.[72]

This decision of the Pontifical Commission seems also to exclude postulants from the jurisdiction of the local superior, when they are outside the religious house, at least if postulants are not to be understood also whenever reference is made in juridical documents to

[68] Cf. Fanfani, *De Iure Religiosorum,* n. 415. Vermeersch-Creusen, *Epitome,* II, n. 582.

[69] *Supra,* p. 140.

[70] *PCI,* 16 iun. 1931—*AAS,* XXIII (1931), 353.

[71] Cf. canons 848, 850.

[72] "Ratio discriminis haec esse potuit, quod pro prioribus, jus superioris ratione personae, pro posterioribus vero ratione loci, sit concessum."—Vermeersch, "Annotationes,"—*Periodica,* XXI (1932), 38.

novices. In this study it has already been maintained that postulants are subject to the jurisdiction of the local superior when they are present in the religious house, because they are to be enumerated among those who are there *causa educationis,* and not because they can be included under the word *novitiis* of canon 514, § 1. Wherefore it is now maintained that in view of the reply of the Pontifical Commission, the local superior cannot administer Viaticum and Extreme Unction to postulants who are ill outside the religious house, unless he obtains the permission of the pastor or other priest who has been granted parochial rights in the place where the postulants are.

In concluding the treatment of the administration of the Holy Eucharist by the local superior, the writer wishes also to note that even though the local superior has the right of administering the Holy Eucharist to his subjects, ordinarily it is not his right to decide whether or not any of these subjects who have been ill a month without certain hope of speedy recovery may receive Holy Communion twice a week even though they may have taken medicine or liquid food beforehand. To give such counsel is the right of the confessor.[73] Moreover, the local superior may well keep in mind always the prescription of canon 865, which warns against the delaying of the administration of Holy Viaticum to the sick and urges vigilance in administering Viaticum while the infirm person has the full use of his faculties.

Article III. Penance

A. Legislation Previous to the Code

1. Members of the Community

A study of the legislation regarding the minister of the Sacrament of Penance both before and after the Council of Trent (1545-1563) and up to the time of the promulgation of the present Code [74] cannot fail to show the student how strictly the decree of the IV

[73] Cf. canon 858, § 2.

[74] Cf. McCormick, *Confessors of Religious,* The Catholic University of America Canon Law Studies, n. 33 (Washington, D. C.: The Catholic University of America, 1926), pp. 1-30.

General Council of the Lateran (1215) prescribing confession to one's own pastor (*proprio sacerdoti*) or to his delegate was carried out as regards religious.[75] The local superior was considered the *proprius sacerdos* for all the religious of his convent, and for those servants (*familiares*) who resided there and who were supported by the institute.[76] Though it was customary that several confessors be appointed for each convent by the superiors of the Order, the local superior always retained his own ordinary penitential jurisdiction over his subjects. In 1593 Clement VIII (1592-1605) had prohibited him from using that jurisdiction unless a subject desired absolution from a reserved sin, or spontaneously and of his own accord asked the superior to hear his confession.[77] In the same constitution the Pope commanded all superiors to depute two or three or even more confessors to administer to the religious as their ordinary confessors. In some Orders the local superior had no power to depute these confessors. Ordinarily the novice master alone could hear the confessions of the novices, but the same Pope permitted the local superior to hear them, either personally or by delegate, once or twice a year.[78]

Usually the local superior was forbidden by particular law to delegate others outside of the Order or from the secular clergy to hear the confession of one of his subjects. Clement IV (1265-1268) had prohibited religious except in cases of necessity from confessing to those who were not members of the same Order.[79] Benedict XI (1303-1304) in the constitution, "*Inter cunctas,*" [80] had also prohibited all religious from confessing to any priest other than one of their own Order, if the Constitutions forbade them to do so. Perhaps this decision of Benedict XI was the basis for the assertion

[75] Canon 12. C. 12, X, *de poenitentiis et remissionibus*, V, 38—Schroeder, *Disciplinary Decrees*, pp. 259, 570.

[76] Cf. Suarez, *De religione*, tr. VIII, lib. II, cap. XV, n. 3. Donatus, *Rerum Regularium*, tom. IV, tr. V, q. 12, n. 1. Vermeersch, "De Unitate Confessarii Ordinarii Apud Moniales et Sorores,"—*Periodica*, V (1913), (1)-(12).

[77] Const. "*Sanctissimus,*" 26 maii 1593, §§ 2, 3—*Fontes*, n. 177.

[78] Const. "*Cum ad regularem,*" 19 mart. 1603—*Fontes*, n. 189.

[79] Const. "*Virtute conspicuos,*" 21 iul. 1265, § 24—*BRT*, III, 736.

[80] 17 febr. 1304—c. 1, *de privilegiis*, V, 7, in Extravag. com.

by many writers [81] that if the Constitutions of the institute did not forbid a superior to delegate others to hear the confessions of his subjects, he could delegate any priest, even a secular priest, to administer the Sacrament of Penance to them. This opinion was confirmed in a response of the Sacred Congregation of Bishops and Regulars, wherein it was maintained that the conventual prior of the Augustinian Order could delegate any other priest approved by the local ordinary to hear the confessions of his subjects.[82] The same Congregation, in this response, referred the petitioner to the Constitutions and Statutes of each Order or institute for the practice to be observed in the Order or institute.

It can be concluded, therefore, that even before the present Code the ordinary jurisdiction of the local superior to hear the confessions of his own subjects and to delegate others to do so was generally recognized. Among the subjects of the local superior were the novices, the professed, and those servants who were actually considered members of the religious family.[83]

2. Women Religious

Very early legislation on the confessors of nuns is wanting, though it is believed that usually the nuns confessed to the local priests.[84] At least from the time of the IV General Council of the Lateran (1215) many of the monasteries of nuns were subject to a regular prelate, who held the place of the proper pastor for the nuns subject to him.[85] In such cases the regular superior appointed the confessor for the nuns. The Council of Trent [86] likewise directed that ordinary

[81] Cf. *Piscien. seu Ordinis Eremitarum S. Augustini,* 3 iun. 1864—*Fontes,* n. 1992. Bizzarri, *Collectanea,* p. 722, note 1.

[82] Cf. *Piscien. seu Ordinis Eremitarum S. Augustini,* 3 iun. 1864—*Fontes,* n. 1992.

[83] Cf. Clemens X, const. *"Superna,"* 21 iun. 1670—*Fontes,* n. 246. S. C. C. *Parisien.,* 30 mart. 1594—*Fontes,* n. 2266.

[84] Cf. McCormick, *Confessors of Religious,* p. 75.

[85] Donatus, *Rerum Regularium,* tom. III, tr. XIII, q. 23, n. 1. Passerinus, *De Statibus,* Q. CLXXXVII, art. I, n. 822.

[86] Sess. XXV, *de regularibus,* c. 10—Schroeder, *Canons and Decrees,* 224, 491.

and extraordinary confessors be provided for them "by the bishop and other superiors" (*ab episcopo et aliis superioribus*), and later Popes [87] continued to issue pronouncements urging a strict adherence to the Council's prescription that the bishops and regular prelates provide these ordinary and extraordinary confessors for the nuns. Though the Council did not explicitly demand the approbation of the bishop for those confessors who had been appointed for the nuns by the regular superiors, such approbation was required by Gregory XV (1621-1623),[88] and this was the practice until the promulgation of the new Code as regards the confessors of nuns subject to regulars.[89] They were designated by the regular superior to whom the nuns were subject, and then approved by the bishop.

It is of particular interest in this study to know what superior, general, provincial, or local, was referred to in these Papal constitutions and in the legislation of the Council of Trent (1545-1563). A careful search of Papal constitutions of the periods both before and after the Council of Trent, as well as of the writings of canonists who have treated in detail the subject of the confessors of nuns,[90] has failed to reveal whether or not any local superior of the regulars ever had any of the monasteries of nuns subject to him. Some of the Papal constitutions found in the *Bullarium* of the Order of

[87] Gregory XV, const. "*Inscrutabile*," 5 febr. 1622—*Fontes*, n. 199; Innocent XIII, const. "*Apostolici ministerii*," 23 maii 1723, § 21—*Fontes*, n. 280; Benedict XIII, const. "*In supremo*," 23 sept. 1724, §§ 17, 18—*Fontes*, n. 283; Benedict XIV, const. "*Pastoralis curae*," 5 aug. 1748—*Fontes*, n. 388.

[88] Const. "*Inscrutabile*," 5 febr. 1622—*Fontes*, n. 199, § 5. Cf. Donatus, *Rerum Regularium*, tom. III, tr. XIII, q. 5, n. 4. The Council did demand the approbation by the bishop before a regular confessor could hear the confessions of seculars.—Sess. XXIII, *de ref.*, c 15—Schroeder, *Canons and Decrees*, 173, 444.

[89] Piatus, *Praelectiones*, I, qu. 591, 3°; Prümmer, *Manuale I. E.*, qu. 232, r. 4.

[90] Cf. especially Donatus, *Rerum Regularium*, tom. III, tr. XIII, qq. 1-58; Passerinus, *De Statibus*, Q. CLXXXVII, art. I, nn. 815-931; Ferreres, *Prompta Bibliotheca*, s. v. "Moniales"; Piatus, *Praelectiones*, qq. 589-610; Pallottini, *Collectio Omnium Conclusionum et Resolutionum quae in causis propositis apud Sacram Congregationem Cardinalium S. Concilii Tridentini Interpretum Prodierunt ab eius institutione anno MDLXIX ad MDCCCLX, distinctis titulis alphabetico ordine per materias digestas* (18 vols., Romae, 1868-1895), s. v. "Moniales." Hereafter cited as Pallottini.

Preachers, for example, are addressed to and refer to the major superiors of the Order; [91] others use only the word "Priores" without qualification.[92] The Council of Trent (1545-1563) used only "Superiores," [93] and the Papal constitutions issued after the Council of Trent refer only to the "Superiores Regulares," [94] and the "Praelati regulares." [95] Donatus [96] and Passerinus [97] do not particularize either, studiously repeating the general regulations "praelatus regularis," and "superior regularis." Pallottini [98] refers to a decree of the Sacred Congregation of the Council, March 10, 1663, which has reference to a monastery of nuns subject to the provincial; and other writers, when referring to the confessor of nuns sometimes designate the general and provincial superior by name but never the local superior.

From an examination of the Papal constitutions and of the authors consulted, it is impossible to determine whether or not the nuns were subject to the local superior. It is the opinion of the writer that the local superior who would be considered a minor local superior in the present legislation had no monasteries of nuns subject to the ordinary jurisdiction which he had as local superior of a religious convent of men. That the local superior could have been delegated by the provincial to act in his name is beyond doubt, but such delegation could likewise be given to any religious as well as to a local superior.

Lacking any example in common law of ordinary jurisdiction exercised over nuns by a local superior of men, one may conclude

[91] Cf. Clemens IV, const. *"Affectu sincero,"* 6 febr. 1267—*BOP,* I, 481; Potthast, *Regesta,* n. 19935. Boniface VIII, const. *"Apostolicae Sedis,"* 18 ian. 1297—*BOP,* II, 52.

[92] Cf. Innocent IV, const. *"Licet olim,"* 4 apr. 1246—*BOP,* I, 161; Potthast, *Regesta,* n. 12055. Boniface IX, const. *"Sacrae religionis,"* 27 apr. 1402—*BOP,* II, 446.

[93] Sess. XXV, *de regularibus,* c. 10.

[94] Cf. Gregory XV, const. *"Inscrutabile,"* 5 febr. 1622, § 5—*Fontes,* n. 199; Innocent XIII, const. *"Apostolici ministerii,"* 23 maii 1723, § 21—*Fontes,* n. 280.

[95] Benedict XIII, const. *"In supremo,"* 23 sept. 1724—*Fontes,* n. 283.

[96] *Rerum Regularium,* tom. III, tr. XIII, qq. 1-58.

[97] *De Statibus,* Q. CLXXXVII, art. I, nn. 815-931.

[98] S. v. "Moniales," § 1, n. 57.

that the local superior as superior of an individual house did not have any ordinary jurisdiction over those who resided "extra septa monasterii." It would seem more consonant with the nature of the jurisdiction of the provincial or general superior as not being confined to a local house,[99] but extending over a whole province or Order, to have had monasteries of nuns subject to his jurisdiction, rather than to the jurisdiction of the local superior.

The conclusion that the nuns were subject to the provincial or general directly rather than to any local superior was beyond doubt in regard to the Dominican Order, though the provincial could institute a conventual prior as his vicar.[100] The priest who was given charge of the nuns was often called the vicar of the provincial, or the prior,[101] but even though called prior he was not necessarily prior of any convent of men, and often devoted all of his time to the care of the nuns. At least one example of subjection to a provincial superior in more recent times can be seen in a letter of a provincial to the Sacred Congregation of Bishops and Regulars.[102]

3. The Laity

Though the local superior according to the present legislation of the Church has no ordinary jurisdiction which would render him competent to administer the Sacrament of Penance to lay persons other than those who reside in the religious house according to canon 514, § 1, a brief account of the jurisdictional power which he

[99] This is not to deny that the local superior's jurisdiction was also personal, that is, could be exercised over his subjects, even though they were not actually present in the house, but only to point out that it does not seem according to the nature of the local superior as *local* to have had religious subject to him who did not reside at least habitually in that superior's convent. Nuns would surely come under this latter classification.

[100] Cf. *Const. S. O. P.* (1886), §§ 715-716.

[101] Cf. *Analecta Sacri Ordinis Fratrum Praedicatorum seu Vetera Ordinis Monumenta Recentioraque Acta* (Romae, 1893—); ab anno 1907: *Analecta Sacri Ordinis Fratrum Praedicatorum,* II, 103, *in fine.* Hereafter cited as *Analecta S. O. P.*

[102] Cf. S. C. Ep. et Reg., *Ordinis Praedicatorum,* 12 oct. 1892—*Analecta S. O. P.,* I, 289.

formerly exercised even over seculars will render the present practice of the Church clearer in contrast.

In the formative period of monasticism the priest-monks were occasionally invited by the local bishops or pastors to hear the confessions of lay people. After the IV General Council of the Lateran (1215) the pastor of the penitent could have given the religious permission to hear the confession of the faithful. Always, however, there remains the question as to the source of the jurisdiction given to such religious. It is beyond the scope of this work to attempt to add further to the arguments in the dispute as to whether jurisdiction came immediately from the Pope, or was given by the bishop, when a religious was presented to the local ordinary by his regular superior.[103] It is sufficient to note here that some of the Papal constitutions seem to support the contention that the religious received jurisdiction directly from the Holy See, after being approved by their superiors.[104] In 1300, however, Boniface VIII (1294-1303) demanded the approval of the bishop even after the superior had chosen the confessor,[105] but Benedict XI (1303-1304), revoking the constitution *"Super cathedram,"* asked only that the religious be deputed by their own superiors.[106] Clement V (1305-1314) [107] and John XXII (1316-1334) [108] renewed the law demanding that the religious be approved by the bishop even after their election by the competent religious superior. Pope Leo X (1513-1521) at the V General Council of

[103] Cf. Donatus, *Rerum Regularium,* tom. IV, tr. IV, qq. 31-33. Piatus, *Praelectiones,* II, Q. 225.

[104] Greg. IX, const. *"Quoniam abundavit,"* 21 apr. 1227—*BOP,* I, 18; Potthast, *Regesta,* n. 7880. *Idem,* const. *"Quoniam abundavit,"* 10 maii 1227—*BOP,* I, 19; *Regesta,* n. 7896. Martin IV, const. *"Ad fructus uberes,"* 10 ian. 1282—*BOP,* II, 1; Potthast, *Regesta,* n. 21821. Rodericus, *Nova Collectio et Compilatio Privilegiorum Apostolicorum Regularium Mendicantium et non Mendicantium praesertim in quibus ipsae Religiones communicant* (ed. ult. Antverpiae, 1623), p. 32. Hereafter cited as Rodericus, *Collectio.*

[105] Const. *"Super cathedram,"* 18 febr. 1300—c. 2, *de sepulturis,* III, 6, in Extravag. com.; Potthast, *Regesta,* n. 24913.

[106] Const. *"Inter cunctas,"* 17 febr. 1304—c. 1, *de privilegiis,* V, 7, in Extravag. com.; Potthast, *Regesta,* n. 25370.

[107] Const. *"Dudum,"* 6 maii 1312—c. 2, *de sepulturis,* III, 7, in Clem.

[108] Const. *"Frequentes,"* 23 ian. 1327—c. un. *de iudiciis,* II, 1, in Extravag. com.

the Lateran (1512-1517) ruled that "religious superiors must present the religious whom they had chosen for hearing confessions to the bishops, if these request such presentation"; [109] and in the Council of Trent (1545-1563) it was definitely stated that no one, even though a regular, could hear the confessions of seculars unless he held a parochial benefice or was approved by the bishop, all privileges and customs to the contrary notwithstanding.[110] The law of the Council of Trent was reiterated by many of the Popes and Sacred Congregations from the sixteenth century, even until the promulgation of the Code of Canon Law into which it was incorporated in canon 875, § 1.[111]

Of principal interest in this study is the question of what superior gave jurisdiction to the religious, if the Order had received the privilege of doing so without seeking jurisdiction from the local ordinary, and what superior approved or presented the religious to the bishop when such presentation became necessary. An examination of two Papal constitutions, both of which begin with the words *"Quoniam abundavit,"* [112] in which Gregory IX (1227-1241) gave faculties to the Friars Preachers to hear the confessions of the faithful, shows that the Pope made no mention of the necessity of approbation by any superior, though such approbation was no doubt understood. The constitution *"Ad fructus uberes,"* [113] makes mention of the master general and the priors provincial, to whom Martin IV permitted the faculties given therein. The later constitutions all used the words "magistri," "Ministri," "Priores provinciales," "Provinciales Ministri," and "Custodes," but no explicit reference has been found in any of them to the "priores conventuales," to the "guardiani" or to the "superiores locales." Leo X (1513-1521) used

[109] Const. *"Dum intra,"* 19 dec. 1516, § 6—*Fontes,* n. 72.

[110] Sess. XXIII, *de ref.,* c. 15; Cf. Schroeder, *Canons and Decrees,* pp. 173, 444.

[111] Cardinal Gasparri in a footnote to canon 874, § 1 refers to thirteen Papal constitutions and to twenty-one documents of various Sacred Congregations, all of which directly or indirectly reaffirm the necessity of the bishop's approval of any confessor who wishes to hear confessions of seculars.

[112] 21 apr. 1227—*BOP,* I, 18; Potthast, *Regesta,* n. 7880. 10 maii 1227 —*BOP,* I, 19; Potthast, *Regesta,* n. 7896.

[113] Martin IV, 10 ian. 1282—*BOP,* II, 1; Potthast, *Regesta,* n. 21821.

only the word "superiores." [114] The Council of Trent [115] made no mention of the necessity of presentation by the superior, but it is generally agreed that the Council presupposed this condition, since it required the approbation of the local ordinary, and since it did not revoke the previous Papal constitutions, which as a rule required at least the approval or presentation of the religious to the bishop by his superior.[116] Most of the declarations of the Sacred Congregation of Bishops and Regulars and of the Sacred Congregation of the Council referred to as sources in canon 874, § 1 generally refer to the necessity of obtaining the bishop's approbation, but do not make reference to the local religious superior.[117] Reference however is made in two decrees of the Sacred Congregation of Bishops and Regulars to the power of the general and of the provincial over these subjects in relation to the faculties for confessions, but no explicit mention is made of the conventual or local superior.[118]

As regards jurisdiction for the confessions of seculars, therefore, it may be concluded that the local superior's power seems to have been very limited. First of all he had no power to grant the jurisdiction itself, except perhaps during the short time (1304-1213) that the constitution of Benedict XI [119] was in force. Secondly it is at least probable that before the V General Council of the Lateran (1512-1517) he could not select the confessors who were later to be presented to the

[114] (In Conc. Lateranen. V), const. *"Dum intra,"* 19 dec. 1516, § 6—*Fontes,* n. 72.

[115] Sess. XXIII, *de ref.*, c. 15.

[116] Cf. Donatus, *Rerum Regularium,* tom. IV, tr. IV, q. 32, nn. 2-4. Piatus, *Praelectiones,* II, q. 234.

[117] S. C. Ep. et Reg. refers to the local prior as administering the Holy Eucharist to his subjects, but does not mention him explicitly when referring to the jurisdiction necessary for the minister of the Sacrament of Penance. (*Zagrabien.*, 14 dec. 1674—*Fontes,* n. 1809.) The S. C. C. refers to a guardian who maintained that he did not need the approbation of the bishop, and then declares the confessions he had heard invalid (*Patavina,* 11 dec. 1683—*Fontes,* n. 2878). These are the only two sources found which refer at all to the local superior.

[118] *"Clericorum Regularium,"* 2 iul. 1627—*Fontes,* n. 1729; *"Ordinis Praedicatorum,"* 2 mart. 1866—*Fontes,* n. 1996.

[119] *"Inter cunctas,"* 17 febr. 1304—c. 1, *de privilegiis,* V, 7, in Extravag. com.

bishop for his approbation, since the constitutions *"Super cathedram"* and *"Dudum"* mention only the general and provincial superiors. Thirdly, after the V General Council of the Lateran, and until the present Code, even the local superior could choose the confessors, and present them to the bishop, unless prohibited from doing so by his own Constitutions, since Leo X (1513-1521) in the constitution *"Dum intra"* made no distinction among superiors when he prescribed that they should present their religious to the bishop when the latter requested such presentation. The Council of Trent did not directly prescribe a presentation by any superior, but as already stated,[120] this presentation was presupposed, and in most of the religious Orders, in practice, even up until the promulgation of the new Code, the presentation was made either by the provincial or by the local superior. Particular law could of course require that the provincial alone present the religious to the bishop,[121] but ordinarily such a duty was given to the local superior. Finally the right to present the religious to the bishop should not be confused with either the actual granting of the jurisdiction on the part of the bishop (at least after the Council of Trent), or with the right of a board of examiners to examine and approve those who, having successfully undergone such an examination, were considered qualified to receive jurisdiction for the hearing of confessions.

4. Reservation of Sins

Concerning the local superior's power to reserve sins, authors do not agree. Before the decree of Clement VIII (1592-1605), limiting the number of cases which prelates could reserve to themselves,[122] the local superiors of the Franciscans had received from Alexander VI (1492-1503) the faculty of reserving sins in certain cases,[123] and this

[120] *Supra*, p. 152.

[121] Donatus (*Rerum Regularium*, tom. IV, tr. IV, q. 29, n. 1), writing in the seventeenth century, stated "In meo enim Ordine (Praedicatorum) . . . dicitur quod confessores tam saecularium quam fratrum debent approbari a patrum Consilio, et P. Provinciali pro tempore . . ." He does not explicitly exclude or include the local superior.

[122] *"Sanctissimus,"* 26 maii 1593—*Fontes*, n. 177.

[123] Const. *"Intelleximus,"* 24 iul. 1501—Rodericus, *Collectio*, p. 212.

privilege was not taken away by the decree of Clement VIII.[124] Suarez [125] taught that the local superiors could reserve sins even after the decree if they had that power before the decree was issued. Schmalzgrueber (+1735) seems to be of the same opinion since he writes that the regular prelate can reserve sins even of novices.[126] Other writers maintained that the power to reserve sins belonged only to provincial and general superiors. This was the opinion of Ferraris, who writes that this opinion was the common and certain one in his time,[127] and also of Thesaurus (+1655).[128] Prümmer, writing just previous to the Code of Canon Law, maintained that even the local superior could reserve sins.[129] Certainly this was true of a conventual prior in the Order of Preachers.[130]

In the opinion of the writer the disagreement seems to be based on the manner in which the various authors regarded the jurisdictional power of the local superiors. Those who maintained that he had quasi-episcopal power were usually in favor of his power to reserve sins, while those who denied such power in the local superior, denied also his power to reserve sins. The dispute is only of historical interest now, however, since the present legislation not only excludes the local superior, but the provincial superior as well.[131]

5. Special Faculties

(a) To Absolve From Reserved Sins

Authors have treated extensively the absolution of reserved sins and censures, but since most of the material considered pertains to the

[124] Donatus, *Rerum Regularium,* tom. IV, tr. V, q. 5, n. 2.

[125] *De religione,* tr. VIII, lib. II, cap. XVIII, n. 14. Donatus also acknowledges the local prior's power to reserve sins,—*op. cit.*, tom. IV, tr. V, q. 37, n. 1.

[126] *Ius Ecclesiasticum Universum* (5 vols. in 12, Romae, 1843-1845), lib. III, tit. XXXI, § 6, nn. 88-89.

[127] *Prompta Bibliotheca,* s.v. "Praelatus Regularis," n. 56, "Reservatio Casuum," n. 11.

[128] *De Poenis Ecclesiasticis Praxis Absoluta et Universalis* (ed. nova ab Ubaldo Giraldi, Romae, 1760), p. 38. Cited *De Poenis Ecclesiasticis* hereafter.

[129] *Manuale I. E.*, q. 152.

[130] *Const. S. O. P.* (1886), § 591.

[131] Canon 896.

question of the privileges of religious in general, it is proposed to summarize here only the points pertaining to the local superior, as a prelate, except in a few instances. The faculties which he has to absolve in common with all other religious will not be treated.

In 1474, Sixtus IV (1471-1484) confirmed privileges previously given by many Popes to the Dominican Order, and stated again that the conventual prior could absolve his subjects "ab excessibus et censuris . . . nisi talia forent propter quae essent ad Sedem Apostolicam merito destinandi. . . . " Continuing, the same Pope listed only three such sins for which recourse was to be had to the Holy See.[132]

In 1479 the same Pope permitted any Dominican or Franciscan religious with the permission of his superior to choose once in his life any confessor who would be able to absolve the religious from all excesses and sins committed by him.[133] Leo X (1513-1521) granted the same faculty to the confessors of the Poor Clares, "a Praelatis deputati."[134] In these two privileges no power was given directly to the local superior to absolve from the reserved sins or censures, but his permission was required before the confessor chosen or appointed could make use of the privilege, which extended to every sin whatsoever, even one reserved to the Holy Father.[135]

By a decree of Clement VIII (1592-1605), March 13, 1601, the local superior was given the power to delegate any confessor to absolve from sins reserved within the Order.[136] In virtue of the often quoted constitution of St. Pius V, *"Romani Pontificis,"*[137] the conventual prior was given the same faculties to absolve his subjects as bishops had over their clergy and laity. This included the faculty to absolve from all occult cases, even those reserved to the Holy See.[138]

[132] Const. *"Regimini universalis,"* 31 aug. 1474—*BRT*, V, 217; *BOP*, III, 516; Rodericus, *Collectio*, I, 146.

[133] Const. *"Sacri Praedicatorum,"* 26 iul. 1479—*BRT*, V, 278; *BOP*, III, 578.

[134] Const. *"Dum praecelsa,"* 19 iun. 1515—Rodericus, *Collectio*, p. 266.

[135] Cf. Piatus, *Praelectiones*, I, q. 482, 1°.

[136] Cf. Piatus, *Praelectiones*, I, q. 474, n. 4.

[137] 21 iul. 1571—*BRT*, VII, 931.

[138] Cf. Conc. Trident., sess. XXIV, *de ref.*, c. 6.

(b) To Absolve From Reserved Penalties

In general it may be said that the privileges given to the local superior to absolve his subjects from reserved excommunications, suspension, and interdict were very extensive. Boniface VIII (1294-1303) in 1296 granted the conventual priors the faculty of absolving their subjects from all excommunications, suspensions, and interdicts "a jure vel a judice generaliter promulgatas . . . nisi adeo gravis fuerit et enormis excessus, quod sint ad eandem Sedem merito destinandi." [139] This privilege was confirmed by John XXII (1316-1334),[140] by Gregory XI (1370-1378) [141] and by Sixtus IV (1471-1484) [142] At a later date (1479) the privilege was restricted to the generals of the Orders,[143] but even after that time was regarded as in force for those who had enjoyed the privilege previous to the reign of Sixtus IV (1471-1484).[144]

The Council of Trent (1545-1563) gave bishops the power of absolving from all Papal reserved cases, if these were occult.[145] Local superiors could also use this faculty in virtue of the constitution of St. Pius V (1566-1572), *"Romani Pontificis,"* originally given to the Dominican Order.[146]

All such faculties were generally conceded to be within the power of the local superior before the issuance of the constitution, *"Apostolicae Sedis,"* of Pius IX (1846-1878).[147] After the issuance of this constitution the local superior could not absolve from any cases included in the constitution which were reserved *speciali modo* or *simpliciter* to the Holy See [148] except possibly from the excommuni-

[139] Const. *"Virtute conspicuos,"* 19 iun. 1296—*BOP*, II, 48; Potthast, *Regesta*, n. 24344.

[140] Const. *"Virtute conspicuos,"* 15 febr. 1317—*BOP*. II, 132.

[141] Const. *"Virtute conspicuos,"* 6 mart. 1374—*BOP*, II, 278.

[142] Const. *"Regimini universalis,"* 31 aug. 1474—*BOP*, III, 516; *BRT*, V, 217.

[143] Sixtus IV, const. *"Sacri Praedicatorum,"* 26 iul. 1479—*BOP*, III, 578; *BRT*, V, 278.

[144] Cf. Passerinus, *Tractatus De Electione Canonica*, cap. XXVI, n. 14.

[145] Sess. XXIV, *de ref.*, c. 6.

[146] 21 iul. 1571—*BRT*, VII, 931; *BOP*, V, 283.

[147] 12 oct. 1869—*Fontes*, n. 552.

[148] Asked whether regular prelates could absolve from cases *simpliciter reservatis* mentioned in the constitution, the Sacred Apostolic Penitentiary re-

cation incurred for striking a religious.[149] Soon after the constitution some authors held that regular superiors could absolve those of their subjects who could not go personally to Rome for absolution;[150] but after the declaration of the Sacred Council of the Inquisition issued on the 23 June 1886, it was evident that the local superior could do so only in urgent cases and with the duty of imposing recourse to the Holy See within a month.[151]

Since regulars can absolve from censures reserved in common law to bishops, according to the teaching of St. Alphonsus[152] who quotes numerous authors in favor of his opinion, the local superior can do so also. Piatus declares that it is certain that prelates can absolve their subjects from such censures in virtue of a declaration of the Sacred Congregation of the Holy Office, March 22, 1881.[153]

B. *Present Legislation*

1. Ordinary Jurisdiction

Canon 873, § 2 grants to all exempt religious superiors ordinary jurisdiction to hear the confessions of their subjects. Among their subjects are included novices and others mentioned in canon 514, § 1.[154] The jurisdiction is granted *ad normam constitutionum*, and consequently its limits will usually be defined in the particular law

plied: "Negative, salvis illis facultatibus quae promanant ex rescriptis particularibus ad tempus concessis."—*ASS*, IX (1885), 314.

[149] Cf. Piatus, *Praelectiones*, I, qu. 762, 5°.

[150] Cf. D'Annibale, *In Constitutionem Apostolicae Sedis Commentarii* (4. ed., Prati, 1894), p. 225. Téphany, *Constitution Apostolicae Sedis Commentaire* (Tours, 1883), n. 23, 1°.

[151] *ASS*, XIX (1886), 46. This decree was to prevail even if the penitent was forever impeded from going to Rome personally for absolution—S. C. S. Off., 17 iun. 1891; *ASS*, XXIV (1892), 745; *Fontes*, n. 1137.

[152] *Theologia Moralis* (ed. absolutissima, 9 vols., Vesontione, 1832), VIII, n. 99.

[153] *Praelectiones*, I, qu. 487, 4°; qu. 763, 5°, *nota*. Cf. Ojetti, *Synopsis Rerum Moralium et Iuris Pontificii* (2 vols., Prati, 1904-1905), I, 275-276. D'Annibale, *In Constitutionem Apostolicae Sedis Commentarii*, n. 348, p. 424, note 1. "Decisions du Saint-Siège mentionées dans Statuts Synodaux d'Ostie et Velletri," *Nouvelle Revue Théologique*, Paris, 1869—, XXVI (1894), 318.

[154] Cf. canon 875, § 1.

of the institute. Since the Code does not distinguish what religious superiors have the power, it must be admitted that all religious superiors, even the local superior, has ordinary jurisdiction to hear the confessions of his subjects,[155] unless the Constitutions of an exempt institute should restrict this use of ordinary jurisdiction to the major superiors.

A limitation is placed on the use of this jurisdiction even in common law, for canon 518, § 2 warns superiors not to hear the confessions of their subjects, unless they seek out the service of the superior of their own accord. Even in the latter case the superior is not to permit his subjects the habitual use of such a concession, and under no circumstances is he to attempt to induce a subject to confess to him.[156] The reason for such a prohibition is no doubt based on the desire of the Church to give the superiors who must also exercise jurisdiction and dominative authority in the external forum an opportunity to do so freely and without fear of violating the sacramental seal.[157]

2. Delegation of Jurisdiction

The local superior in a clerical exempt religious institute not only has ordinary jurisdiction to hear the confessions of his subjects, but he also has the right to designate confessors for his subjects, unless

[155] On the contrary, Augustine (*Commentary,* IV, 259) says that "the *superiors* mentioned are those who are called *majores,* hence the general or provincials of exempt Orders or congregations and their vicars, who hold a position similar to the provincial." Such a statement can only be true in regard to those Orders which would expressly exclude the local superior, since the canon as it stands must be interpreted to include all who come under the name "superior." Cf. Blat, *Commentarium,* lib. III, pars I, p. 216; Cappello, *De Sacramentis,* II, pars I, n. 386; Claeys-Bouuaert-Simenon, *Manuale Iuris Canonici ad Usum Seminariorum* (Vol. I, 3. ed., 1930; Vol. II, 1931; Vol. III, 3. ed., 1931, Gandae et Leodii: apud auctores in Seminariis Gandavensi et Loediensi), II, n. 123. Hereafter cited as *Manuale Iuris Canonici.* Pejška, *Ius Canonicum Religiosorum,* p. 392; Berutti, *Institutiones,* III, n. 38, I; Schaefer, *De Religiosis,* n. 166, 3.

[156] Canon 518, § 3.

[157] Cf. canon 890, § 2; Clemens VIII, decr. *"Sanctissimus,"* 26 maii 1593, § 4 —*Fontes,* n. 177.

this faculty is reserved in the Constitutions to the major superiors.[158] Moreover, if the confessors designated by the local superior do not already possess jurisdiction over the religious, the local superior himself can delegate jurisdiction to them. This jurisdiction extends not only to the professed, but also to the novices and all others who reside in the religious house "diu noctuque causa famulatus aut educationis aut hospitii aut infimae valetudinis." In a previous article the meaning and extension of these terms of canon 514, §1 have been pointed out.[159] It will suffice here to note that the religious superior can delegate any other priest, either of his own or of another Order, or of the secular clergy to hear the confessions of any of his subjects. Again, because no restriction of superiors is made in the Code, it is maintained that the words "proprius superior" used in this canon, include the local superior, unless the Constitutions of any particular Order would exclude him from the exercise of this power.[160]

In view of the controversy existing in the law previous to the Code, as to whether or not the priest delegated by the religious superior needed the approbation of his own ordinary, one might ask: can the local superior delegate a religious of another Order who is not approved for hearing confessions in that Order, or even a priest of his own Order who had not fulfilled the requirements necessary to receive faculties "ex iure Ordinis," or finally, a secular priest who is not approved by his own bishop or by the ordinary of the place where the confession is to be heard? In canon 875, § 1 the Code does not mention explicitly any of the qualifications demanded in the priest whom the superior wishes to delegate, and certainly does not demand that the

158 Canon 518, § 1. Cf. Berutti, *Institutiones*, III, n. 36. Larraona, "Commentarium Codicis"—*CpR*, X (1929), 251, III. Even though the local superior cannot reserve sins in the Order, the confessors whom he deputes or delegates, according to this canon, receive from the law itself the power to absolve from sins reserved in the Order—Larraona, *loc. cit.*, p. 259; *e contra*, Schaefer, *De Religiosis*, n. 166, who says that the deputed confessors must receive this power from the competent superior.

159 Cf. *supra*, chap. VIII, art. II, pp. 139-144.

160 Blat, *Commentarium*, III, n. 220. Claeys-Bouuaert-Simenon, *Manuale Iuris Canonici*, II, 110. Pejška, *Ius Canonicum Religiosorum*, p. 293. Larraona, "Commentarium Codicis," *CpR*, X (1929), 251, note (12).

delegated priest be approved by his own ordinary.[161] A declaration of the Sacred Congregation of Bishops and Regulars, which is given as one of the sources of canon 875, § 1, allowed the prior of the Augustinians to delegate another priest "dummodo sacerdos fuerit ex approbatis ab ordinario loci," [162] and likewise some pre-Code authors declared that the priest delegated by the regular superior had to have the approbation of the local ordinary.[163] Nevertheless this condition is not retained in the present law, and unless the Constitutions of a particular Order should determine otherwise, it does not seem necessary that the local superior should be obliged to delegate only a priest who has previously received the approbation of his own ordinary, local or religious.[164]

In conferring jurisdiction upon others to hear the confessions of his subjects, the local superior is obliged to abide by the prescriptions of canon 877, § 1, and thus he is to confer jurisdiction only on one who is fit to receive it. Ordinarily if a secular or religious priest has been approved by his own ordinary, a local superior could feel secure in considering him as "idoneus" in the sense of canon 877, § 1, and would not be compelled to examine him again. If the priest to be delegated is not so approved, the local superior is all the more obligated to ascertain for himself that the priest has the necessary fitness. Canon 877 makes mention of an examination by which a priest's fitness is to be judged. It does not seem probable that the local superior would ordinarily be called upon to give such an examination, at least when he is delegating another priest in a particu-

[161] On the contrary, canon 1338, § 1, explicitly states that a secular cleric, or a cleric of another religious institute, may be delegated by the (local) religious superior to preach to the community, "*dummodo* a proprio ordinario vel superiore fuerint idonei judicati."

[162] *Piscien. seu Ordinis Eremitarum S. Augustini,* 3 iun. 1864—*Fontes,* n. 1992.

[163] Cf. Santi, *Praelectiones Iuris Canonici* (4. ed., cura Leitner, 5 vols. in 3, Ratisbonae, 1904-1905), III, tit. XXXVII, nn. 14-18. Vermeersch, *De Religiosis,* I, n. 416, 2. It must be admitted, however, that even in the old legislation it was at least doubtful that a priest whom a religious superior wished to delegate needed the approbation of his own ordinary beforehand.

[164] Modern authors do not require the local ordinary's approbation. Cf. Vermeersch-Creusen, *Epitome,* II, n. 145, 2. Cappello, *De Sacramentis,* Vol. II, pars I, n. 418, 5°.

lar case. However, he is bound to determine the fitness of the priest to be delegated, even if such a determination can be reached in no other way than by an examination. It may be noted also that the superior is not obliged to demand that the priest delegated make a profession of faith as required on similar occasions by reason of canon 1406, § 1, 7°.[165]

In granting jurisdiction the local superior has no power according to the present law to reserve sins to himself. This power, though probably exercised even by the local superior under the pre-Code legislation, is now reserved to the supreme governmental agencies (the master, or minister, or superior general) of the Order alone.[166]

3. The Local Ordinary

Canon 874 grants the local ordinary the right to delegate jurisdiction to priests to hear the confessions of all who are present in his diocese, religious as well as seculars. Religious priests, however, are warned not to use the faculties received from the bishop without at least the presumed permission of their own superior, exception being made for the use of canon 519, which allows a religious in institutes of men to approach any confessor approved by the local ordinary, "ad suae conscientiae quietem."

The same canon in its second paragraph urges the local ordinaries not to grant jurisdiction habitually to religious who are not presented to him by their own superior, and not to deny faculties without a grave reason to those who are presented by their own superior.

Canon 524, § 1 recognizes the right of the superior of a religious priest to give or to deny permission for such a subject to be deputed as ordinary or extraordinary confessor for religious women.

With the prescriptions of these two canons in mind, one may ask what superior is competent to give a religious permission to use diocesan faculties, either of a general nature,[167] or the special faculties given for confessions of religious women? [168] What superior pre-

[165] Pejška, *Ius Canonicum Religiosorum*, p. 294.

[166] Canon 896. This canon thus restricts the application of canon 893, § 1.

[167] Canon 874, § 1.

[168] Canon 524, § 1.

sents the religious to the bishop? Any true superior, even a local superior, can certainly give the permission.[169] The Code makes no distinction and does not reserve the right to the higher or major superior. After a careful study of the legislation from the thirteenth century up to the present time as expressed in the various papal constitutions and in the Council of Vienne (1311), the V General Council of the Lateran (1512-1517), and in the Council of Trent (1545-1563), one must come to the conclusion that even now in the Code, no change has been made in regard to the competent superior who presents the religious, and that consequently the local superior can do so. It has already been seen that as far back as the V General Council of the Lateran, the word "superior" had been used without qualification, even as it is now in the Code. One is therefore led to the same conclusion, viz., that since no distinction of superiors is made in the canon, any true superior, even the local superior, may be competent to present a religious to the bishop.[170] Again, particular law may reserve such a right to the provincial or general superior.

In regard to the superior's permission, necessary for the use of faculties conceded to a religious by the bishop, it may be noted that even without any such permission the use of the faculties will always be valid, even though it may be illicit.[171] The local superior can also prohibit the use of the jurisdiction given one of his subjects by the bishop, but again the subject who continues to hear confessions after such a prohibition would administer the Sacrament validly, and would not incur any irregularity, since he has jurisdiction, even though its use has been rendered illicit by his own local superior.[172]

[169] Cf. Blat, *Commentarium,* lib. III, pars I, p. 219.

[170] The local superior may "present" his subjects personally or by letter. Fanfani, *De Iure Religiosorum,* n. 143, (B).

[171] Cf. S. C. Ep. et Reg., *Ordinis Praedicatorum,* 2 mart. 1866—*Fontes,* n. 1996. In the instance of a confession being made in accordance with canon 519, the action of the religious priest in hearing the confession will be both valid and licit—cf. Blat, *Commentarium,* lib. III, pars I, p. 219; Fanfani, *De Iure Religiosorum,* n. 145, p. 163. Authors teach that a religious who makes use of diocesan faculties without at least the presumed permission of his superiors, cannot use any privileges which have been given to regulars as such in the administration of the Sacrament of Penance.

[172] S. C. Ep. et Reg., *Ordinis Praedicatorum,* 2 mart. 1866—*Fontes,* n. 1996.

ARTICLE IV. HOLY ORDERS

The religious superior primarily entrusted with the rights and duties in regard to the ordination of religious is the major superior, for of all the canons pertaining to ordination, only one, perhaps, has direct reference to the local superior.[173] In the present legislation the provincial or other major superior has the duty of issuing the dismissorial letters,[174] and the right of prohibiting a religious from receiving Orders,[175] of dispensing from certain irregularities,[176] of issuing testimonial letters,[177] of shortening the length of the ordination retreat under certain circumstances,[178] of determining whether or not the ordination retreat must be repeated,[179] of attesting to the fact that the religious has made the prescribed retreat,[180] and, finally, of transmitting to the pastor of the place of baptism the notice that subdiaconate has been conferred upon the religious concerned.[181]

Such action on the part of the legislator is a distinct change from that in force before 1918.[182] Up to that time the local superior of exempt religious, regarded as a prelate exercising quasi-episcopal power, had the right to issue dismissorial and testimonial letters, if

173 Canon 1001, § 4. This canon states that it is the duty of the local superior to inform the bishop that a secular priest has made his retreat in the religious house; even this canon does not give the local superior the right to inform the bishop that a religious has made his retreat, for this is also reserved to the major superior.

174 Canon 964, 2°.

175 Canon 970.

176 Canon 990, § 1.

177 Canon 995, § 1.

178 Canon 1001, § 1.

179 Canon 1001, § 2.

180 Canon 1001, § 4.

181 Canon 1011.

182 Frequently, however, the Constitutions of an Order in use previous to the promulgation of the Code reserved some of these rights to the general and provincial superior. In the Dominican Order the provincial issued the dimissorials "post praesentationem sibi factam a Superiore Conventus cum Patrum Consilio," but the local prior could do so also with the consent of the provincial. (*Const. S. O. P.* [1866], n. 1137).

he was not prohibited from doing so by particular law,[183] of forbidding his subjects to receive Orders,[184] and of dispensing in the external forum from whatever irregularities a bishop could dispense his subjects.[185]

It is evident, however, that in practice the general or provincial will often be obliged to depend upon the local superior for much of the information needed concerning the qualifications of candidates for Orders. Being in closer contact with the subjects, the local superior will be better informed concerning the qualifications of those to be promoted to Orders. However, the right and duty of expressing a final judgment to the ordaining prelate always remains with the general or provincial superior.[186]

Appendix — Matrimony

The local superior will not be called upon very frequently to exercise any direct authority in regard to the Sacrament of Matrimony. As superior he may be called upon to grant permission to one of his subjects to act as *vicarius substitutus* for a pastor,[187] but, as has been noted before, in chapter VII, article IX, F, the religious acting in this capacity will validly and licitly assist at marriages which are celebrated within the parish even before he has the permission of his local superior to act as vicar,[188] as long as he has the approval of the local ordinary. Such a vicar can also give a particular priest permission to assist at a particular marriage, also after the approval of the local ordinary, and before the approval of his local superior.[189]

183 Cf. Passerinus, *De Statibus,* Q. CLXXXIX, art. X, n. 852. Gasparri, *Tractatus Canonicus de Sacra Ordinatione* (2 vols., Parisiis, 1893-1894), II, n. 743, and n. 919. Prümmer, *Manuale I. E.,* qu. 235, 2, note 2.

184 Passerinus, *De Statibus,* Q. CLXXXIX, art. X, n. 864.

185 Conc. Trident. sess. XXIV, *de ref.,* c. 6. S. Pius V, const. "*Romani Pontificis,*" 21 iul. 1571—*BRT,* VII, 931. Gasparri, *op. cit.,* I, n. 228. All of these functions are now reserved, in common law at least, to the major superiors.

186 Canon 993, 5°.

187 Canon 465, § 4.

188 Cf. *PCI,* 14 iul. 1922, V—*AAS,* XIV (1922), 527.

189 Cf. *PCI,* 20 maii 1923—*AAS,* XVI (1924), 114.

CHAPTER IX

OTHER RIGHTS AND DUTIES UNDER THE LAW *"DE REBUS"*

THE legislation on the Sacraments forms a major part of the legislation contained in the Third Book of the Code. It is followed by five other divisions of the same book. Only some of the titles of the divisions, "De Locis Sacris," "De Cultu Divino," and "De Magisterio Ecclesiastico" will be treated in this chapter, since the local superior's power to dispense his subjects from the observance of feasts and from the law of fast and abstinence, as well as from non-reserved vows and oaths, has been treated already. The same may be said for the subject of temporal goods, as the legislation on the acquisition and administration of temporal goods, as it affects the local superior, was treated in detail in article V of chapter VII. There seems to be no further legislation applicable to the office of the local superior in the treatment of ecclesiastical benefices as it appears in this Third Book of the Code which has not been referred to already in article IX of chapter V.

ARTICLE I. CHURCHES AND ORATORIES

The right of blessing sacred places which belong to religious, of blessing and of laying the corner stone of a church or public oratory of religious and of blessing church bells for religious is reserved to the major superior,[1] but the local superior may be delegated to perform such rites.[2] Augustine,[3] in conformity with his teaching that even local superiors who have ordinary ecclesiastical jurisdiction enjoy the status of ordinaries, writes that guardians and conventual priors may bless churches and altars either themselves or through others. It has already been shown that priors and guardians are not

[1] Cf. canons 1156; 1163; 1169, § 1.

[2] Cf. canon 1156.

[3] *Commentary,* VI, 6.

ordinaries, even though they have ordinary jurisdiction. They do not, therefore, have the right in common law to bless sacred places unless delegated to do so by their own major superiors.

In virtue of a privilege granted to the Franciscan Order by Leo X (1513-1521), the regular prelates of the Order, including the guardians, were permitted to bless "coemeteria, ac capitula, et oratoria . . . ac paramenta et ornamenta, ac alia quaecumque ad divinum cultum et usum vestrum necessaria . . ."[4] This privilege, it would seem, can still be used by those local superiors of the Orders which enjoyed it before the Code.[5]

If it should become necessary to reconcile a violated church attached to a religious house, which church was not previously consecrated but only blessed, the local superior may perform the ceremony if he is also the rector of the church.[6] If the church was previously consecrated, the ceremony of reconciliation is reserved to the major superior,[7] but, in case of grave and urgent necessity, even a consecrated church may be reconciled by a local superior who is also the rector of the church.[8] The Code likewise allows the rector of a church to give permission to others to extradite those who have sought asylum in a church edifice.[9] The local superior could therefore grant such a permission in regard to a church of which he is the rector.

Article II. Ecclesiastical Burial

A. *Cemeteries*

The right of exempt religious to possess their own cemeteries, previously acknowledged under the law of the decretals,[10] is re-

[4] Const. *"Religionis honestas,"* 3 febr. 1514—Rodericus, *Collectio,* pp. 253-254. Cf. Reiffenstuel, *Jus Canonicum Universum,* lib. III, tit. XL, n. 9.

[5] Cf. Coronata, *Institutiones,* II, n. 726.

[6] Canon 1176, § 1.

[7] Canon 1176, § 2.

[8] Canon 1176, § 3.

[9] Canon 1179.

[10] C. 16, X, *de excessibus praelatorum et subditorum,* V, 31; c. 2, *de sepulturis,* III, 6, in Extravag. com.; c. 2, *de sepulturis,* III, 7, in Clem.; c. un., *de iudiciis,* II, 1, in Extravag. com.

affirmed in the Code of Canon Law.[11] Religious institutes have a right to bury their own subjects in their cemeteries and also to allow the burial of the faithful there, if previous to death they will have chosen to be buried in these cemeteries. The local superior's duties in regard to the administration of affairs connected with a cemetery attached to a religious house are pointed out generally in the canons under title XII of the Code, "De Sepultura Ecclesiastica," and specifically in canons 1209, § 1, and 1211, and possibly in canon 1228, § 2.

With the written permission of the religious superior, the faithful are allowed to construct burial vaults in cemeteries belonging to regulars, and to alienate them.[12] Such a right seems to imply that the local superior can give this permission, unless the particular law of the institute would determine otherwise.[13] At times it might be necessary also for the local superior to forbid certain epitaphs, inscriptions, or modes of ornamentation chosen by the faithful for the embellishment of monuments, but not consonant with Catholic doctrine or piety.[14]

All religious, and consequently the local superior also, are warned not to attempt in any way to induce the faithful to vow or to promise to choose a cemetery of the religious as a burial place.[15] The laity are to be left free to choose, either personally or through a representative,[16] to be buried in such places, but are in no way to be forced to vow or to promise to do so. The purpose of the law, no doubt, is to prevent the renewal of the very serious quarrels between the parochial and religious priests over the question of burial rights. But if any of the faithful will have chosen to be buried in a cemetery attached to the religious house, the permission of the religious

[11] Canon 1208, § 2.

[12] Canon 1209, § 1. Alienation as used in this canon is to be understood as "a conveyance for burial purposes." (Augustine, *Commentary*, VI, 110.)

[13] Augustine, *Commentary*, VI, 110. Coronata, *Institutiones*, II, n. 793, III, (d), and n. 802, 5°, (b), B.

[14] Canon 1211.

[15] Canon 1227.

[16] Cf. S. C. C., *Dianen.*, 9 iul. 1921—*AAS*, XIII (1921), 534.

superior, local or major, according to the prescriptions of the Constitutions, is required in order that the body may be interred there.[17]

B. *Funeral Rites*

Ecclesiastical burial consists in the bringing of the body to the church, in the performance of the obsequies there, and in the final transportation of the body to the place of interment.[18] The faithful are ordinarily brought for burial to their own parish church unless the deceased has legitimately chosen another church,[19] but professed religious and novices are buried from the church or oratory of the religious house, or at least from a church or oratory of their own religious institute.[20] However, novices have the right of choosing another church, but in all cases where a subject, even a novice, of the religious superior is concerned at least the right of saying the liturgical prayers when the body is taken from the place of death, and the right of transporting the body to the church of burial are always that of the religious superior.[21] Servants who die in the religious house and who were actually in the service of the religious and lived permanently within the confines of the religious house may also be buried from the church or oratory of the religious house.[22] According to an interpretation of the Pontifical Commission, postulants and apostolic students do not enjoy the right given in canon 1221 to the professed, to novices, and to servants, even though such postulants or apostolic students were cared for in their illness by the local superior as provided for in canon 514, §1,[23] nor do others who have resided there as guests, students, or patients.[24] However, if the postulants or apostolic students or servants who die outside the religious house had chosen burial from the church of religious before death, they would, if the choice was made legitimately, be

[17] Canon 1228, § 2.
[18] Cf. canons 1204, 1215.
[19] Cf. canons 1216, 1223.
[20] Canon 1221, § 1.
[21] Canon 1221, § 1. Cf. Coronata, *Institutiones*, II, n. 805, 3°, (e).
[22] Canon 1221, § 3.
[23] *PCI*, 20 iul. 1929—*AAS*, XXI (1929), 573.
[24] Canon 1222.

permitted burial in the religious church, as would any of the faithful in similar circumstances.[25]

In clerical exempt institutes the local superior enjoys whatever rights and duties are given to religious superiors in all the canons listed under the title, "De Sepultura Ecclesiastica." No distinction is made by the legislator in regard to the superiors mentioned, except that in canon 1228, § 2 it is stated that the superior designated by the Constitutions of each institute has the right of granting consent to the choice of burial in a cemetery of religious made by one permitted in law to do so. In regard to the burial of his own subjects, of the professed, of novices who have not chosen to be buried elsewhere, and of servants as provided for in canon 1221, § 3, but not of postulants or of apostolic students, it will be the right of the local superior to say the liturgical prayers when the body is removed from the place of death (*ius levandi*), to accompany it to the religious church or oratory (*ius deducendi*), to conduct the funeral services in the church (*ius exsequia celebrandi*), and to transport the body to the grave (*ius comitandi*).[26] These rights belong to the local superior even if the religious does not die within the religious house, as long as the superior provides for the transportation of the body to the church or oratory of the religious house.[27] In regard to the burial of the faithful in general, including servants who die outside of the religious house, postulants, and apostolic students, if these choose to be buried from the church or oratory of the religious, the local superior will have the right of conducting the funeral services in the church and of leading the body to the grave, but the competent pastor must be granted the *ius levandi* and the *ius deducendi*.[28]

If it should happen that one of the faithful chooses to be buried from the parochial church attached to a religious house, the right of conducting the funeral in the church and at the grave will belong to the religious pastor of the church, and not to the local superior unless he is at the same time pastor of the parochial church and superior of the house.[29]

[25] Canons 1223, § 1, 1225. Cf. Coronata, *Institutiones,* II, n. 800, (c).

[26] Cf. canons 1204, 1231, § 2.

[27] Cf. canons 1221, § 2; 1218, § 3.

[28] Cf. canon 1230, § 3.

[29] Canons 609, § 1; 415, § 2, 3°.

Mention may be made of a privilege granted to the Dominican Order and to the Franciscan Order, permitting the faithful, when dying, to ask for and to receive the habit of the Order, and then to be buried from the church of the Order whose habit they had received.[80] A necessary condition for the exercise of the privilege was that the habit be given by the superiors of the Order, among whom was included the local superior, "per Priorem . . . aut Guardianum."[81] This privilege was confirmed and placed among the decrees of the V General Council of the Lateran (1512-1517) by Pope Leo X (1513-1521).[82] It is still in force, and may be invoked by the relatives of the deceased tertiary, for instance, who would desire that the funeral should take place from a church of the Order, even though the deceased did not make an explicit choice of such a church during life.[83]

Article III. Custody and Worship of the Blessed Sacrament

As head of the community the local superior is ordinarily the one who is charged with the custody of the Blessed Sacrament, whether It be reserved in the church attached to the religious house,[84] or in the oratory of the convent itself. Such a duty involves the observance of all the liturgical prescriptions in regard to the custody of the Blessed Sacrament, and notably the obligation of seeing to the ornamentation of the altar of the Blessed Sacrament,[85] and the custody of the tabernacle key.[86] The Sacred Congregation of the Sacraments in an Instruction issued on May 26, 1938,[87] was most explicit in reaffirming the grave obligation of guarding the key of the tabernacle. The priest to whom it is entrusted must provide for the ful-

[80] Sixtus IV, const. *"Sacri Praedicatorum,"* 26 iul. 1479,—*BOP,* III, 578; *BRT,* V, 278.

[81] Passerinus, *De Statibus,* Q. CLXXXVII, art. IV, n. 372.

[82] Const. *"Dum intra,"* 19 dec. 1516—Schroeder, *Disciplinary Decrees,* pp. 507, n. 9, 647, n. 9.

[83] Cf. Coronata, *Institutiones,* II, n. 800, 3°, (c), *in fine.*

[84] Cf. canons 609, § 1; 415, § 3, 1°; canon 1265, § 1.

[85] Canon 1268, § 4.

[86] Canon 1269, § 4.

[87] *AAS,* XXX (1938), 198.

fillment of this obligation. Consequently, the local superior will have to take charge of the key, and to see to it that it is not lost, or that it does not fall into the hands of externs.

Article IV. Images, Relics, Processions

The local superior will sometimes be obliged to see to the observance of the canonical regulations governing the veneration of images and relics, especially providing that no unusual image be exposed for veneration in the religious church or oratory.[38] Rectors of churches and others are warned to be vigilant lest sacred relics be exposed to profanation or lost because of the carelessness of those placed in charge of them, or even kept in an indecorous manner.[39] In arranging for religious processions, the local superior should remember that except during the octave of Corpus Christi, his community is not permitted, without the permission of the local ordinary, to hold a procession outside of the church or oratory or of the confines of the cloister. Finally, the right of blessing the sacred vestments and vessels used in the liturgical functions celebrated in the religious church or oratory belongs to the local superior or to a priest delegated by him.[40]

Article V. Preaching

The right and duty of teaching Catholic doctrine to the faithful is recognized as part of the jurisdictional power conferred by the Church upon her prelates. Much of the teaching is done in the form of catechetical instruction and through the medium of sermon preaching. It will be necessary therefore to determine to what extent the local superior's jurisdiction applies in this matter.

A. *Legislation Before the Code*

The Roman Pontiffs, the Councils, and the Doctors of the Church had from the earliest times spoken of the necessity and utility of preaching the Word of God. This sacred duty, they maintained, was

[38] Canon 1279, § 1.
[39] Canon 1289, § 2.
[40] Canon 1304, 5°.

always the *ex officio* duty of the bishop of the diocese, but when the IV General Council of the Lateran (1215) in its tenth canon decreed "that bishops provide suitable men, powerful in work and word, to exercise with fruitful result the office of preaching,"[41] the bishops turned especially to the Franciscan and Dominican Friars to fulfill this wish of the Council. It was not long until the question of their authority and jurisdiction to preach was to be more clearly defined. Since preaching is an act of jurisdiction, such jurisdiction is granted by those who have charge of the common and public good of the church, usually, therefore, the Pope and the bishops of the individual dioceses. Due to the extra-diocesan character of their work, the mendicants had received extensive privileges directly from the Popes, who invariably granted the superiors of the Orders the power and authority to designate and approve those who would enjoy the faculty of preaching the word.[42]

The legislation of the Council of Trent embodied much of the previous legislation within its second chapter of the fifth session, on reform: "Regulars of whatever order unless they have been examined by their superiors regarding life, morals, and knowledge, and approved by them, may not without their permission preach even in the churches of their order. . . ."[43]

Again, as in the study of the documents concerning jurisdiction for the hearing of the confessions of the faithful, it is the purpose of the author to try to determine whether or not the jurisdiction, permission, or approbation, required for preaching to the faithful, could be given by the local superior. Since generally the same Papal constitutions which treated of jurisdiction for the Sacrament of

[41] Cf. Schroeder, *Disciplinary Decrees*, pp. 251, 566; c. 15, X, *de officio iudicis ordinarii*, I, 31.

[42] Cf. Gregory IX, const. *"Quoniam abundavit,"* 21 apr. 1227—Potthast, *Regesta*, n. 7880; *BOP*, I, 18. Gregory IX, const. *"Prohibente,"* 31 maii 1237—Rodericus, *Collectio*, p. 11. Alexander IV, const. *"Prohibente,"* (no date given) —Rodericus, *Collectio*, p. 24. Clement IV, const. *"Quidem temere,"* 20 iun. 1265 —*BOP*, I, 455; Potthast, *Regesta*, n. 19216. Martin IV, const. *"Ad fructus uberes,"* 10 ian. 1282—*BOP*, II, 1; Potthast, *Regesta*, n. 21821. (Cf. also the constitutions: *"Super cathedram," "Inter cunctas,"* and *"Dudum,"* cited *supra*, p. 150.

[43] Cf. Schroeder, *Canons and Decrees*, p. 27.

Penance[44] treated the matter of jurisdiction for preaching to the faithful, and in almost the same manner, it will readily be seen that the conclusions as to the competency of the local superior over preaching will parallel the same conclusions reached in regard to penitential jurisdiction. It is probable therefore that before the V General Council of the Lateran, the local superior was not competent to give his subjects approbation or permission to preach. The constitutions *"Supra cathedram," "Inter cunctas,"* and *"Dudum"* mention only the general and provincial superiors.[45] But there is reason to believe that after the V General Council of the Lateran (1513-1521) wrote that no religious was to undertake the office of exercise the office of preaching to the faithful, and was competent to inform the local ordinaries of the qualifications of his own religious. In the eleventh session of the V General Council of the Lateran, Leo X (1513-1521), wrote that no religious was to undertake the office of preaching "nisi prius per superiorem suum respective diligenter examinatus."[46]

The Council of Trent would not permit regulars to preach "nisi a suis superioribus . . . examinati et approbati fuerint, ac de eorum licentia."[47] Since the Council did not make any distinction among superiors it would seem that the Council had reference also to the local superior. The legislation of the Council on this matter remained in force until the promulgation of the canons which now govern the conferring of jurisdiction to preach. It may be said, therefore, that before the promulgation of the Code, unless the Constitutions of a particular Order ruled otherwise,[48] even a local

[44] Cf. *supra*, pp. 150-153.

[45] Cf. what has already been written concerning the wording of these primary Papal documents, *supra*, pp. 151-152.

[46] Const. *"Superna majestatis,"* 19 dec. 1516—*Fontes*, n. 71; Schroeder, *Disciplinary Decrees*, pp. 505, 645.

[47] Sess. V, *de ref.*, c. 2.

[48] In the Dominican Order the examination and approbation of religious for preaching was reserved in the formative period of the Order to the provincial (cf. Martin IV, const. *"Ad fructus uberes,"* 10 ian. 1282—*BOP*, II, 1; Potthast, *Regesta*, n. 21821). After a short time the religious was obliged to undergo an examination before a board of examiners deputed by the provincial. Nevertheless even after passing such an examination, the subject was obliged

superior could approve his subjects for preaching. Such is also the conclusion of Passerinus who, after admitting that the duty of examining and approving religious was reserved in some Orders to the general and to the provincial, stated that in common law even the local superior was able to approve his subjects.[49]

B. *Present Legislation*

The duties of the local superior in regard to the catechetical instruction of his own subjects have already been treated.[50] With reference to the faithful in general the local superior is to aid the bishop, inasmuch as he is bound to instruct the faithful in his own church, either personally or through others, and even to supply the bishop with religious who can teach the faithful, if in the judgment of the local ordinary such help is needed in the diocese.[51] The superior is not to offer assistance, however, if to do so would be detrimental to regular discipline.[52]

The rights and duties of the local superior in regard to sermon preaching are clearly outlined in the Code. As was the procedure in regard to the jurisdiction necessary for the hearing of confessions, the Code permits the religious superior to grant faculties to his own subjects and to all others of the secular or regular clergy, but with this difference that, as to the concession of delegation for preaching, the recipients must be approved by their own proper ordinary or superior. This faculty can only be used in favor of the professed, the novices, and those who reside habitually in the religious house as servants, guests, students, or the infirm.[53]

To preach to the general faithful even in churches belonging to regulars a cleric needs jurisdiction from the local ordinary.[54] Con-

to secure the *licentia* of his local superior before he could preach in a particular diocese—Passerinus, *De Statibus*, Q. CLXXXVII, art. I, n. 1038.

[49] *De Statibus*, Q. CLXXXVII, art. I, n. 1037.

[50] *Supra*, chap. VII, art. II.

[51] Cf. canon 1334.

[52] Canon 1334.

[53] Canon 1338, § 1; Blat (*Commentarium*, lib. III, pars IV, p. 262) states that the superior can only give this faculty for a particular case, basing his opinion on the words "in casu" which are used in this canon. The interpretation does not seem at all justified.

[54] Canon 1338, § 2.

sequently a religious cannot receive such jurisdiction from his own local superior, unless the local ordinary has given the superior the faculty to delegate others. The Code also presupposes that a religious will generally be presented to the bishop by his superior.[55] It is also stated that a religious cannot licitly use the faculty he has received from the local ordinary unless he has the permission of his own superior,[56] a repetition of the legislation passed in the Council of Trent (1545-1563).[57]

It will be necessary to determine again whether or not the local superior is competent to give the faculties just referred to. It will be remembered that in pre-Code law the writer thought it probable that at least after the V General Council of the Lateran (1512-1517), the local superior could approve his subjects for this ministry. This right is placed beyond all doubt now, if the Constitutions designate the local superior as capable of exercising it, since canon 1338, § 1 allows individual Constitutions to determine what superior will exercise the power given.[58] The writer is in complete agreement with Coronata who says that even if the Constitutions of an Order do not determine the superior, the local superior is to be regarded as capable of giving the jurisdiction and the necessary permission referred to in canons 1338, § 1, and 1339, § 2,[59] and of presenting his own subjects to the local ordinary as provided for in canon 1339, § 1.[60] The legislator did not distinguish and consequently no distinction or exclusion of superiors should be made.

The local superior's right to delegate others to preach to his subjects involves not only giving permission to preach, but the actual concession of jurisdiction, an action justified because of the jurisdictional capacity of the local superior, recognized in canon 501, § 1.

In granting clerics jurisdiction to preach, the local superior is gravely bound not to give the faculty to those whose character and

[55] Cf. canon 1339, § 1.

[56] Canon 1339, § 2.

[57] Sess. V, *de ref.*, c. 2.

[58] Cf. Blat, *Commentarium*, lib. III, pars IV, p. 261.

[59] *Institutiones*, II, n. 921 (b).

[60] Cf. Blat, *Commentarium*, lib. III, pars IV, p. 263.

doctrinal qualifications are not sufficiently established.[61] Generally, the local superior can determine the qualification by learning whether or not a cleric has been approved by his own ordinary or superior, either by seeking this information from others, or by examining the testimonials which the cleric may have. If the cleric is approved, the local superior can usually presume that he has the necessary qualifications. It might become necessary to examine the cleric, at least in summary fashion.[62] The cleric whether diocesan or regular must have been previously approved by his own ordinary or religious superior, for this is one of the conditions placed in the canon as necessary for the licitness of the concession of jurisdiction.

Finally, it may be noted that should a local superior be requested by a pastor of a diocese, other than that in which the religious house is located, to supply a priest to preach in his church, the superior should give the name of the priest he is willing to send, and not merely promise to send someone of the priests of the convent, since the pastor according to canon 1341, § 2 has the obligation of seeking the permission of the local ordinary before he can invite an extra-diocesan priest to preach to the faithful of his parish. The local ordinary in turn will sometimes request information concerning the doctrine, piety, and character of the proposed preacher. Canon 1341, § 1 directs him to seek the information from the proper Ordinary, who in the case of religious is the major superior, and not the minor local superior.[63]

[61] Canon 1340, § 1.

[62] Coronata (*Institutiones,* II, n. 921, [b]) writes that a religious superior cannot submit a secular cleric or a religious of another Order to an examination, but must give the faculty only to one who is already approved by his own ordinary. It would seem that this statement is not to be understood as denying the faculty of examining a cleric once he has been approved by his own ordinary or superior, but only with reference to examining a cleric who has not been examined by his own ordinary.

[63] Cf. Keene, *Religious Ordinaries and Canon 198,* The Catholic University of America Canon Law Studies, n. 135 (Washington, D. C.: The Catholic University of America Press, 1942), p. 91. The Sacred Consistorial Congregation in n. 11 of the "*Normae pro Sacra Praedicatione*" (*AAS,* IX [1917], 330) refers to the ordinary and the regular superior, but the word "superior" if viewed in the light of canon 1341, § 1, refers to the major superior, and not to the minor local superior.

Article VI. Censorship and Prohibition of Books

Religious who wish to publish books or periodicals are obliged to submit them to the censorship of the local ordinary, but before requesting such an examination they must obtain the permission of their own major superior.[64] Evidently therefore the local superior cannot give this permission, nor can he give his subjects permission to contribute articles to, or to direct the publication of secular papers or periodicals, or to publish books on secular subjects. Such a permission must also be obtained from the major superior.[65]

The juridical act of prohibiting books in religious Orders is reserved to the general or highest superior of the Order, though provincials and other major superiors may do so if there is need of prompt action.[66] Therefore the local superior may not, in virtue of his jurisdictional power, prohibit his subjects from reading certain books. He may however forbid a subject to read a book, in virtue of his dominative authority and his general duty of caring for the spiritual welfare of his subjects.[67] Such a prohibition however will not obtain the juridical effect recognized by the Church in the case of books prohibited by those to whom this duty is officially entrusted.

[64] Canon 1385.

[65] Canon 1386, § 1.

[66] Canon 1345, § 2.

[67] Cf. Goyeneche, "Consultationes," *CpR*, IX (1928), 427.

CHAPTER X

COERCIVE POWER

The final chapter of this dissertion completes the treatment of the rights and duties of the local superior which emanate from his executive power. Practically all of the material considered from chapter VII to chapter IX has been based on the administrative power of the local superior. There remains only a consideration of coercive jurisdiction.

The writer feels that it is his principal task in this final chapter to point out the *existence* of penal jurisdiction in the office of the local superior, and to stress again the foundation upon which it is based, namely the jurisdiction granted him in canon 501, § 1. The *extent* of the local superior's coercive power depends in great measure on the solution of certain difficulties inherent in the problem of the extent of all extrajudicial coercive power of ecclesiastical superiors. These difficulties will be enumerated and a preference shown for one solution or the other but the reader will be referred to *ex professo* treatments of these problems for a more detailed study.

It may be pointed out also that in practice the local superior will seldom have occasion to make use of many of the more grave coercive measures which are inherent in his jurisdictional power. Generally, the ordinary constitutional coercive penances and punishments, and, in extreme cases, the imposition of a precept to be observed in virtue of the subject's vow of obedience, will be sufficient sanction for the good government of his community. Nevertheless, a consideration of the coercive power which is fundamentally present in the jurisdiction which the legislator has annexed to the office of the local superior will serve to give a more complete knowledge of both the office and of the jurisdiction attached to it.

Article I. Legislation Before the Code

Whatever coercive power the local superior had under pre-Code legislation, its source like all his jurisdictional power, may be traced to papal grants of exemption. In virtue of his jurisdictional power the local superior was able to enforce his precepts by means of ecclesiastical penalties. Examples of the exercise of penal jurisdiction by the local superiors, or of the recognition of his possession of such power are few, and authors seem to speak only in general terms on the subject, content to state the principle that coercive power was a necessary attribute flowing from the quasi-episcopal status of the local religious superior.

St. Raymond of Pennafort taught that not only bishops but also prelates "qui praesunt Ecclesiis, ut abbates et similes, possunt excommunicare majori excommunicatione." [1] He based this opinion on decretal legislation.[2] From another passage in his *Summa,* the conclusion might lawfully be drawn that he regarded the conventual prior among regulars as equal in coercive jurisdiction to the abbot of a monastery, for he concludes that the prior can absolve his subjects from the excommunication incurred for striking a religious, a faculty granted in decretal law to abbots.[3] St. Alphonsus (+1787) taught that the local superior could impose ecclesiastical censures,[4] and seems to base his opinion on decretal law.[5] Thesaurus (+1655) [6] and Passerinus (+1677) [7] also regarded the local superior as possessed of coercive jurisdiction. Yet Donatus (+1661), a contemporary of Passerinus, denies the power of the conventual prior to invoke the more grave ecclesiastical penalties, principally because, according to Donatus, he, though a prelate, did not have the quasi-episcopal jurisdiction necessary for imposing these grave penalties.[8] Despite this opinion of Donatus, it can safely be said, in view of the opinion of the authors just quoted, that local superiors possessed quasi-episcopal jurisdiction, and likewise the power to excommuni-

[1] *Summa,* lib. III, tit. XXXIII, § VII, p. 392.

[2] C. 3, X, *de officio iudicis ordinarii,* I, 31.

[3] *Ibidem,* p. 390.

[4] *Theologia Moralis,* lib. VI, cap. I, n. 10.

[5] C. 3, X, *de officio iudicis ordinarii,* I, 31.

[6] *De Poenis Ecclesiasticis,* p. 37.

[7] *Tractatus de Electione Canonica,* cap. XXVI, n. 4: "Praelati locales, cum habeant jurisdictionem quasi episcopalem, et in foro contentioso possunt excommunicare, et censuras ferre. . . ."

[8] *Rerum Regularium,* pars II, tr. IX, qu. 12, nn. 2-3.

cate and suspend their subjects.[9] This power, if not possessed by common law, was at least held in virtue of privilege, particularly in virtue of the constitution, "*Romani Pontificis*" of St. Pius V.[10]

Bouix sums up the common teaching of pre-Code authors as follows: "Potest nempe regularis praelatus, qui uni dumtaxat conventui praeest, excommunicationis, suspensionis, et interdicti personalis poenam in subditos animadvertere, nisi ex iure particulari suae religionis prohibeatur." [11]

Particular legislation in each Order would also have to be examined to determine whether or not the local superior could inflict these penalties judicially or extra-judicially.[12] In this matter the Instruction of the Sacred Congregation of Bishops and Regulars, issued on June 11, 1880,[13] though addressed to local ordinaries, could have served as a guiding norm for even local superiors in their extra-judicial exercise of coercive power.

Article II. Present Legislation

In the fifth book of the Code of Canon Law the legislator again recognizes [14] and defines the limits of the coercive power of the Church, and gives general and particular norms concerning delicts and penalties. Delinquent subjects of the Church may be punished with either medicinal penalties (censures: excommunication, interdict, suspension)[15] or with vindicative penalties (interdict, suspension, privation of ecclesiastical offices) [16] or with penal remedies

[9] The local superior in the Order of Preachers had the power to suspend "ex informata conscientia" but in virtue of a decree of the S. C. of Bishops and Regulars, 21 iun. 1697, he could not place an interdict on a church subject to him. (*Const. S. O. P.* [1886], nn. 420, 588.) He was also recognized as possessing quasi-episcopal jurisdiction in his own convent. (*Const. S. O. P.* [1886], n. 589.)

[10] 21 iul. 1571—*BRT*, VII, 931.

[11] *De Jure Regularium*, II, 439.

[12] In the Order of Preachers the conventual prior could proceed both judicially or extrajudicially against delinquent subjects.—*Const. S. O. P.* (1886), n. 588.

[13] *Fontes*, n. 2005; *ASS*, XIII (1880), 324-336.

[14] Canon 2214, § 1.

[15] Canon 2255, § 1.

[16] Twenty-four vindictive penalties are listed in canons 2291, 2298.

(admonition, rebuke, precept, vigilance) [17] or with canonical penances (recitation of determined prayers, fasts, etc.).[18] Some of these penalties are contained in the law itself, while others may be imposed by precept. All may be inflicted judicially, and at least some extrajudicially.

In all the penal legislation of the Code, the fundamental question for the purpose of this study is whether or not the local superior in clerical exempt religious Orders participates in the right to make use of the coercive power of the Church. Is he one of the active subjects of such power?

A. *The Existence of Coercive Jurisdiction*

In the opinion of the present writer, it must be admitted that the local superior in clerical exempt religious institutes has coercive jurisdiction, and that this power includes the ability to annex canonical penalties, including censures, to the precepts which he can give in virtue of his jurisdictional power. This opinion is based fundamentally on canon 501, § 1, which gives ecclesiastical jurisdiction over both *fora* to all religious superiors of clerical exempt religious institutes, to be used according to the norms established by the common law, or by the Constitutions of the particular institute. In virtue of canon 501, § 1, which recognizes the fundamental jurisdiction of the local superior, it must be concluded also that the jurisdiction therein conceded extends to everything to which jurisdiction generally extends, unless some particular jurisdictional function is taken away from the local superior, either by the common law or by his own Constitutions.[19] Since coercive power is one of the functions of jurisdictional power,[20] it must be within the competency

[17] Canon 2306.

[18] Canon 2313. It is to be noted that penal remedies and penances are not properly speaking canonical *penalties,* nor are they called "poenae" in the enumeration given in canon 2216, as are censures and vindictive penalties.

[19] According to Schaefer, *De Religiosis,* n. 107, note 72, in the Capuchin Order canonical penalties can be inflicted only by the major superior.

[20] "Nam jurisdictio sine modica correctione nulla est"—S. Raymundi de Pennafort, *Summa,* tit. XXIII, § 2, p. 367. Cf. c. 28, 29, X, *de officio et potestate iudicis delegati,* I, 29.

of the local superior unless taken away or restricted, either in common law or in the Constitutions. Furthermore, since the ability to inflict canonical penalties is one of the functions of coercive power, the local superior must be able to inflict such penalties, again unless limited either in the Code or in his own Constitutions. These two sources, common and particular law, must therefore be consulted in determining whether or not the coercive power of the local superior implied in canon 501, § 1, has been taken away or restricted.

Presupposing, therefore, that the local superior has jurisdiction in the external forum,[21] in any examination of the canons of the Code, one must recognize immediately that there are no canons which explicitly or implicitly take away *all* coercive jurisdiction from the local superiors. Undoubtedly, however, his coercive power is limited in the Code, e. g., the local superior cannot suspend "ex informata conscientia," [22] nor can he impose any of the penal remedies or canonical penances.[23] On the other hand, the assertion that he has coercive power receives its greatest support from canon 2220, § 1. This canon states that those who have the power to make laws or to impose precepts can also annex penalties to the laws or precepts. It is evident that the legislator is referring to the power of imposing jurisdictional precepts, and of annexing canonical penalties, since those who can command only in virtue of dominative power certainly cannot annex a canonical penalty to their commands inasmuch as they lack jurisdiction, a fundamental requisite for the infliction of any canonical penalty.[24]

But a necessary condition for the application of canon 2220, § 1, to the local superior is that he be competent to impose a jurisdictional precept. Can he do so? It is not explicitly stated in any canon of the Code that he can. It will be necessary to consult in-

[21] Canon 501, § 1. Cf. *supra*, chap. IV.

[22] In canons 2186-2194 the exercise of this power is given only to ordinaries, local or religious, and therefore not to local superiors. Cf. Noval, *De Processibus*, I, n. 758, 4.

[23] In canons 2301-2313 the Code frequently uses the word "ordinaries," using "superior" only once (canon 2309, § 6). Noval (*loc. cit.*) therefore concludes that the power to impose penal remedies and penances *vi iurisdictionis* does not pertain to the religious superior who is not an ordinary.

[24] Cf. Blat, *Commentarium*, V, 57.

dividual Constitutions to see if he can in virtue of particular law. However, it must be recalled that an explicit grant of particular acts of jurisdiction need not be made in the Code, or in the Constitutions. In order that the local superior be able to exercise any act of jurisdiction it is sufficient that that particular act be not taken away or limited either in the Code or in the Constitutions, since jurisdiction in general is granted him in canon 501, § 1. The power to enact jurisdictional precepts is not taken away or limited in the Code. Therefore if it is not taken away or restricted, for example, to major superiors, by constitutional law, the local superiors must be said to have the power to impose jurisdictional precepts. Moreover, one can argue that if the local superior is given jurisdictional authority to rule his subjects, necessarily including the right to command the actions of his subjects, he must also be given the power to enforce these commands, and therefore in view of the principle "accessorium sequitur principale" the coercive power of command, as an accessory to the jurisdictional authority, should also be jurisdictional itself. Thus, if the local superior has jurisdictional authority over his subjects, the power in virtue of which he enforces that authority, namely, by the imposition of precepts, will be jurisdictional also.

Chelodi [25] denies the fact that in common law local superiors have coercive power, and both Cappello [26] and Chelodi [27] oppose the statement that even local superiors can inflict censures *ex iure communi.* Chelodi restricts canon 501, § 1 to major superiors and states that local superiors do not seem to have from common law the power to give a precept to which they can annex a true canonical penalty. Cappello states that it is not evident from canon 501, § 1 that these superiors have the power of giving such a precept. Both authors refer to the legislation previous to the Code, Chelodi stating that "Iure antiquo haec facultas eis non erat certa (cf. Wernz, [*Ius Decretalium*], III, 692), in iure novo non apparet satis probata, nisi

[25] *Ius de Personis*, p. 419, note 1.

[26] *Tractatus Canonico-Moralis de Censuris iuxta Codicem Iuris Canonici* (3. ed. recognita et emendata, Taurinorum Augustae: Marietti, 1933), n. 11, nota (8). Hereafter cited *De Censuris.*

[27] *Ius Poenale et Ordo Procedendi in Iudiciis Criminalibus iuxta Codicem Iuris Canonici* (3. ed., aucta et emendata, Tridenti: Libreria Editrice Moderna A. Ardesi, 1933), p. 27, nota 1. Hereafter cited *Ius Poenale.*

expresse in eorum constitutionibus contineatur," [28] while Cappello writes: "In iure antiquo haec facultas erat valde dubia. Cf. Wernz, [*Ius Decretalium*], III, n. 692." [29]

Salucci [30] flatly denies that the local superior can impose a precept to which is annexed a canonical penalty. He quotes canon 2220, § 1, and then states that the local superior, not having the power to enact a law or to impose a precept in a juridical sense, cannot even threaten his subjects with a penalty. Nor, he continues, can the local superior do so in virtue of his jurisdiction in the external forum, since, he says, jurisdiction in the external forum does not *per se* imply the power to impose or inflict penalties. As proof of this latter statement he gives the example of the vicar general who according to canons 366 and 368 has ordinary jurisdiction, and yet by reason of canon 2220, § 1 cannot inflict canonical penalties without a special mandate. Finally, Salucci asks, how can the power of inflicting penalties be denied to a vicar general, who is called an Ordinary, and then be conceded to a simple guardian, "che rispetto al primo può appena mettersi alla stregua di un parroco?" [31]

On the contrary, other authors do not hesitate to include the local superiors among those who, as participants in the jurisdictional power of the Church, can attach censures and other canonical penalties to the precepts which they can impose upon their subjects. Claeys Bouuaert-Simenon,[32] and O'Brien [33] attribute coercive power in general to the local superior; Vermeersch-Creusen [34] say that he can attach canonical penalties and censures to his precepts; other au-

[28] Chelodi, *Ius Poenale, loc. cit.*

[29] *De Censuris, loc. cit.*

[30] *Il Diritto Penale Secondo il Codice di Diritto Canonico* (2 vols., Subiaco: Typografia dei Monasteri, Vol. I, 1926; Vol. II, 1930), I, 102-103, nota 1.

[31] *Loc. cit.*

[32] *Manuale Iuris Canonici,* III, n. 520.

[33] *The Exemption of Religious in Church Law* (Milwaukee: Bruce, 1942), pp. 43-44.

[34] *Epitome,* I, n. 574, 4, and III, n. 411, 1. In the first of these references the authors speak of "Prelati religiosi" but previously state that even the local superior is a prelate. Cf. *op. cit.,* I, n. 573.

thors, including Noval,[35] Fanfani,[36] Coronata,[37] Raus,[38] Cerato,[39] and Cipollini [40] state expressly that the local superior can attach censures to the precepts which he imposes upon his subjects. Ferreres [41] states that "regular superiors" can attach penalties to their precepts, Crnica [42] that "regular superiors" can inflict censures, and Noldin-Schönegger [43] that "superiors" can impose censures. Since these last three authors do not exclude the local superior in their use of the general term "superior" one may conclude that they wish to include him also.

The extrinsic authority of these authors may therefore be added to the intrinsic reasons previously offered for admitting jurisdictional coercive power in the local superior.[44] Moreover, the opinions of Chelodi, Cappello and Salucci who deny that the local superior has coercive power in common law, may be refuted.

Chelodi states that local superiors cannot exercise legislative, judicial, or coercive power.[45] Throughout this study the writer has consistently maintained that in virtue of canon 501, § 1 these three functions of jurisdictional authority belong to the local superior unless

[35] *De Processibus,* I, n. 758; "De Ratione Corrigendi et Puniendi sive in Judicio sive extra Jure Codicis J. C."—*JP,* III (1923), 208-209. The author does not make explicit mention of the "local superior" but refers to "Superior religiosorum non Ordinarius sed Religionis Clericalis exemptae . . ." (*art. cit.,* p. 208), among whom is certainly included the local superior, as is evident from the example given by the same author on p. 209. With reference to the judicial power of the local superior in the Order of Preachers, referred to by the author, cf. *supra,* p. 52, note 7.

[36] *De Iure Religiosorum,* n. 55, (C), I, (c).

[37] *Institutiones,* IV, n. 1693.

[38] *Institutiones Canonicae juxta Novum Codicem Juris pro Scholis vel ad Usum Privatum Syntheticae Redactae* (2. ed., Lugduni: Vitte, 1931), n. 447.

[39] *Censurae Vigentes Ipso Facto a Codice Iuris Canonici Excerptae* (2. ed. recognita, Patavii, 1921), n. 6, p. 13.

[40] *De Censuris Latae Sententiae Iuxta Codicem Iuris Canonici* (Taurini: Marietti, 1925), p. 11.

[41] *Institutiones,* II, n. 974.

[42] *Modificationes in Tractatu de Censuris per Codicem Iuris Canonici Introductae* (S. Mauritii Agauensis, 1919), p. 15.

[43] *De Censuris* (30. ed., Oeniponte: Rauch, 1936), n. 11.

[44] *Supra,* pp. 181-183.

[45] *Ius de Personis,* p. 419, nota 1.

taken away or restricted in the Code of Canon Law or in particular Constitutions. It has already been shown that legislative power in regard to its principal function, the enactment of law, is not within the competence of the local superior, but that the local superior need not have such power to exercise other jurisdictional functions.[46] Moreover, the Code itself, while as a general rule reserving judicial power to the provincial superior, recognizes this power even in the local superior if the Constitutions of his Order declare him competent to act as judge in first instance.[47] From what has been written already concerning coercive power in the local superior one can readily deny the assertion of Chelodi that the local superior has no coercive jurisdiction.[48] Though he does not give as a reason for his statement the fact that he regards canon 501, § 1 as applicable to major superiors alone, the reader can gather as much from the opinion expressed in the text to which the present footnote is appended. Yet, the legislator does not distinguish. Why should the interpreter? One of the reasons Chelodi does give is that coercive power would pre-suppose quasi-episcopal power in the local superior.

Both Chelodi [49] and Cappello [50] declare that the local superior cannot impose censures *ex iure communi*. This statement has already been refuted and will not be dealt with here.[51] It will be sufficient to note that the Code nowhere speaks of quasi-episcopal jurisdiction and it is not demanded as a necessary foundation for coercive power.[52] Thus their opinion can be denied because on the one hand the Code, while not expressly designating local superiors as active subjects of this power, does not expressly name any others, except to exclude the vicar general unless he has a special mandate.[53] On the other hand, the Code does grant coercive power to

[46] *Supra*, chap. V, art. II, p. 41.

[47] Canon 1579, § 1. Cf. *supra*, p. 52.

[48] *Supra*, pp. 181-183.

[49] *Ius Poenale*, p. 27, nota 1.

[50] *De Censuris*, n. 11, nota (8).

[51] *Supra*, chap. X, art. II, p. 181.

[52] Cf. Wernz-Vidal, *Ius Canonicum*, III, n. 95, nota 15.

[53] Cf. canon 2220, §§ 1, 2.

local superiors when it grants them general jurisdiction in canon 501, § 1. Included in this coercive power is the ability to enforce their jurisdictional authority with jurisdictional penalties.[54]

It is true that both Cappello and Chelodi deny that local superiors can give a precept and annex a canonical penalty to it in virtue of canon 501, § 1, but they do so merely by making the denial and giving no reason for it other than the statement that under the law prior to the Code the power of the local superior to give such a precept was not certain, or was highly dubious.[55] Both authors then quote Wernz as an authority for their interpretation of pre-Code law. But both the reason given and the authority quoted cannot be used in support of their opinion because in pre-Code law noted authors recognized the local superiors as possessing quasi-episcopal jurisdiction.[56] Generally it was held that their jurisdiction was possessed in virtue of privileges granted by the Popes. Suarez [57] refers to various passages in the decretals as examples of the local superior's coercive jurisdiction but in another passage he seems to state definitely that the quasi-episcopal coercive power of regular prelates was given them "non quidem jure communi sed speciali . . . " ; but other authors [58] likewise based it on the decretals, which gave jurisdictional power to local abbots and priors. Nor would the fact that the local superiors had jurisdiction in pre-Code law only by privilege argue against their having it now by common law for even Chelodi himself freely admits that in virtue of canon 501, § 1, clerical exempt institutes for the first time possess ecclesiastical jurisdiction by common law.[58a] This canon expressly states that "*Superiores* . . . habent iurisdictionem. . . . " If the religious institutes possess jurisdiction now in virtue of common law, such jurisdiction resides in their superiors, even the local superiors, in virtue of the legislation of canon 501, § 1.

Finally, it is difficult to understand how both Chelodi and Cap-

[54] Cf. *supra*, p. 183.

[55] Chelodi, *Ius Poenale, loc. cit.;* Cappello, *De Censuris, loc. cit.*

[56] Cf. *supra*, chap. IV, art. III, p. 31, note 20.

[57] *De religione*, tr. VIII, lib. II, cap. IX, n. 3.

[58] Cf. *supra*, p. 179.

[58a] *Ius de Personis*, n. 252, (d).

pello can interpret the words of Wernz [59] as favoring their opinion that in the old law the power of the local superior to give precepts and to annex canonical penalties to them was "valde dubia" or "non erat certa." First of all, Wernz makes no explicit mention whatsoever of a precept or of a local superior in the references cited, nor can it be said that he does so even implicitly in view of the following passage taken from the paragraph referred to both by Cappello and Chelodi:

"Denique potestas coercitiva vi iurisdictionis quasi-episcopalis regularibus Praelatis exemptis . . . generatim eadem ratione competit, qua Episcopis est concessa, nisi speciales limitationes sive ex iure communi sive ex iure particulari religionis sint appositae. Quare Praelati exempti . . . certe possunt personis sibi subditis infligere censuras. . . . " [60]

Why these words do not apply to the local religious superior is certainly not explained either by Chelodi or by Cappello. In view of the fact that in a previous paragraph Wernz [61] recognizes the local superior as a prelate with quasi-episcopal jurisdiction, it must be said that he also wishes to include the local superior in the words "regularibus Praelatis" and "Praelati exempti" of the passage quoted.

What is to be said of the opinion of Salucci? He expressly denies that a local superior can impose a precept to which is annexed a canonical penalty, even in virtue of his jurisdiction in the external forum since, says this author, jurisdiction in the external forum does not *per se* imply the power to impose or inflict penalties.[62]

The present writer denies absolutely the assertion of Salucci, and the reasons he gives in support of it. Jurisdiction in the external forum does *per se* imply the power to impose or inflict canonical penalties because jurisdiction implies power to give a command with the consequent power to enforce such a law or command with suitable and proportionate sanctions. In virtue of his jurisdictional power the local superior has the ability to impose jurisdictional pre-

[59] *Ius Decretalium,* III, n. 692.

[60] *Loc. cit.*

[61] *Ibidem,* n. 683.

[62] *Il Diritto Penale Secondo il Codice di Diritto Canonico,* I, 102-103, nota 1.

cepts[63] and to annex penalties to these precepts.[64] It is, therefore, entirely *per accidens* that a superior possessing jurisdiction should not also possess the power to impose ecclesiastical penalties since in itself the concept of jurisdiction embraces coercive jurisdictional power or the power to enforce authoritatively whatever laws or precepts a superior exercising jurisdiction may make.

Salucci attempts to prove his statement by showing that in virtue of canon 2220, § 2 the vicar general, without a special mandate, cannot inflict penalties and yet he has ordinary power in the diocese. However, the fact that the vicar general has not the power of inflicting penalties in no way proves that such power does not *per se* pertain to jurisdiction. All it proves is that the legislator here restricts the exercise of the ordinary jurisdiction given the vicar general in canon 366, § 1, and in canon 368, § 1.[65] The vicar general, and he alone, despite his ordinary jurisdiction, does not possess the power to inflict penalties. Any grant of jurisdiction by the Church is a free gift, subject entirely to whatever limitations the Supreme Pontiff may see fit to put upon its use. If, for obvious reasons, the vicar general is given jurisdiction in the diocese but needs the permission of the bishop to enact penalties, such a limitation prevents the use of a power which he ordinarily would have in virtue of his ordinary jurisdiction. Canonists, contending that the vicar general, even with a mandate, exercises not delegated but ordinary power, maintain that this power is still fundamentally included in the ordinary jurisdiction which the vicar general has at all times.[66] Were one to grant that the vicar general can only impose penalties in virtue of delegated power given him in the mandate of the bishop, the fact that ordinarily and *per se* jurisdiction and the coercive juris-

[63] Cf. *supra*, chap. V, art. III, p. 45.

[64] Canon 2220, § 1.

[65] Restriction of the vicar general's power in some way at least would be expected from the very wording of the canon which guarantees his ordinary jurisdiction: "Vicario Generali, vi officii, ea competit in universa dioecesi iurisdictio in spiritualibus ac temporalibus, quae ad Episcopum iure ordinario pertinet, exceptis iis quae Episcopus sibi reservaverit, vel *quae ex iure requirant speciale Episcopi mandatum*."—Canon 368, § 1.

[66] Cf. Roelker, "The Vicar General and the Special Mandate," *The Jurist*, II (1942), 358.

dictional power to inflict penalties go together would still be true and applicable in all other cases, unless the Code restricted the use of coercive power by other superiors as it has done in the case of the vicar general.

Finally, Salucci does not think that a vicar general "who is truly an ordinary" should be denied the power to impose and inflict penalties, and yet that such power should be given "a simple guardian." Such a comparison can be based only on a lack of understanding of the fundamental nature of ecclesiastical jurisdiction as participated by prelates other than the Pope and bishops of the Church, and of the office of a vicar general and of a local superior of a clerical exempt religious community. First of all, the Church may give her jurisdictional power to any superior without reference to any laws or customs involving dignity, precedence, or position. If the good of the Church can be served by giving jurisdiction to one superior and not to another, even if the former is inferior in rank to the latter, there is nothing to prevent the legislator from conceding jurisdiction to the one and not to the other. An examination of the nature of the two offices will also show a reason for the legislator's action. The vicar general is juridically one with the bishop; he acts essentially in the name of another. As such he is called a "vicar" and his jurisdiction, though ordinary, is vicarious.[67] On the other hand, the local superior acts in his own name and with ordinary jurisdiction which is proper and not vicarious. Since the ordinary jurisdiction of both is not of the same nature, neither will it extend to the same effects. The jurisdiction of the local superior, as ordinary and proper, is to be compared to that of the bishop of the diocese and not to the ordinary but vicarious jurisdiction of the vicar general.

Since the bishop of a diocese has all the coercive power consequent upon his ordinary jurisdiction and necessary for the effective government of the diocese, and since the government of the diocese pertains primarily and directly to him personally, the good of the Church is sufficiently maintained in that diocese by reserving the power to inflict penalties to the bishop, who, in turn, may permit the vicar general to use such power whenever the needs of the diocese

[67] Roelker, *art. cit.*, 346-348.

demand this. The local superior is likewise personally responsible for the good of his own community. To him is entrusted directly the right and duty of guiding his subjects to the end of the Church; to him is usually given the right to constitute his own vicar and to delegate jurisdictional authority to him. Why should he not be given the power to enforce his authority effectively, since his community is exempt from the jurisdiction of the bishop, and since there is no other superior in that particular local community who possesses such power?

The comparison which Salucci makes between the coercive power of the local superior and that of the pastor is gratuitous and not at all in conformity with the actual nature of the powers of both. The pastor has no ordinary jurisdiction in the external forum other than what is conceded to him in individual cases in the Code.[68] Nowhere is it stated in the Code that a pastor has the fundamental jurisdiction granted to the local superior in canon 501, § 1. Of the pastor it may be said that he has no ordinary jurisdiction in the external forum other than what the Code expressly gives him, but of the local superior, that he has jurisdiction in the external forum excepting where the Code or his Constitutions take away or limit its use.

In summary, therefore, it is maintained that the local superior in clerical exempt religious institutes, *in virtue of common law*, exercises coercive jurisdiction in both the internal and external *fora*, embracing also the power to attach canonical penalties, including censures, to the precept which he gives. This statement is based on the prescriptions of canons 501, § 1, and 2220, § 1, and upon the extrinsic authority of many canonists, despite the objections of others, whose contrary arguments can readily be refuted.

B. *The Extent of Coercive Jurisdiction*

It has been shown in the previous article that the local superior has coercive power, that is, he can inflict canonical penalties. Ordinarily, to inflict penalties implies both the power to establish them and the power to apply them. Has the local superior such power? The answer to this question must depend on what the legis-

[68] Cf. Vermeersch-Creusen, *Epitome*, I, n. 501.

lator has explicitly or implicitly decided in the Code, and on how individual Constitutions have applied the law of the Code in any particular religious Order.

Since the legislator makes no distinction in canon 2220, § 1, as to the type of penalty which the superior who can impose a precept can inflict, from that canon alone one would have to conclude that the local superior can establish any penalty which can be inflicted *per modum praecepti,* that is, extrajudicially.[69] Canon 1933, § 4 enumerates the penalties which can be inflicted extrajudicially, namely, excommunication, suspension, and interdict, and also states that canonical penances and penal remedies may be inflicted in the same way. The canon does not distinguish whether or not these extrajudicial penalties can be constituted as *latae* or *ferendae sententiae,* or whether the suspension or interdict can be inflicted as a censure or as a vindicative penalty. Consequently, it would seem that the penalties can be established either as *latae* or *ferendae sententiae,*[70] and that the suspension or interdict can be established either as a vindicative penalty or as a censure.[71]

But the general prescription given in canon 2220, § 1, that a superior who can impose a precept can attach a canonical penalty to the precept (ordinarily restricted to extrajudicial infliction in the local superior),[72] when particularized to some extent by the application of canon 1933, § 4, is still not devoid of difficulties. By comparing canons 2220, § 1, and 1933, § 4, only, one could conclude that the local superior can inflict canonical penances, penal remedies, excommunication, suspension, and interdict, either *latae* or *ferendae sententiae,* and that he can inflict suspension and interdict either as a censure or as a vindicative penalty. Such a conclusion cannot be true when considered in the light of other canons of the Code, and might not give a complete summary of the extent of the local su-

[69] If the local superior has judicial power, in virtue of constitutional prescription, as provided for in canon 1579, § 1, he will also be able, within the limits of his judicial competence, to establish and apply canonical penalties judicially. Since, as a rule, a local superior is not granted ordinary judicial power, penalties will be regarded only with respect to extrajudicial procedure.

[70] Cf. canon 2225; Coronata, *Institutiones,* III, n. 1453.

[71] Cf. Blat, *Commentarium,* IV, 452; Coronata, *Institutiones,* III, n. 1453.

[72] Cf. canon 1579, § 1.

perior's coercive power, if the enumeration given in canon 1933, § 4 is not a taxative one. Has the Code restricted the power of the local superior, and taken away his jurisdiction in virtue of which he inflicts the penances, penal remedies, and penalties listed in canon 1933, § 4? Are the penalties therein the only penalties which a local superior may inflict? Of the penalties which he would ordinarily be considered capable of inflicting, can he inflict them if the penalty has not been constituted previously by his own precept, but rather in the law itself?

The answer to these questions will depend on the solution given to the same problems as applied to any superior who exercises extrajudicial coercive power. Since such problems have already been thoroughly treated,[73] the writer does not feel it necessary to repeat the matter here, but only to apply the more probable conclusions to the authority of the local superior.

The Code restricts the local superior's power to make use of canon 1933, § 4 to its fullest extent, first of all, because it seems to allow only those who are ordinaries [74] to impose canonical penances and penal remedies. In the canons 2306-2313, which treat of these remedies and penances, the legislator makes frequent reference to the ordinary,[75] but uses the word "Superior" only once.[76] Therefore he would seem to exclude the local superior who is not an ordinary. Consequently a local superior cannot give a canonical *monitio, correptio,* or *praeceptum,*[77] or place a subject under canonical vigi-

[73] Cf. Noval, *De Processibus,* nn. 754-761; *idem,* De Ratione Corrigendi et Puniendi sive in Judicio sive extra Jure Codicis J. C."—*JP,* II (1922), 147-156, III (1923), 36-40, 204-210; Roberti, "Quaenam Poenae Applicari Possint per Modum Praecepti,"—*Apollinaris,* IV (1931), 294-300; Coronata, *Institutiones,* III, n. 1453; Esswein, *The Extrajudicial Coercive Powers of Ecclesiastical Superiors,* The Catholic University of America Canon Law Studies, n. 127 (Washington, D. C.: The Catholic University of America Press, 1941), pp. 110-114.

[74] Cf. canon 198, § 1.

[75] Cf. canons 2307; 2308; 2309, § 3; 2311; 2313, § 2.

[76] Canon 2309, § 6. Considering the context in which the word appears, it seems to be used also in reference to an ordinary.

[77] Even though a local superior cannot make use of the canonical precept of canon 2310, which is a penal remedy, he can nevertheless impose a precept which is "quoddam iussum aut quaedam prohibitio sive sine annexione alicuius

lance, if by these terms reference is made to the penal remedies of canons 2306-2313.

A second restriction on the complete use of canon 1933, § 4 is placed when the legislator reserves the suspension *ex informata conscientia* also to ordinaries,[78] while a third is commonly placed by those authors who state that regular prelates may not impose a local interdict, but only a personal one.[79]

Another restriction would be considered to have been placed by the law itself according to the opinion of Noval,[80] Coronata,[81] and Esswein,[82] who say that a superior cannot apply any penalty at all *per modum praecepti,* unless he himself has constituted the penalty *per modum praecepti.* Roberti, on the contrary, holds that any penalty at all may be inflicted *per modum praecepti* as long as the legislator has not declared that it must be applied judicially.[83] The writer believes that Esswein has analyzed the various opinions in a manner conformable to the rules of interpretation of penal legislation, that is, restrictively and not extensively.[84] Consequently, he believes that this interpretation, which is that of Noval and Coronata, should be applied to the local superior, also. Therefore, the local superior can only apply those penalties extrajudicially which he or his predecessor has established *per modum praecepti.* Wherefore he has no authority to give a precept threatening a *latae* or *ferendae sententiae* penalty concerning matter commanded or forbidden under penalty in the law itself. If a penalty is threatened in the law as *latae sententiae,* it will take effect as soon as the law is transgressed,[85] or in some cases after the penalty has been declared to

poenae, sive etiam cum poena adnexa, quae in hoc casu est quid accessorium praecepto . . ." Noval, *De Processibus,* n. 761.

78 Canon 2186.

79 Cf. Coronata, *Institutiones,* IV, n. 1785.

80 *De Processibus,* n. 755 and n. 756; *idem,* "De Ratione Corrigendi et Puniendi sive in Judicio sive extra Jure Codicis J. C."—*JP,* III (1923), p. 205.

81 *Institutiones,* III, n. 1453.

82 *The Extrajudicial Coercive Powers of Ecclesiastical Superiors,* p. 114.

83 "Quaenam Poenae Applicari Possint per Modum Praecepti,"—*Apollinaris,* IV (1931), 297-299.

84 Cf. canon 2219, § 1.

85 Cf. canons 2217, § 1, 2°; 2223, § 4.

have been incurred.[86] If it is threatened as *ferendae sententiae* by the law itself, the person concerned must be canonically warned and given time to repent. If he continues contumacious, the *ferendae sententiae* penalty can then be inflicted.[87] In either case, since there is involved a penalty established by law, the local superior cannot act, since he has no power to give the canonical admonition of canon 2307, which seems to be the admonition required in canon 2233, § 2, and since ordinarily he will not possess the judicial power required to inflict the penalties thus established in law as either *latae* or *ferendae sententiae*.

Presupposing, therefore, that the local superior can inflict *per modum praecepti* only those penalties which he has constituted *per modum praecepti,* and these either as *latae* or *ferendae sententiae,* additional problems arise. Canon 2233, § 2 states that no censure is to be inflicted without a canonical warning. But it has already been stated that the local superior cannot give the warning of canon 2307. Is he, therefore, disqualified from threatening and inflicting a *ferendae sententiae* censure? In view of a response of the Pontifical Commission, which declared that a censure can be inflicted immediately without a new warning upon proof of the offense once the censure has been imposed as *ferendae sententiae per modum praecepti,*[88] the local superior must be regarded as competent to inflict a *ferendae sententiae* censure which he himself has established even though he cannot give the canonical admonition of canon 2307. The precept threatening the censure is a warning in itself, and consequently there is no need of the procedure provided in canon 2307.

A final problem may be presented as follows. Are the *latae sententiae* censures which a local superior attaches to his precepts reserved or not? The difficulty is based on the fact that the censures in this case are both *latae sententiae* and *ab homine*. Since they are *ab homine* they would seem to be reserved at all times,[89] but since they are also *latae sententiae* they should only be reserved when the

[86] Cf. canons 2354, § 2; 2372.

[87] Canon 2233, § 2.

[88] *PCI,* 14 iul. 1922—*AAS,* XIV (1922), 530.

[89] Cf. canon 2245, § 2.

reservation is expressly mentioned in the precept.[90] Moriarty has treated the problem thoroughly [91] and concludes that in view of the *dubium iuris* involved and of the extrinsic authority of canonists the *latae sententiae* penalty attached to a particular precept is not reserved.[92] Consequently, with reference to the local superior it can be said that the censures which he inflicts will be reserved only when he explicitly states in the precept with which he established the *latae sententiae* censure that its absolution is reserved to himself.

In summary, it may be stated that as regards the extent of his coercive jurisdiction, the minor local superior in clerical exempt religious institutes who has no judicial power can:

(1) establish (*statuere*) whatever canonical penalties can be established *per modum praecepti.* These include excommunication *latae vel ferendae sententiae;* suspension and personal interdict *latae vel ferendae sententiae* and either as a censure or as a vindicative penalty—always provided that these penalties are not already established by law.

(2) apply (*infligere, applicare*) the penalties which he has constituted, either by declaring a *latae sententiae* penalty to have been incurred, or by inflicting extrajudicially a *ferendae sententiae* penalty previously threatened by precept.

(3) apply penalties constituted by his predecessor if they were constituted in a legitimate document or before two witnesses, as required by canon 24.

(4) punish with some just penalty a delict committed by one of his subjects even though such a delict is not punished in law, or even though he did not by precept threaten the punishment, when scandal has been given, or if the seriousness of the violation of law demands it.[93]

The same superior cannot:

[90] Cf. canon 2245, § 4.

[91] *The Extraordinary Absolution from Censures,* The Catholic University of America Canon Law Studies, n. 113 (Washington, D. C.: The Catholic University of America, 1938), pp. 91-106.

[92] *Ibidem,* p. 104.

[93] Canon 2222, § 1.

(1) establish by precept either *latae vel ferendae sententiae* a penalty already constituted in law, whether such a penalty be explicitly stated as reserved to ordinaries or not.

(2) inflict a canonical penance or penal remedy.

(3) inflict suspension *ex informata conscientia.*

(4) apply a penalty constituted in law as *ferendae sententiae,* or declare a *latae sententiae* penalty which also was constituted in law.[94]

On the contrary if such a superior has been granted the power to proceed judicially by his own Constitutions in accordance with the provisions of canon 1579, § 1, he can, in addition to the extrajudicial power just mentioned, judicially inflict whatever penalties require infliction by a judicial process. Thus, such a superior could inflict *ferendae sententiae* penalties and declare *latae sententiae* penalties even if either should be constituted in the law.

Against the conclusions upheld in this chapter affirming the coercive jurisdiction of local religious superior in clerical exempt religious institutes, it might be objected that religious subjects are placed in a precarious position if not only religious ordinaries but even the minor local superior can establish and inflict by precept such very grave canonical penalties as excommunication and suspension. Such power in the hands of a minor local superior, it might be said, is open to serious abuse. The objection may be answered in a fourfold manner:

(1) The Church's coercive jurisdiction is not something which can be exercised arbitrarily, according to the inclinations of any ecclesiastical superior. If the minor local superior abuses such power, the Code itself has provided for his punishment in canon 2404, wherein it is stated that if, in the prudent judgment of the ordinary (religious) a local superior has misused his coercive power, he can be punished by the higher superior according to the seriousness of the offense.

(2) There is no more reason to believe that this power will be

[94] Noval gives a similar summary in *De Processibus,* n. 758; *idem,* "De Ratione Corrigendi et Puniendi sive in Judicio sive extra Jure Codicis J. C"—*JP,* III (1923), 208-210.

misused by a local superior than by a provincial superior. Often there may be less reason for so believing, since the local superior, ordinarily in closer personal contact with his own religious subjects than is the major superior, would be in an even better position to judge the seriousness of a violation of law on the part of a subject, and the necessity of inflicting a canonical penalty.

(3) The subject is not without protection in the law itself. In most cases he can have recourse to a higher superior, either against the very establishment of the precept threatening the penalty; or, allowing the precept to stand, against the penalty threatened; or, finally, against the infliction of a penalty already applied. If he has recourse against a precept threatening a censure, his recourse will suspend both the precept and the threatened censure;[95] if a vindicative penalty has been threatened, he may also have recourse, but the law does not determine what effect the recourse will have. If he has recourse, not against the precept threatening a censure but only against the censure threatened, the censure will not be suspended if it has been threatened in regard to matter in which the law does not admit recourse as having a suspensive effect; but if in regard to matter in which a suspensive effect is admitted, the threat of censure will have no effect.

If a penalty has already been inflicted, the subject can still have recourse but with regard to the effect of recourse a distinction must be made. The effect of recourse against a censure inflicted is *in devolutivo* only, whereas the effect of recourse against a vindicative penalty inflicted is *in suspensivo.*

(4) The fact that a local superior can exercise coercive jurisdiction should serve to emphasize the serious obligation incumbent upon subjects who elect them of choosing only prudent and well-qualified religious to fulfill such an office, or to emphasize the same obligation incumbent upon major superiors, if it devolves upon them to appoint or to approve the election of a local superior.

[95] Cf. canon 2243, § 2.

CONCLUSIONS

The following opinions are offered as a summary of the present study:

1. The minor local superior in religious Orders of men has both dominative and jurisdictional authority. His jurisdiction may be traced historically to the privilege of exemption, and is recognized in the present legislation fundamentally in canon 501, § 1. It extends to everything to which jurisdiction extends, unless the common or particular law reserves certain functions to the higher superior.

2. He is a prelate because of the jurisdiction he exercises in the external forum, but he is not a religious ordinary, since he is not a major religious superior.

3. His jurisdictional authority is exercised in the direction of his subjects to the end of the Church, his dominative power in the direction of his subjects to the end of the religious institute.

4. The local religious superior does not exercise strict legislative power in an Order, for the reason that the exercise of such power is reserved to the general chapters or to the supreme moderator, but not for the reason that the community over which he rules is incapable of receiving a law.

5. Whenever the Code uses the word *superior* alone, without qualifying it as *superior maior* or in some equivalent way, the local superior is also referred to, unless particular law or the nature of the matter concerned restrict application of the word to major superiors.

6. The local superior can issue a *celebret*. He can administer Holy Communion and Extreme Unction to his subjects, including novices, whether they are ill within or without the religious house. He may do so also for postulants as long as they are within the house, but not when they are outside the religious house, unless he has the permission of the pastor concerned. He can delegate other priests, religious or secular, to hear the confessions of his subjects.

7. He has coercive jurisdiction, or the power of annexing canonical penalties, including censures, to his precepts, but he can only apply or inflict these penalties when he himself has previously established them by precept. He cannot establish or apply *per modum praecepti* a penalty already established in the law.

BIBLIOGRAPHY

Sources

Acta Apostolicae Sedis, Commentarium Officiale, Romae, 1909—

Acta et Decreta, Concilii Plenarii Baltimorensis III, Baltimorae, 1886.

Acta Sanctae Sedis, 41 vols., Romae, 1865-1908.

Bullarium Ordinis FF. Praedicatorum, ed. a T. Ripoll, recognitum a A. Bremond, 8 vols., Romae, 1729-1740.

Bullarum Diplomatum et Privilegiorum Sanctorum Romanorum Pontificum Taurinensis Editio, 24 vols. et Appendix, Augustae Taurinorum, 1857-1872.

Codex Iuris Canonici, Pii X Pontificis Maximi iussu digestus Benedicti Papae XV auctoritate promulgatus, ed. Petri Card. Gasparri, Civitate Vaticana: Typis Polyglottis Vaticanis, 1930.

Codicis Iuris Canonici Fontes cura Emi. Petri Card. Gasparri editi, 9 vols., Romae (later Civitate Vaticana): Typis Polyglottis Vaticanis, 1923-1939. Vols. VII-IX *ed. cura et studio Emi. Iustiniani Card. Serédi.*

Collectanea in usum Secretariae Sacrae Congregationis Episcoporum et Regularium, cura A. Bizzarri, Romae, 1885.

Collectanea S. Congregationis de Propaganda Fide, 2 vols., Romae, 1907.

Concilii Plenarii Baltimorensis II., in Ecclesia Metropolitana Baltimorensi, a Die VII. ad Diem XXI., Octobris, A. D., MDCCCLXVI., Habiti, et a Sede Apostolica Recogniti, Decreta, Baltimorae, 1880.

Constitutiones Fratrum S. Ordinis Praedicatorum, ed. nova, Parisiis, 1886.

Constitutiones Fratrum S. Ordinis Praedicatorum, Romae: Apud Domum Generalitiam, 1932.

Corpus Iuris Canonici, Editio Lipsiensis 2, 2 vols., Richter-Friedberg, Lipsiae, 1879-1881. Editio anastatice repetita, 1922.

Corpus Iuris Civilis, 3 vols., Berolini: apud Weidmannos, 1912-1920:

Vol. I, ed. stereotypa tertia decima, *Institutiones,*—Paulus Krueger; *Digesta,* —Theodorus Mommsen, retractavit Paulus Krueger.

Vol. II, ed. stereot. nona, *Codex Iustinianus,*—P. Krueger.

Vol. III, ed. stereot. quarta, *Novellae,*—Rudolphus Schoell; opus Schoellii morte interceptum absolvit Guilelmus Kroll.

Decreta Authentica Congregationis Sacrorum Rituum, 6 vols., Romae, 1898-1927.

Jaffe, Philippus, *Regesta Pontificum Romanorum ab condita Ecclesia ad annum post Christum natum MCXCVIII, ed. 2, correctam et auctam auspiciis Gulielmi Wattenbach curaverunt S. Loewenfeld, F. Kaltenbrunner, P. Ewald,* 2 vols. in 1, Lipsiae, 1885-1888.

Mansi, J. D., *Sacrorum Conciliorum Nova et Amplissima Collectio,* 53 vols. in 59, Paris, Leipzig, Arnhem, 1901-1927.

Pallottini, Salvator, *Collectio Omnium Conclusionum et Resolutionum quae in causis propositis apud Sacram Congregationem Cardinalium S. Concilii Tridentini Interpretum Prodierunt ab eius institutione, anno MDLXXIX ad MDCCCLX, distinctis titulis alphabetico ordine per materias digestas,* 18 vols., Romae, 1868-1895.

Potthast, Augustus, *Regesta Pontificum Romanorum, inde ab A. post Christum natum MCXCVIII ad A. MCCCIV,* 2 vols., Berolini, 1874-1875.

Schroeder, Henry J., *Canons and Decrees of the Council of Trent,* St. Louis: Herder, 1941.

Reference Works

Acta Congressus Iuridici Internationalis, 5 vols., Romae: Apud Custodiam Librariam, Pont. Instituti Utriusque Iuris, 1935-1937.

Alphonsus Liguori, St., *Theologia Moralis,* ed. absolutissima, 9 vols., Vesontione, 1832.

Bachofen, Augustine, *Compendium Juris Regularium,* New York, 1903.

[Bachofen], Charles Augustine, *A Commentary on the New Code of Canon Law,* 8 vols., Vol. II, 4. ed., 1923; Vol. III, 3. ed., 1922; Vol. IV, 2. ed., 1921; Vol. VI, 2. ed., 1923; Vol. VIII, 1922, St. Louis: Herder.

———, *The Canonical and Civil Status of Catholic Parishes in the United States,* St. Louis: Herder, 1926.

Benedictus XIV, *De Synodo Diocesana,* 2. ed., 4 vols., Mechliniae, 1842.

Berutti, Christophorus, *Institutiones Iuris Canonici,* 6 vols., Vol. III, Taurini-Romae: Marietti, 1936.

Beste, Udalricus, *Introductio in Codicem,* Collegeville, Minn.: St. John's Abbey Press, 1938.

Blat, Albertus, *Commentarium Textus Codicis Iuris Canonici,* 6 vols., lib. II, *De Personis,* 2. ed., 1921; lib. III, *De Rebus,* Pars I, 1920, Partes II-VI, 1923; lib. IV, *De Processibus,* 1927; lib. V, *De Delictis et Poenis,* 1924; Romae.

Bouix, Dominicus, *Tractatus de Jure Regularium,* 3. ed., 2 vols., Parisiis, 1883.

Bouscaren, T. Lincoln, *The Canon Law Digest,* 2 vols., and *Supplement—1941,* Milwaukee: Bruce, 1934-1941.

Butler, Cuthbert, *Benedictine Monachism,* 2. ed., New York, 1924.

———, *The Lausiac History of Palladius,* Texts and Studies, VI, 2 vols., Cambridge, 1898.

Cappello, Felix, *Tractatus Canonico-Moralis de Sacramentis,* 3 vols. in 6, Vol. I, 2. ed., 1928; Vol. II, Pars I, 2. ed., 1929, Taurinorum Augustae: Marietti.

———, *Tractatus Canonico-Moralis de Censuris iuxta Codicem Iuris Canonici,* 3. ed recognita et emendata, Taurinorum Augustae: Marietti, 1933.

Cerato, Prosdecimus, *Censurae Vigentes Ipso Facto a Codice Iuris Canonici Excerptae,* 2. ed. recognita, Patavii, 1921.

Chelodi, Ioannes, *Ius de Personis iuxta Codicem Iuris Canonici*, ed. altera a Sac. Ernesto Bertagnolli recognita et aucta, Tridenti: Libr. Edit. Tridentum, 1927.

———, *Ius Poenale et Ordo Procedendi in Iudiciis Criminalibus iuxta Codicem Iuris Canonici*, 3. ed. aucta et emendata, Tridenti: Libreria Editrice Moderna A. Ardesi, 1933.

Cicognani, Hamletus J., *Commentarium ad Librum I Codicis*, Romae: Ex Schola Typographica "Pio X," 1925.

Cipollini, Albertus, *De Censuris Latae Sententiae iuxta Codicem Iuris Canonici*, Taurini: Marietti, 1925.

Claeys-Bouuaert, F.-Simenon, G., *Manuale Iuris Canonici ad Usum, Seminariorum*, Vol. I, 3. ed., 1930; Vol. II, 1931; Vol. III, 3. ed., 1931, Gandae et Leodii: apud auctores in Seminariis Gandavensi et Leodiensi.

Codex pro Postulatoribus, 4. ed., Romae: Apud Libreria del Collegio S. Antonio, 1929.

Coronata, Matthaeus Conte a, *Institutiones Iuris Canonici ad Usum Utriusque Cleri et Scholarum*, 5 vols., Taurini (Italia): Marietti, 1928-1936.

Creusen, Joseph - Ellis, Adam C. - Garesché, Edward F., *Religious Men and Women in the Code*, 3. ed., Milwaukee: Bruce, 1940.

Crnica, Antonius, *Modificationes in Tractatu de Censuris per Codicem Iuris Canonici Introductae*, S. Mauritii Agauensis, 1919.

D'Annibale, Josephus, *In Constitutionem Apostolicae Sedis Commentarii*, 4. ed., Prati, 1894.

Delatte, Paul, *The Rule of St. Benedict*, New York: Benziger Bros., 1921.

De Meester, Alphonsus, *Juris Canonici et Juris Canonico-Civilis Compendium*, ed. nova, 3 vols. in 4, Brugis, 1921-1928.

Dictionnaire de Droit Canonique, Tom. I-II, publié sous la direction de R. Naz, Paris VI: Librairie Letouzey et Ané, 1935-1937.

Doheny, William J., *Practical Problems in Church Finance*, Milwaukee: Bruce, 1941.

Donatus, Hyacinthus, *Rerum Regularium Quadripartita Praxis Resolutoria*, 4 vols., Neapoli, 1652-1661.

Engel, Ludovicus, *Collegium Universi Iuris Canonici*, Salisburgi, 1726.

Esswein, Anthony, *The Extrajudicial Coercive Powers of Ecclesiastical Superiors*, The Catholic University of America Canon Law Studies, n. 127, Washington, D. C.: The Catholic University of America Press, 1941.

Fagnanus, Prosper, *Commentaria in Quinque Libros Decretalium*, 5 vols. in 3, Coloniae Allobrogum, 1759.

Fanfani, Ludovicus, *De Iure Parochorum ad Normam Codicis Iuris Canonici*, Taurini-Romae: Marietti, 1924.

———, *De Iure Religiosorum ad Normam Codicis Iuris Canonici*, 2. ed., Taurini-Romae: Marietti, 1925.

Ferraris, Lucius, *Prompta Bibliotheca Canonica, Iuridica, Moralis, Theologica, necnon Ascetica, Polemica, Rubricistica, Historica,* 11 vols., Venetiis, 1782-1794.

Ferreres, Joannes, *Institutiones Canonicae,* 2. ed., 2 vols., Barcinonae, 1920.

Fontana, Vincentius - Lo - Cicero, Cajetanus, *Constitutiones, Declarationes et Ordinationes Capitulorum Generalium Sacri Ordinis Fratrum Praedicatorum,* Romae, 1862.

Gasparri, Petrus, *Tractatus Canonicus de Sacra Ordinatione,* 2 vols., Parisiis, 1893-1894.

———, *Tractatus Canonicus de Sanctissima Eucharistia,* 2 vols., Parisiis, 1897.

Gasquet, F. A., *English Monastic Life,* 2. ed. rev., New York, 1904.

Génicot, Eduardus-Salsmans, I., *Institutiones Theologiae Moralis,* 10. ed., 2 vols., Bruxellis, 1922.

Haddan, Arthur West-Stubbs, William, *Councils and Ecclesiastical Documents Relating to Great Britain and Ireland,* 3 vols. in 4, Oxford, 1869-1873.

Hefele, Carolus-Leclercq, Henricus, *Histoire des Conciles,* 10 vols. in 19, Paris: Letouzey et Ané, 1907-1938.

Kearney, Raymond A., *The Principles of Delegation,* The Catholic University of America Canon Law Studies, n. 55, Washington, D. C.: The Catholic University of America, 1929.

Keene, Michael, *Religious Ordinaries and Canon 198,* The Catholic University of America Canon Law Studies, n. 135, Washington, D. C.: The Catholic University of America Press, 1942.

Lega, Michael, *Praelectiones in Textum Iuris Canonici, De Iudiciis Ecclesiasticis,* 4 vols., Romae, 1896-1901.

McCormick, Robert, *Confessors of Religious,* The Catholic University of America Canon Law Studies, n. 33, Washington, D. C.: The Catholic University of America, 1926.

McManus, James, *The Administration of Temporal Goods in Religious Institutes,* The Catholic University of America Canon Law Studies, n. 109, Washington, D. C.: The Catholic University of America, 1937.

Maroto, Philippus, *Institutiones Iuris Canonici ad Normam Novi Codicis,* 2 vols., Tom I, Matriti, 1919.

Michalicka, Wenceslas, *Judicial Procedure in Dismissal of Clerical Exempt Religious,* The Catholic University of America Canon Law Studies, n. 19, Washington, D. C.: The Catholic University of America, 1923.

Michiels, Gommarus, *Normae Generales Iuris Canonici,* 2 vols., Lublin, Polonia: Universitas Catholica, 1929.

———, *Principia Generalia de Personis in Ecclesia,* Lublin, Polonia, Universitas Catholica, 1932.

Migne, J. P., *Patrologiae Cursus Completus, Series Latina,* 221 vols., Parisiis, 1844-1864.

Moriarty, Francis, *The Extraordinary Absolution from Censures,* The Catholic University of America Canon Law Studies, n. 113, Washington, D. C.: The Catholic University of America, 1938.

Noldin, H.-Schönegger, A., *De Censuris,* 30. ed., Oeniponte: Rauch, 1936.

Noval, Josephus, *Commentarium Codicis Iuris Canonici,* lib. IV, *De Processibus,* 2 vols., Pars I, *De Iudiciis,* 1920; Pars II, *De Causis Beatificationis Servorum Dei et Canonizationis Beatorum,* 1932; Pars IV, *De Modo Procedendi in Nonnullis Expediendis Negotiis vel Sanctionibus Poenalibus Applicandis,* 1932; Augustae Taurinorum-Romae, Marietti.

O'Brien, Joseph D., *The Exemption of Religious in Church Law,* Milwaukee: Bruce, 1942.

Ojetti, Benedictus, *Commentarium in Codicem Iuris Canonici,* 4 vols., Romae: apud Aedes Universitatis Gregoriani, 1927-1931.

———, *Synopsis Rerum Moralium et Iuris Pontificii,* 2 vols., Prati, 1904-1905.

Ottaviani, Alaphridus, *Institutiones Iures Publici Ecclesiastici,* 2 vols., Romae: apud Aedes Facultatis Iuridicae ad S. Apollinaris, 1925.

Passerinus, Petrus Maria de Sextula, *De Hominum Statibus et Officiis,* ed. nova, 3 vols., Lucae, 1732.

———, *Tractatus de Electione Canonica,* ed., post Romanam prima in Germania, Coloniae Agrippinae, 1694.

Pejška, Josephus, *Ius Canonicum Religiosorum,* 3. ed., Friburgi Brisgoviae: Herder, 1927.

Piatus, Montensis, *Praelectiones Iuris Regularis,* 3. ed., 2 vols., Tornaci, 1906.

Pistocchi, Marius, *De Bonis Ecclesiae Temporalibus,* Taurini (Italia): Marietti: 1932.

Prümmer, Dominicus, *Manuale Iuris Ecclesiasticae,* Tom. II, *Ius Regularium Speciale,* Friburgi Brisgoviae, 1907.

———, *Manuale Iuris Canonici in Usum Scholarum,* 6. ed., Friburgi Brisgoviae: Herder, 1938.

Raus, P. J. B., *Institutiones Canonicae iuxta Novum Codicem Iuris pro Scholis vel ad usum Privatum Syntheticae Redactae,* 2. ed., Lugduni: Vitte, 1931.

Raymond of Pennafort, St., *Summa,* ed. nova, Veronae, 1744.

Reiffenstuel, Anacletus, *Jus Canonicum Universum,* 5 vols. in 7, Parisiis, 1864-1882.

Rodericus, Emmanuel, *Nova Collectio et Compilatio Privilegiorum Apostolicorum Regularium Mendicantium et non Mendicantium praesertim in quibus ipsae Religiones Communicant,* editio ultima, Antverpiae, 1623.

Salucci, Raffaele, *Il Diritto Penale Secondo il Codice di Diritto Canonica,* 2 vols., Subiaco: Typografia dei Monasteri, 1926-1930.

Santi, Franciscus, *Praelectiones Iuris Canonici,* 4. ed., cura Martini Leitner, 5 vols. in 3, Ratisbonae, 1904-1905.

Schaaf, Valentine, *The Cloister,* The Catholic University of America Canon Law Studies, n. 13, Washington, D. C.: The Catholic University of America, 1921.

Schaefer, Timotheus, *De Religiosis ad Normam Codicis Iuris Canonici,* 3. ed., Romae: S. A. L. E. R., 1940.

Schmalzgrueber, Franciscus, *Ius Ecclesiasticum Universum,* 5 vols. in 12, Romae, 1843-1845.

Schroeder, Henry J., *Disciplinary Decrees of the General Councils*, Text, Translation, and Commentary, St. Louis: Herder, 1937.

Smith, Mariner, *The Penal Law for Religious*, The Catholic University of America Canon Law Studies, n. 98, Washington, D. C.: The Catholic University of America, 1935.

Suarez, Franciscus, *Opera Omnia*, ed. nova, 28 vols., Tom. I-IV a D. M. André; Tom. V-XXVI a Carolo Berton, Parisiis, 1856-1878.

Tamburini, Ascanius, *De Jure Abbatum et Aliorum Praelatorum*, 3 vols. in 2, Coloniae Agrippinae, 1691.

Téphany, Joseph-Marie, *Constitution Apostolicae Sedis Commentaire*, Tours, 1883.

Thesaurus, Carolus, *De Poenis Ecclesiasticis Praxis Absoluta et Universalis*, ed. nova et aucta ab Ubaldo Giraldi, Romae, 1760.

Thomas Aquinas, St., *Doctoris Angelici Opera Omnia iussu impensaque Leonis XIII, P. M. edita*, Romae, 1882—; *Summa Theologica*, Romae, 1888-1906.

Toso, Albertus, *Ad Codicem Iuris Canonici Commentaria Minora*, 5 vols., Vol. II, Romae, 1922.

van Etten, Gregorius, *Compendium Privilegiorum Regularium Praecipue Ordinis Eremitarum S. Augustini*, Romae, 1900.

Van Hove, A., *Commentarium Lovaniense in Codicem Iuris Canonici*, Vol. I, Tom. II, *De Legibus Ecclesiasticis*, Mechliniae-Romae: Dessain, 1930.

Verhoeven, Marianus, *De Praxi a Parochis Observanda in Celebratione Missae pro Populo*, Hasseleti, 1849.

Vermeersch, A., *De Religiosis, Institutis et Personis*, 2 vols., Brugis, 1902-1904.

Vermeersch, A.-Creusen, J., *Epitome Iuris Canonici cum Commentariis ad Scholas et ad Usum Privatum*, 3. ed., 3 vols., Mechlinae—Romae: Dessain, 1927-1928.

Vromant, G., *De Bonis Ecclesiae temporalibus ad usum praesertim Missionariorum et Religiosorum*, Louvain: Editions du Muséum Lessianum, 1927.

Wernz, Franciscus X., *Ius Decretalium ad usum Praelectionum in Scholis Textus Canonici sive Iuris Decretalium*, 6 vols. in 7, Romae-Prati, 1899-1913.

Wernz, F.-Vidal, Petrus, *Ius Canonicum ad Codicis Normam Exactum*, 7 vols. in 8, Romae: apud Aedes Universitatis Gregorianae, 1923-1938.

ARTICLES

Blat, A., "De Potestate Superiorum in Religionibus secundum Codicem I. C.,"—*CpRM*, XVI (1935), 321-353.

———, "De Ordinarii Potestate Delegandi Iuxta Canones 1043 et 1044,"—*Angelicum*, XV (1938), 35-47.

Canuto, A., "De regimine domus studiorum in religione clericali exempta ad normam can. 588,"—*Apollinaris*, IX (1936), 19-39.

Goyeneche, S., "Consultationes,"—*CpR*, VI (1925), 357-364; IX (1928), 427-433; XIII (1932), 100-105.

Hannan, J., "Ex-Seminarian and Novice,"—*The Jurist*, II (1942), 380-382.

Hilling, N., "Über den Gebrauch des Ausdrucks *iurisdictio* im kanonischen Recht während der ersten Hälfte des Mittelalters,"—*AKKR*, CXVIII (1938), 165-170.

Hüfner, A., "Das Rechtsinstitut der klösterlichen Exemtion in der abendländischen Kirche,"—*AKKR*, LXXXVI (1906), 302-318; LXXXVII (1907), 71-86; 270-284; 462-469; 599-636.

Larraona, A., "Commentarium Codicis,"—*CpR*, IV (1923), 39-46; 72-76; 107-112; VI (1925), 425-431; IX (1928), 100-109; X (1929), 33-38; 248-259; XII (1931), 353-359.

———, "Consultationes,"—*CpR*, II (1921), 110-114, 297.

———, "Responsa Minora,"—*CpR*, II (1921), 114-115.

———, "De Potestate Dominativa Publica in Iure Canonico,"—*ACII*, IV, 145-180.

Noval, J., "De Ratione Corrigendi et Puniendi sive in Judicio sive extra Jure Codicis J. C.,"—*JP*, II (1922), 147-156; III (1923), 36-40; 204-210.

Ojetti, B., "Praelatus in Codice I. C. quisnam sit,"—*Periodica*, XVII (1928), 229*-231*.

Pauwels, J., "De missa religiosis praescripta,"—*Periodica*, XIII (1925), (20)-(28).

———, "Annotationes,"—*Periodica*, XIII (1925), 119-120.

Ramos, D., "De Conditione Saecularium in Domibus Religiosorum,"—*CpR*, VII (1925), 136-140.

Roberti, F., "Quaenam poenae applicari possint per modum praecepti,"—*Apollinaris*, IV (1931), 294-300.

Roelker, E., "The Vicar General and the Special Mandate,"—*The Jurist*, II (1942), 346-362.

Van de Kerckhove, M., "De Notione Jurisdictionis in Jure Romano,"—*JP*, XVI (1936), 49-65.

———, "De Notione Jurisdictionis apud Decretistas et Priores Decretalistas,"—*JP*, XVIII (1938), 10-14.

Vermeersch, A., "De Unitate Confessarii Ordinarii apud Moniales et Sorores,"—*Periodica*, V (1913), (1)-(12).

———, "Annotationes,"—*Periodica*, XII (1923), 155-157; XXI (1932), 38-40.

Vromant, G., "De Regimine Paroeciarum et Quasi-Paroeciarum Religiosis Sodalibus Concreditarum,"—*JP*, XIII (1933), 274-284.

Anonymous, "Decisions du Saint-Siège mentionées dans Statuts Synodaux d'Ostie et Velletri,"—*Nouvelle Revue Théologique*, XXVI (1894), 318.

Anonymous, "Annotationes,"—*Periodica*, VII (1914), 70; VIII (1919), 40.

Periodicals

Analecta Sacri Ordinis Fratrum Praedicatorum seu Vetera Ordinis Monumenta Recentioraque Acta, Romae, 1893—; ab anno 1907: *Analecta Sacri Ordinis Fratrum Praedicatorum*.

Apollinaris, Romae, 1928—

Archiv für katholisches Kirchenrecht, Innsbruck, 1857-1861; Mainz, 1862—

Commentarium pro Religiosis, Romae, 1920—; ab anno 1935: *Commentarium pro Religiosis et Missionariis.*

Jurist, The, Washington, D. C., 1941—

Jus Pontificium, Romae, 1921—

Nouvelle Revue Théologique, Paris, 1869—

Periodica de Re Canonica et Morali utili praesertim Religiosis et Missionariis, Bruges, 1905—; ab anno 1927: *Periodica de Re Canonica, Morali, Liturgica.*

Unio Thomistica, Romae, 1924—; ab anno 1925: *Angelicum.*

ABBREVIATIONS

AAS—Acta Apostolicae Sedis.

ACII—Acta Congressus Iuridici Internationalis.

AKKR—Archiv für katholisches Kirchenrecht.

Analecta S. O. P.—Analecta Sacri Ordinis Fratrum Praedicatorum.

ASS—Acta Sanctae Sedis.

BOP—Bullarium Ordinis FF. Praedicatorum.

BRT—Bullarum Diplomatum et Privilegiorum Romanorum Pontificum Taurinensis Editio.

CpR—Commentarium pro Religiosis.

CpRM—Commentarium pro Religiosis et Missionariis.

Const. S. O. P. (1886)—*Constitutiones Sacri Ordinis Fratrum Praedicatorum*, Parisiis, 1886.

Const. S. O. P. (1932)—*Constitutiones Sacri Ordinis Fratrum Praedicatorúm*, Romae, 1932.

Fontes—Codicis Iuris Canonici Fontes cura . . . Gasparri editi.

Hefele—*Histoire des Conciles.*

J (K-E-L)—Jaffé (Kaltenbrunner, Ewald, Loewenfeld).

JP—Jus Pontificium.

Mansi—*Sacrorum Conciliorum Nova et Amplissima Collectio.*

MPL—Migne, *Patrologia Latina.*

N.—*Novellae* (Iustinianae).

Pallottini—*Collectio Omnium Conclusionum et Resolutionum*, etc.

PCI—Pontificia Commissio ad Codicis Canones authentice interpretandos.

Periodica—Periodica de Re Canonica et Morali utili praesertim Religiosis et Missionariis.

Regesta—Potthast, *Regesta Pontificum Romanorum.*

S. C. C.—Sacra Congregatio Concilii.

S. C. de Prop. Fide—Sacra Congregatio de Propaganda Fide.

S. C. Ep. et Reg.—Sacra Congregatio Episcoporum et Regularium.

S. C. S. Off.—Sacra Congregatio Sancti Officii.

S. R. C.—Sacrorum Rituum Congregatio.

ALPHABETICAL INDEX

Abbot,
as local superior, 12;
authority of, 12-13, 26, 36.
Administration, acts of ordinary, 71-73.
Admonition, as penal remedy, 181, 193, 195.
Alienation,
definition of, 75;
religious pastor and, 114.
Alms, solicitation of, 67.
Altar,
blessing of, 165;
ornamentation, of, 170.
Annuities, 76.
Apostate religious, 125.
Apostolic Benediction, imparting of, 139 note [55].
Augustinian Order,
conventual prior in, 37 note [45], 146, 160.
Authority,
during time of visitation, 63;
in an imperfect society, 2;
in a perfect society, 2;
jurisdictional, division of, 56;
of local superior in the Code, 26-39.

Baptism,
administration of, 128;
sponsors at, 128-129.
Beatification, process of, 55.
Bells, blessing of, 163.
Bishop,
coercive power of, 190-191;
exemption from authority of, 16-22, 26;
religious chosen as, 124;
rôle of,
in appointment of,
confessors of religious, 161;
parochial vicars, 109-111;
religious pastor, 109;
in early monasteries, 13-15;
in faculties for preaching, 174;
in permission for investments, 77;
in removal of religious pastor or vicar, 109;
in solicitation of alms, 68;
supervision of religious pastor by, 115-116.
Blessed Sacrament,
custody of, 112, 137 note [47], 170;
visits to, 96.
Blessing of,
altars, 165;
church bells, 165;
sacred places, 165;
sacred vessels, 171;
vestments, 171.
Bonds, issuance of, 76.
Books,
censorship of, 177;
prohibition of, 177;
publication of, 177.
Burial of,
apostolic students, 168-169;
the faithful, 167, 169;
the infirm, 168-169;
novices, 168-169;
postulants, 81, 168-169;
religious, 168-170;
servants, 168-169;
tertiaries, 170.
Burial vaults, 167.

Canonical penances, 181, 192, 193.
Canonization, process of, 55.
Cardinals, religious chosen as, 124.
Cases, solution of moral and liturgical, 93.
Catechetical instruction, 60, 108, 171, 174.
Celebret, superior competent to issue, 130-132.

Cemeteries,
of religious, 166-168;
choice of, by lay people, 167.
Censorship of books, 177.
Censures,
ab homine, 195-196;
latae sententiae, 195-196;
reserved, 195-196.
Chapter,
admission of novices by the, 82-83;
definition of, 63;
general, 102;
local, 63, 64, 75.
Christian doctrine, instruction in, 60.
Church,
capitular, 112;
religious,
administration of goods of, 112;
care of, 112;
reconciliation of violated, 166;
reservation of Blessed Sacrament in, 170.
Cloister,
canonical legislation concerning, 102;
entrance into, 102-104;
penalties for violation of, 104;
reasons for egress from, 105-106.
Coercive power,
existence of, 181-191;
extent of, 191-198;
source of, 178.
Conferences,
bi-monthly to community, 60, 61;
to lay-brother novices, 60;
to professed lay-brothers and servants, 60.
Confession,
of religious,
pre-Code legislation, 94, 146-149;
present legislation,
faculties for, 157-161;
after serious external fault, 99;
weekly, 91-97;
of seculars,
pre-Code legislation, 149-153;
present legislation, 161-162.
Confessor,
extraordinary, 146-147;
ordinary, 145, 146, 158.
Confirmation,
administration of, 128;
sponsors at, 128-129.
Conscience, examination of, 97.
Constitutions,
means of perfection, 94;
public reading of, 59;
regulations of, concerning,
acquisition of temporal goods, 66;
administration of temporalities, 71, 72, 73;
admission to the novitiate, 82-83;
admission to profession, 90;
advice of the council, 64-66;
alienation of goods, 75, 76;
annual retreat, 96;
assistance at community Mass, 96;
burial of the faithful, 167-168, 169;
coercive power of the local superior, 181-183;
common precepts, 46, 47;
confines of the cloister, 102;
daily celebration of Mass, 134;
delegation to hear confessions, 159, 160;
designation of pastors and parochial vicars, 109, 111, 116;
designation of priests for parochial work, 107;
dismissal of novices, 85, 123;
dismissal of the professed, 124;
dispensations for students, 92;
donations, 79-80;
egress from the cloister, 104-105;
examination of conscience, 97;
extent of jurisdiction, 30;
government of the novitiate, 86, 87;

individual precepts, 47;
investments, 114;
judicial power, 52-53, 197;
jurisdiction for confessions, 146, 157-158, 160;
jurisdiction for preaching, 173-174, 175;
jurisdiction of local chapter, 64;
legislative power, 42, 43, 44;
limitation of jurisdiction, 27-29, 181-183, 186, 191;
local superior acting in name of community at ecclesiastical trial, 54;
membership in local council, 64;
Missa pro communitate, 135;
observance of spiritual exercises, 94, 95, 96;
reception of the professed, 88;
reception of visitors, 104;
recitation of the Rosary, 96;
religious visiting another religious house, 38;
residence, 57, 58;
rite of profession, 88;
solicitation of alms, 68;
solution of moral and liturgical cases, 93;
subjection of *moniales,* 38;
those obliged to choral recitation of the office, 118;
visits to the Blessed Sacrament, 96-97.

Conventual Mass,
obligation of, 117-118;
those dispensed or impeded from, 118.

Council,
admission of novices by, 82;
advice of, 64;
consent of, 64, 75;
definition of, 63;
dismissal of novices by, 123;
local, 63-64;
manner of acting, 66.

Councillors,
advice of, 64;
consent of, 63.

Debts, responsibility for, 78.

Declaration,
before temporary profession, 89;
before solemn profession, 89;
before subdiaconate, 89.

Decrees of the Holy See,
on cases reserved to the Holy Office, 60;
on manifestation of conscience, 60;
reading of, 58-59;
on the solicitation of alms, 68;
on testimonial letters, 60;
on the training of candidates for the priesthood, 60.

Dismissal,
judicial process in, 126;
of novices, 85, 123;
of religious in solemn vows, 126;
of religious in temporary vows, 125-126.

Dispensation,
as an act of jurisdiction, 50;
local superior's power of,
in pre-Code legislation, 47;
in present legislation, 41, 47-49;
from choral obligation, 91-92, 121;
from community exercises, 91;
from fast and abstinence, 48, 81, 86;
from non-reserved vows, 48-49, 81, 86;
from an oath, 49, 81, 86;
from observance of feasts, 48, 81, 86;
from public vow, 49.

Dominative power,
distinction between jurisdiction and, 9-11;
division of, 9;
during time of visitation, 63;

exercise of, and confession, 158;
in the Code of Canon Law, 8, 26-29;
meaning, 7-8;
of local chapter, 64;
over postulants, 81;
private, 9;
public, 9.
Dominican Order, 149, 155, 163, 170, 172.
Donations, competency of local superior regarding, 79-80.

Easter Communion, 136-137.
Epitaphs, 167.
Examination before conferring of jurisdiction,
for hearing confessions, 160-161;
for preaching, 176.
Exclaustration, indult of, 124.
Excommunication, 179, 180, 192.
Exemption, 15-22.
Exercises of piety, 96.
Extreme Unction, administration of,
to the faithful, 138;
to novices, 86, 139, 140;
to postulants, 81, 140-142, 143-144;
to the professed, 128, 139-140, 143.

Familiares,
baptism of, 129;
and the bi-monthly conference, 61;
Holy Eucharist and the, 138, 139;
marriages of, 129;
preaching to, 174.
Fast,
as canonical penance, 181;
dispensation from, 48.
Franciscan Order, 153, 166, 170, 172.
Fugitive religious, 125.

Guardian, 25, 165, 166, 170, 190.
Guest, cf. *hospitii.*

Habit, religious,
causes for temporary laying aside of, 101;
laying aside of, 100.
Holy Communion, cf. Holy Eucharist.
Holy Eucharist,
administration of, *devotionis causa,*
privately, 137-138;
publicly, 137;
administration of, as Viaticum, cf. Viaticum;
daily reception of, 91, 97-99;
fast prescribed before, 144;
frequent reception of, 94, 97-99;
received by the sick, 99, 137.
Holy Orders, 91, 163-164.
Hospitii,
burial of, 168, 169;
preaching to, 174;
Viaticum and Extreme Unction for, 139-140.

Images,
alienation or transfer of, 76;
veneration of, 171.
Infirm,
administration of Sacraments to, 139;
burial of, 168-169;
preaching to, 174.
Interdict, 180, 192, 194.
Investments,
of parish funds, 114;
permission of bishop for, 77;
religious pastor and, 114.

Judge of first instance, 52-54, 186.
Judicial power,
in Code of Canon Law, 52-55, 186, 197;
in pre-Code law, 51-52.
Judicial process in dismissal of religious, 126.
Jurisdiction,
delegation of,
for hearing of confessions, 158-159;
for preaching, 172-176;
division of,
contentious, 7;

delegated, 6-7;
delegated *a iure,* 50;
in external forum, 6, 34, 182, 188;
in internal forum, 6;
ordinary, 6, 32, 39, 50, 158, 189;
personal, 7, 39, 54;
proper, 7, 32, 39;
quasi-episcopal 31-33, 179, 186-187;
territorial, 7, 54;
universal, 7;
vicarious, 7, 32, 39;
voluntary, 7;
distinction between dominative power and, 9;
during time of the visitation, 63;
history of,
in Roman law, 3;
after St. Gregory the Great, 3;
in latter half of 12th century, 3;
after 1215, 3-4;
in Code of Canon Law, 4-5, 26-39;
limitation of, 27-29, 181-183, 186, 191;
of local chapter, 64;
meaning of, 4-6;
penal, 178-198;
in a perfect society, 2, 3;
required for preaching, 107, 172-176.

Key of tabernacle, custody of, 112, 170-171.

Law, definition of, 40, 42, 43.
Legislative power,
of general chapter, 40;
and imposition of canonical penalties, 182;
of local superior, 34-35, 40-44, 185-186.
Letter-writing, 106.
Liturgical,
cases, solution of, 93;
laws, observance of, 112.

Mass,
attendance at, 96;
celebration of, 96, 133;
conventual, 117, 134;
pro communitate, 135;
pro populo, 135.
Mass stipends, 67, 135-136.
Matrimony, 128, 164.
Meditation, 91, 94, 96.
Mendicants,
and jurisdiction for preaching, 21, 172;
and solicitation of alms, 67-68.
Monasticism, early period of, 12.
Moniales,
confessors of, 147-149;
as subject to regular superior, 38-39.

Notary, use of, in,
imposition of precepts, 45;
judicial trials, 53, 54;
process of beatification and canonization, 55.
Novice master, relationship of, to local superior, 85-87.
Novices,
and absence from the novitiate, 84;
administration of Sacraments to, 139, 140;
admission of, 82;
burial of, 168-169;
confessions of, 157, 159;
dismissal of, 85, 123;
preaching to, 174;
as subjects of local superior, 38, 86;
training of, 83-84.
Novitiate,
admission to, 82-83;
validity of, 83.
Nuns, cf. *moniales.*

Oath,
before judicial trials, 53;
before subdiaconate, 89;
promissory, dispensation from, 49.

Obligations, responsibility for, 78-79.
Office, divine,
  dispensation from, 91-92, 120-121;
  manner of recitation, 119;
  obligation of choral recitation of, 116-121;
  place of recitation of, 120;
  privileges in private recitation of, 121;
  time of recitation of, 119-120.
Offices,
  incompatible, 85-86, 108-109;
  privation of ecclesiastical, 180.
Ordinary, local superior as, 25, 34-35, 36-38.
Ordinary administration, acts of, 71-73.
Ordination, cf. Holy Orders.

Parish,
  religious, 108;
    legacies given to, 112;
    sponsors at baptism in, 129;
    vigilance over funds of, 113.
Parochial work, 106-108.
Pastor,
  coervice power of, 191;
  religious,
    attendance at community exercises by, 112-113;
    burial of faithful by, 169;
    compared with local superior, 191;
    designation of, 109;
    removal of, 109;
    rights and duties of, 112;
    supervision of, by local ordinary, 115-116.
Penal remedies, 180, 192, 193.
Penalty,
  for impeding the visitation, 62;
  for non-residence, 57;
  for violation of the cloister, 104;
  inflicted upon religious pastor, 116.
Penance, Sacrament of, cf. Confession.
Penances, canonical, 181, 192, 193.
Periodicals,
  articles for, 177;
  publication of, 177.
Pious foundations, acceptance of, 67.
Pontifical Commission for Interpretation, 110, 127, 137, 143, 168, 195.
Pope,
  in government of religious Orders, 26;
  jurisdiction of, 27, 40.
Postulancy,
  abbreviation of, 82;
  admission to, 80;
  prolongation of, 82.
Postulants,
  administration of Sacraments to, 140-142;
  admission of, 80;
  burial of, 168-170;
  subjects of the local superior, 38, 81.
Prayer, as a canonical penance, 181.
Preaching,
  jurisdiction required for, 107, 172-176;
  part of teaching office, 171.
Precepts,
  common, 46;
  definition of, 44;
  dominative, 45;
  jurisdictional, 44, 47, 182-185, 187-188, 192;
  particular, 45;
  as penal remedies, 181, 193;
  regarding celebration of Mass according to the intention of the superior, 134.
Precious Objects, alienation of, 76.
Prelates,
  in the Code of Canon Law, 30;
  the local superior as a, 30;
  in pre-Code law, 30.
Prior,
  faculties of, in pre-Code law, 156;
  in Augustinian Order, 37 note [45], 146, 160;
  in monastic congregations, 12, 26;

in the Order of Preachers, 123 note [299], 154, 163 note [182], 180 notes [9], [12];
in religious Orders, 25, 165, 179.
Privileges,
communication of, 31;
in private recitation of office, 121;
in regard to the Sacrament of Penance, 155.
Process in dismissal of religious, 126.
Processions, 171.
Procurator and local superior, relationship between, 69.
Profession, religious.
admission to, 87;
declaration before, 89;
petition before, 89;
prolongation of temporary, 88;
reception of, 88.
Prohibition of books, 177.

Rebuke, as penal remedy, 181.
Reconciliation of violated church, 166.
Records,
of Mass stipends, 135-136;
of pious foundations accepted, 67;
of profession, 88.
Rector,
of church attached to a religious house, 111;
removal of, 111-112.
Relics,
alienation or transfer of, 76;
care of, 171.
Reservation of sins,
in pre-Code legislation, 153-155;
in present legislation, 161.
Residence,
law of, 56-58;
penalty for violation of law of, 58.
Retreat,
annual, 91, 95-96;
made by candidate for the priesthood in religious house, 163 note [178].
"Romani Pontificis," 27, 31, 32, 34, 47, 130, 132, 155, 164, 180.
Rosary, daily recitation of, 96.

Sacred places, blessing of, 165.
School, funds of, 113.
Secularization, indult of, 124.
Servants,
administration of Sacraments to, 139, 142;
burial of, 168-169;
preaching to, 174.
Sponsors at,
Baptism, 128-129;
Confirmation, 128-129.
Students,
administration of the Sacraments to, 139-142, 143;
burial of apostolic, 168-169;
and the cloister, 103;
and the Sacrament of Penance, 159;
preaching to, 174.
Studium,
common life in, 91;
ministerial occupations outside of, 91-93.
Subjects of the local superior, 38-39.
Superior,
general (supreme),
in Code of Canon Law, 24-25, 26;
legislative power of, 42-43;
reservation of sins by, 153-154;
rôle of,
in alienation of property, 74;
in dismissal of religious, 122, 125;
in donations, 79;
major, 24-25, 35, 36-38;
rôle of,
in admission to the novitiate, 82-83;
in admission to profession, 87;
in dismissal of novices, 123;
in dismissal of the professed, 124, 125;

in establishing limits of the cloister, 102;
in issuance of the *celebret,* 130-132;
in ordination of subjects, 163-164;
in prolongation of the novitiate, 84;
in prolongation of the postulancy, 82;
in prolongation of temporary profession, 88;
in retreat obligation, 95;
in transfer of delinquent religious, 126;
in vigilance over parish funds, 114;
in visitation, 62;
provincial, 24;
acceptance of pious foundations by, 67;
alienation of property by, 74;
delegation of jurisdiction by, 37;
designation of notary by, 54;
dismissal of novices by, 123;
investments by, 78;
judicial power of, 52;
recourse to, 65;
minor local,
jurisdiction of, 28, 37, 38, *passim;*
right of vigilance over parish funds by, 113;
relationship of, with neighboring pastor, 108;
relationship of, with novice master, 85-87;
relationship of, with procurator, 69;
rôle of,
in appointment and removal of rector of a church, 111-112;
in appointment and removal of a vicar *cooperator,* 111;
in approval of a vicar substitute, 110;
in burial of religious subjects, 168-170;
in delegation of jurisdiction, 32;
for hearing confessions, 161-162;
for preaching, 172-174, 175-176;
in dismissal of religious, 122, 126;
in fulfillment of Mass obligations, 135;
in issuance of *celebret,* 130-132;
in issuance of testimonial letters, 83;
in observance of the cloister, 102;
in presentation of the vicar adjutant, 111;
in reception of Holy Orders, 163-164;
in reconciliation of a violated church, 166;
in return of apostate and fugitive religious, 126-127;
in right of vigilance over parish funds, 113;
subjects of, 38-39, 146;
as witness in ecclesiastical trial, 54-55.
Suspension, 180, 192;
ex informata conscientia, 180 note [9], 182, 194, 197.

Tabernacle key, custody of, 112, 170-171.
Temporal goods,
acquisition of, 67;
administration of, 71;
alienation of, 73-75.
Tertiaries, burial of, 170.
Trials, ecclesiastical, 51-55.

Vessels, sacred, blessing of, 171.
Vestments, blessing of, 171.
Viaticum, administration of,

to the faithful, 138;
to residents of a religious house,
outside the religious house,
to novices and to the professed, 140, 143;
to postulants, 143-144;
to servants, students, guests, and to the infirm, 143;
within the religious house,
to *familiares*, 138, 139, 140;
to guests, 139, 140;
to the infirm, 139, 142-143;
to servants, 139, 140, 142;
to students, 139, 140-142;
to novices, 139, 140;
to postulants, 140-142;
to the professed, 139, 140.

Vicar,
adjutant, appointment and removal of, 111;
cooperator, appointment and removal of, 111;
econome,
appointment of, 109;
removal of, 111;
forane, 133;
general,
and *celebret*, 132-133;
coercive power of, 184, 189-191;
parochial, designation and removal of, 109;
substitute,
appointment of, 110, 164;
assistance at marriages by, 110;
removal of, 111.

Vigilance,
local superior's right of, 69-70, 113;
as a penal remedy, 181, 193-194;
of provincial over record of Mass stipends, 136.

Vindicative penalty, 180, 192, 196, 198.

Violated church, reconciliation of, 166.

Visitation, canonical, 62-63;
penalties for interference with, 62-63.

Visitors,
celebret required of, 132;
as subject to the local superior, 38.

Vow,
non-reserved, dispensation from, 48-49;
public, dispensation from, 49.

Wage, just and adequate, 72.

BIOGRAPHICAL NOTE

PATRICK M. J. CLANCY was born on February 20, 1912, at Chicago, Illinois. After completing his elementary education at Visitation and St. Rita of Cascia parochial schools, he attended Quigley Preparatory Seminary in Chicago. He matriculated at Providence College, Providence, Rhode Island, in the fall of 1930. After two years of college training, he entered the novitiate of the Order of Preachers at Springfield, Kentucky, where he made his religious profession on August 16, 1933. He received the degree of Bachelor of Arts in June, 1936, at the Dominican House of Studies, River Forest, Illinois. Upon the completion of his philosophical studies, he studied theology for three years at St. Joseph's Priory, Somerset, Ohio, where he was ordained to the priesthood on May 17, 1939. After completing his final year of theology at the Dominican House of Studies, Washington, D. C., he received the degree of Lector of Sacred Theology in the spring of 1940. In the fall of the same year he entered the School of Canon Law at the Catholic University of America, and received the Baccalaureate in June, 1941, and the Licentiate in May, 1942.

CANON LAW STUDIES *

1. Freriks, Rev. Celestine A., C.PP.S., J.C.D., Religious Congregations in Their External Relations, 121 pp., 1916.
2. Galliher, Rev. Daniel M., O.P., J.C.D., Canonical Elections, 117 pp., 1917.
3. Borkowski, Rev. Aurelius L., O.F.M., J.C.D., De Confraternitatibus Ecclesiasticis, 136 pp., 1918.
4. Castillo, Rev. Cayo, J.C.D., Disertacion Historico-Canonica sobre la Potestad del Cabildo en Sede Vacante o Impedida del Vicario Capitular, 99 pp., 1919 (1918).
5. Kubelbeck, Rev. William J., S.T.B., J.C.D., The Sacred Penitentiaria and Its Relation to Faculties of Ordinaries and Priests, 129 pp., 1918.
6. Petrovits, Rev. Joseph, J.C., S.T.D., J.C.D., The New Church Law on Matrimony, X-461 pp., 1919.
7. Hickey, Rev. John J., S.T.B., J.C.D., Irregularities and Simple Impediments in the New Code of Canon Law, 100 pp., 1920.
8. Klekotka, Rev. Peter J., S.T.B., J.C.D., Diocesan Consultors, 179 pp., 1920.
9. Wanenmacher, Rev. Francis, J.C.D., The Evidence in Ecclesiastical Procedure Affecting the Marriage Bond, 1920 (Printed 1935).
10. Golden, Rev. Henry Francis, J.C.D., Parochial Benefices in the New Code, IV-119 pp., 1921 (Printed 1925).
11. Koudelka, Rev. Charles J., J.C.D., Pastors, Their Rights and Duties According to the New Code of Canon Law, 211 pp., 1921.
12. Melo, Rev. Antonius, O.F.M., J.C.D., De Exemptione Regularium, X-188 pp., 1921.
13. Schaaf, Rev. Valentine Theodore, O.F.M., S.T.B., J.C.D., The Cloister, X-180 pp., 1921.
14. Burke, Rev. Thomas Joseph, S.T.D., J.C.D., Competence in Ecclesiastical Tribunals, IV-117 pp., 1922.
15. Leech, Rev. George Leo, J.C.D., A Comparative Study of the Constitution "Apostolicae Sedis" and the "Codex Juris Canonici," 179 pp., 1922.
16. Motry, Rev. Hubert Louis, S.T.D., J.C.D., Diocesan Faculties According to the Code of Canon Law, II-167 pp., 1922.
17. Murphy, Rev. George Lawrence, J.C.D., Delinquencies and Penalties in the Administration and the Reception of the Sacraments, IV-121 pp., 1923.
18. O'Reilly, Rev. John Anthony, S.T.B., J.C.D., Ecclesiastical Sepulture in the New Code of Canon Law, II-129 pp., 1923.

* Below n. 100 only the following numbers are still available: Nn. 3, 4, 9, 25, 34, 57 and 75. Beginning with n. 100 only the following are unavailable: Nn. 100, 101, 102, 104, 105, 107, 108, 109, 111 and 113.

19. Michalicka, Rev. Wenceslas Cyrill, O.S.B., J.C.D., Judicial Procedure in Dismissal of Clerical Exempt Religious, 107 pp., 1923.
20. Dargin, Rev. Edward Vincent, S.T.B., J.C.D., Reserved Cases According to the Code of Canon Law, IV-103 pp., 1924.
21. Godfrey, Rev. John A., S.T.B., J.C.D., The Right of Patronage According to the Code of Canon Law, 153 pp., 1924.
22. Hagedorn, Rev. Francis Edward, J.C.D., General Legislation on Indulgences, II-154 pp., 1924.
23. King, Rev. James Ignatius, J.C.D., The Administration of the Sacraments to Dying Non-Catholics, V-141 pp., 1924.
24. Winslow, Rev. Francis Joseph, O.F.M., J.C.D., Vicars and Prefects Apostolic, IV-149 pp., 1924.
25. Correa, Rev. Jose Servelion, S.T.L., J.C.D., La Potestad Legislativa de la Iglesia Catolica, IV-127 pp., 1925.
26. Dugan, Rev. Henry Francis, A.M., J.C.D., The Judiciary Department of the Diocesan Curia, 87 pp., 1925.
27. Keller, Rev. Charles Frederick, S.T.B., J.C.D., Mass Stipends, 167 pp., 1925.
28. Paschang, Rev. John Linus, J.C.D., The Sacramentals According to the Code of Canon Law, 129 pp., 1925.
29. Piontek, Rev. Cyrillus, O.F.M., S.T.B., J.C.D., De Indulto Exclaustrationis necnon Saecularizationis, XIII-289 pp., 1925.
30. Kearney, Rev. Richard Joseph, S.T.B., J.C.D., Sponsors at Baptism According to the Code of Canon Law, IV-127 pp., 1925.
31. Bartlett, Rev. Chester Joseph, A.M., LL.B., J.C.D., The Tenure of Parochial Property in the United States of America, V-108 pp., 1926.
32. Kilker, Rev. Adrian Jerome, J.C.D., Extreme Unction, V-425 pp., 1926.
33. McCormick, Rev. Robert Emmett, J.C.D., Confessors of Religious, VIII-266 pp., 1926.
34. Miller, Rev. Newton Thomas, J.C.D., Founded Masses According to the Code of Canon Law, VII-93 pp., 1926.
35. Roelker, Rev. Edward G., S.T.D., J.C.D., Principles of Privilege According to the Code of Canon Law, XI-166 pp., 1926.
36. Bakalarczyk, Rev. Richardus, M.I.C., J.U.D., De Novitiatu, VIII-208 pp., 1927.
37. Pizzuti, Rev. Lawrence, O.F.M., J.U.L., De Parochis Religiosis, 1927. (Not Printed.)
38. Bliley, Rev. Nicholas Martin, O.S.B., J.C.D., Altars According to the Code of Canon Law, XIX-132 pp., 1927.
39. Brown, Mr. Brendan Francis, A.B., LL.M., J.U.D., The Canonical Juristic Personality with Special Reference to its Status in the United States of America, V-212 pp., 1927.
40. Cavanaugh, Rev. William Thomas, C.P., J.U.D., The Reservation of the Blessed Sacrament, VIII-101 pp., 1927.

41. Doheny, Rev. William J., C.S.C., A.B., J.U.D., Church Property: Modes of Acquisition, X-118 pp., 1927.
42. Feldhaus, Rev. Aloysius H., C.PP.S., J.C.D., Oratories, IX-141 pp., 1927.
43. Kelly, Rev. James Patrick, A.B., J.C.D., The Jurisdiction of the Simple Confessor, X-208 pp., 1927.
44. Neuberger, Rev. Nicholas J., J.C.D., Canon 6 or the Relation of the Codex Juris Canonici to the Preceding Legislation, V-95 pp., 1927.
45. O'Keefe, Rev. Gerald Michael, J.C.D., Matrimonial Dispensations, Powers of Bishops, Priests, and Confessors, VIII-232 pp., 1927.
46. Quigley, Rev. Joseph A. M., A.B., J.C.D., Condemned Societies, 139 pp., 1927.
47. Zaplotnik, Rev. Johannes Leo, J.C.D., De Vicariis Foraneis, X-142 pp., 1927.
48. Duskie, Rev. John Aloysius, A.B., J.C.D., The Canonical Status of the Orientals in the United States, VIII-196 pp., 1928.
49. Hyland, Rev. Francis Edward, J.C.D., Excommunciation, Its Nature, Historical Development and Effects, VIII-181 pp., 1928.
50. Reinmann, Rev. Gerald Joseph, O.M.C., J.C.D., The Third Order Secular of Saint Francis, 201 pp., 1928.
51. Schenk, Rev. Francis J., J.C.D., The Matrimonial Impediments of Mixed Religion and Disparity of Cult, XVI-318 pp., 1929.
52. Coady, Rev. John Joseph, S.T.D., J.U.D., A.M., The Appointment of Pastors, VIII-150 pp., 1929.
53. Kay, Rev. Thomas Henry, J.C.D., Competence in Matrimonial Procedure, VIII-164 pp., 1929.
54. Turner, Rev. Sidney Joseph, C.P., J.U.D., The Vow of Poverty, XLIX-217 pp., 1929.
55. Kearney, Rev. Raymond A., A.B., S.T.D., J.C.D., The Principles of Delegation, VII-149 pp., 1929.
56. Conran, Rev. Edward James, A.B., J.C.D., The Interdict, V-163 pp., 1930.
57. O'Neill, Rev. William H., J.C.D., Papal Rescripts of Favor, VII-218 pp., 1930.
58. Bastnagel, Rev. Clement Vincent, J.U.D., The Appointment of Parochial Adjutants and Assistants, XV-257 pp., 1930.
59. Ferry, Rev. William A., A.B., J.C.D., Stole Fees, V-136 pp., 1930.
60. Costello, Rev. John Michael, A.B., J.C.D., Domicile and Quasi-Domicile, VII-201 pp., 1930.
61. Kremer, Rev. Michael Nicholas, A.B., S.T.B., J.C.D., Church Support in the United States, VI-136 pp., 1930.
62. Angulo, Rev. Luis, C.M., J.C.D., Legislation de la Iglesia sobre la intencion en la application de la Santa Misa, VII-104 pp., 1931.
63. Frey, Rev. Wolfgang Norbert, O.S.B., A.B., J.C.D., The Act of Religious Profession, VIII-174 pp., 1931

64. ROBERTS, REV. JAMES BRENDAN, A.B., J.C.D., The Banns of Marriage, XIV-140 pp., 1931.

65. RYDER, REV. RAYMOND ALOYSIUS, A.B., J.C.D., Simony, IX-151 pp., 1931.

66. CAMPAGNA, REV. ANGELO, PH.D., J.U.D., Il Vicario Generale del Vescovo, VII-205 pp., 1931.

67. COX, REV. JOSEPH GODFREY, A.B., J.C.D., The Administration of Seminaries, VI-124 pp., 1931.

68. GREGORY, REV. DONALD J., J.U.D., The Pauline Privilege, XV-165 pp., 1931.

69. DONOHUE, REV. JOHN F., J.C.D., The Impediment of Crime, VII-110 pp., 1931.

70. DOOLEY, REV. EUGENE A., O.M.I., J.C.D., Church Law on Sacred Relics, IX-143 pp., 1931.

71. ORTH, REV. CLEMENT RAYMOND, O.M.C., J.C.D., The Approbation of Religious Institutes, 171 pp., 1931.

72. PERNICONE, REV. JOSEPH M., A.B., J.C.D., The Ecclesiastical Prohibition of Books, XII-267 pp., 1932.

73. CLINTON, REV. CONNELL, A.B., J.C.D., The Paschal Precept, IX-108 pp., 1932.

74. DONNELLY, REV. FRANCIS B., A.M., S.T.L., J.C.D., The Diocesan Synod, VIII-125 pp., 1932.

75. TORRENTE, REV. CAMILO, C.M.F., J.C.D., Las Processiones Sagradas, V-145 pp., 1932.

76. MURPHY, REV. EDWIN J., C.PP.S., J.C.D., Suspension Ex Informata Conscientia, XI-122 pp., 1932.

77. MACKENZIE, REV. ERIC F., A.M., S.T.L., J.C.D., The Delict of Heresy in its Commission, Penalization, Absolution, VII-124 pp., 1932.

78. LYONS, REV. AVITUS E., S.T.B., J.C.D., The Collegiate Tribunal of First Instance, XI-147 pp., 1932.

79. CONNOLLY, REV. THOMAS A., J.C.D., Appeals, XI-195 pp., 1932.

80. SANGMEISTER, REV. JOSEPH V., A.B., J.C.D., Force and Fear as Precluding Matrimonial Consent, V-211 pp., 1932.

81. JAEGER, REV. LEO A., A.B., J.C.D., The Administration of Vacant and Quasi-Vacant Episcopal Sees in the United States, IX-229 pp., 1932.

82. RIMLINGER, REV. HERBERT T., J.C.D., Error Invalidating Matrimonial Consent, VII-79 pp., 1932.

83. BARRETT, REV. JOHN D. M., S.S., J.C.D., A Comparative Study of the Third Plenary Council of Baltimore and the Code, IX-221 pp., 1932.

84. CARBERRY, REV. JOHN J., PH.D., S.T.D., J.C.D., The Juridical Form of Marriage, X-177 pp., 1934.

85. DOLAN, REV. JOHN L., A.B., J.C.D., The Defensor Vinculi, XII-157 pp., 1934.

86. HANNAN, REV. JEROME D., A.M., S.T.D., LL.B., J.C.D., The Canon Law of Wills, IX-517 pp., 1934.

87. LEMIEUX, REV. DELISE A., A.M., J.C.D., The Sentence in Ecclesiastical Procedure, IX-131 pp., 1934.
88. O'ROURKE, REV. JAMES J., A.B., J.C.D., Parish Registers, VII-109 pp., 1934.
89. TIMLIN, REV. BARTHOLOMEW, O.F.M., A.M., J.C.D., Conditional Matrimonial Consent, X-381 pp., 1934.
90. WAHL, REV. FRANCIS X., A.B., J.C.D., The Matrimonial Impediments of Consanguinity and Affinity, VI-125 pp., 1934.
91. WHITE, REV. ROBERT J., A.B., LL.B., S.T.B., J.C.D., Canonical Ante-Nuptial Promises and the Civil Law, VI-152 pp., 1934.
92. HERRERA, REV. ANTONIO PARRA, O.C.D., J.C.D., Legislacion Ecclesiastica sobra el Ayuno y la Abstinencia, XI-191 pp., 1935.
93. KENNEDY, REV. EDWIN J., J.C.D., The Special Matrimonial Process in Cases of Evident Nullity, X-165 pp., 1935.
94. MANNING, REV. JOHN J., A.B., J.C.D., Presumption of Law in Matrimonial Procedure, XI-111 pp., 1935.
95. MOEDER, REV. JOHN M., J.C.D., The Proper Bishop for Ordination and Dimissorial Letters, VII-135 pp., 1935.
96. O'MARA, REV. WILLIAM A., A.B., J.C.D., Canonical Causes for Matrimonial Dispensations, IX-155 pp., 1935.
97. REILLY, REV. PETER, J.C.D., Residence of Pastors, IX-81 pp., 1935.
98. SMITH, REV. MARINER T., O.P., S.T.Lr., J.C.D., The Penal Law for Religious, VII-169 pp., 1935.
99. WHALEN, REV. DONALD W., A.M., J.C.D., The Value of Testimonial Evidence in Matrimonial Procedure, XIII-297 pp., 1935.
100. CLEARY, REV. JOSEPH F., J.C.D., Canonical Limitations on the Alienation of Church Property, VIII-141 pp., 1936.
101. GLYNN, REV. JOHN C., J.C.D., The Promoter of Justice, XX-337 pp., 1936.
102. BRENNAN, REV. JAMES H., S.S., M.A., S.T.B., J.C.D., The Simple Convalidation of Marriage, VI-135 pp., 1937.
103. BRUNINI, REV. JOSEPH BERNARD, J.C.D., The Clerical Obligations of Canons 139 and 142, X-121 pp., 1937.
104. CONNOR, REV. MAURICE, A.B., J.C.D., The Administrative Removal of Pastors, VIII-159 pp., 1937.
105. GUILFOYLE, REV. MERLIN JOSEPH, J.C.D., Custom, XI-144 pp., 1937.
106. HUGHES, REV. JAMES AUSTIN, A.B., A.M., J.C.D., Witnesses in Criminal Trials of Clerics, IX-140 pp., 1937.
107. JANSEN, REV. RAYMOND J., A.B., S.T.L., J.C.D., Canonical Provisions for Catechetical Instruction, VII-153 pp., 1937.
108. KEALY, REV. JOHN JAMES, A.B., J.C.D., The Introductory Libellus in Church Court Procedure, XI-121 pp., 1937.
109. McMANUS, REV. JAMES EDWARD, C.SS.R., J.C.D., The Administration of Temporal Goods in Religious Institutes, XVI-196 pp., 1937.

110. Moriarty, Rev. Eugene James, J.C.D., Oaths in Ecclesiastical Courts, X-115 pp., 1937.
111. Rainer, Rev. Eligius George, C.SS.R., J.C.D., Suspension of Clerics, XVII-249 pp., 1937.
112. Reilly, Rev. Thomas F., C.SS.R., J.C.D., Visitation of Religious, VI-195 pp., 1938.
113. Moriarty, Rev. Francis E., C.SS.R., J.C.D., The Extraordinary Absolution from Censures, XV-334 pp., 1938.
114. Connolly, Rev. Nicholas P., J.C.D., The Canonical Erection of Parishes, X-132 pp., 1938.
115. Donovan, Rev. James Joseph, J.C.D., The Pastor's Obligation in Prenuptial Investigation, XII-322 pp., 1938.
116. Harrigan, Rev. Robert J., M.A., S.T.B., J.C.D., The Radical Sanation of Invalid Marriages, VIII-208 pp., 1938.
117. Boffa, Rev. Conrad Humbert, J.C.D., Canonical Provisions for Catholic Schools, VII-211 pp., 1939.
118. Parsons, Rev. Anscar John, O.M.Cap., J.C.D., Canonical Elections, XII-236 pp., 1939.
119. Reilly, Rev. Edward Michael, A.B., J.C.D., The General Norms of Dispensation, XII-156 pp., 1939.
120. Ryan, Rev. Gerald Aloysius, A.B., J.C.D., Principles of Episcopal Jurisdiction, XII-172 pp., 1939.
121. Burton, Rev. Francis James, C.S.C., A.B., J.C.D., A Commentary on Canon 1125, X-222 pp., 1940.
122. Miaskiewicz, Rev. Francis Sigismund, J.C.D., Supplied Jurisdiction According to Canon 209, XII-340 pp., 1940.
123. Rice, Rev. Patrick William, A.B., J.C.D., Proof of Death in Prenuptial Investigation, VIII-156 pp., 1940.
124. Anglin, Rev. Thomas Francis, M.S., J.C.D., The Eucharistic Fast, VIII-183 pp., 1941.
125. Coleman, Rev. John Jerome, J.C.D., The Minister of Confirmation, VI-153 pp., 1941.
126. Downs, Rev. Joseph Emmanuel, A.B., J.C.D., The Concept of Clerical Immunity, XI-163 pp., 1941.
127. Esswein, Rev. Anthony Albert, J.C.D., Extrajudicial Penal Powers of Ecclesiastical Superiors, X-144 pp., 1941.
128. Farrell, Rev. Benjamin Francis, M.A., S.T.L., J.C.D., The Rights and Duties of the Local Ordinary Regarding Congregations of Women Religious of Pontifical Approval, V-195 pp., 1941.
129. Feeney, Rev. Thomas John, A.B., S.T.L., J.C.D., Restitutio in Integrum, VI-169 pp., 1941.
130. Findlay, Rev. Stephen William, O.S.B., A.B., J.C.D., Canonical Norms Governing the Deposition and Degradation of Clerics, XVII-279 pp., 1941.

131. Goodwine, Rev. John, A.B., S.T.L., J.C.D., The Right of the Church to Acquire Property, VIII-119 pp., 1941.

132. Heston, Rev. Edward Louis, C.S.C., Ph.D., S.T.D., J.C.D., The Alienation of Church Property in the United States, XII-222 pp., 1941.

133. Hogan, Rev. James John, A.B., S.T.L., J.C.D., Judicial Advocates and Procurators, XIII-200 pp., 1941.

134. Kealy, Rev. Thomas M., A.B., Litt.B., J.C.D., Dowry of Women Religious, IX-152 pp., 1941.

135. Keene, Rev. Michael James, O.S.B., J.C.D., Religious Ordinaries and Canon 198, V-164 pp., 1942.

136. Kerin, Rev. Charles A., S.S., M.A., S.T.B., J.C.D., The Privation of Christian Burial, XVI-279 pp., 1941.

137. Louis, Rev. William Francis, M.A., J.C.D., Diocesan Archives, X-101 pp., 1941.

138. McDevitt, Rev. Gilbert Joseph, A.B., J.C.D., Legitimacy and Legitimation, X-247 pp., 1941.

139. McDonough, Rev. Thomas Joseph, A.B., J.C.D., Apostolic Administrators, X-217 pp., 1941.

140. Meier, Rev. Carl Anthony, A.B., J.C.D., Penal Administration Procedure Against Negligent Pastors, XI-240 pp., 1941.

141. Schmidt, Rev. John Rogg, A.B., J.C.D., The Principles of Authentic Interpretation in Canon 17 of the Code of Canon Law, XII-331 pp., 1941.

142. Slafkosky, Rev. Andrew Leonard, A.B., J.C.D., The Canonical Episcopal Visitation of the Diocese, X-197 pp., 1941.

143. Swoboda, Rev. Innocent Robert, O.F.M., J.C.D., Ignorance in Relation to the Imputability of Delicts, IX-271 pp., 1941.

144. Dubé, Rev. Arthur Joseph, A.B., J.C.D., The General Principles for the Reckoning of Time in Canon Law, VIII-299 pp., 1941.

145. McBride, Rev. James T., A.B., J.C.D., Incardination and Excardination of Seculars, XX-585 pp., 1941.

146. Król, Rev. John T., J.C.D., The Defendant in Ecclesiastical Trials, XII-207 pp., 1942.

147. Comyns, Rev. Joseph J., C.SS.R., A.B., J.C.D., Papal and Episcopal Administration of Church Property, XIV-155 pp., 1942.

148. Barry, Rev. Garrett Francis, O.M.I., J.C.D., Violation of the Cloister, XII-260 pp,, 1942.

149. Bolduc, Rev. Gatien, C.S.V., A.B., S.T.L., J.C.D., Les Études dans les Religions Cléricales, VIII-155 pp., 1942.

150. Boyle, Rev. David John, M.A., J.C.D., The Juridic Effects of Moral Certitude on Pre-Nuptial Guarantees, XII-188 pp., 1942.

151. Canavan, Rev. Walter Joseph, M.A., Litt.D., J.C.D., The Profession of Faith, XII-143 pp., 1942.

152. Desrochers, Rev. Bruno, A.B., Ph.L., S.T.B., J.C.D., Le Premier Concile Plénier de Québec et le Code de Droit Canonique, XIV-186 pp., 1942.

153. Dillon, Rev. Robert Edward, A.B., J.C.D., Common Law Marriage, X-148 pp., 1942.
154. Dodwell, Rev. Edward John, Ph.D., S.T.B., J.C.L., The Time and Place for the Celebration of Marriage.
155. Donnellan, Rev. Thomas Andrew, A.B., J.C.D., The Obligation of the Missa pro Populo, VII-131 pp., 1942.
156. Eltz, Rev. Louis Anthony, A.B., J.C.L., Cooperation in Crime.
157. Gass, Rev. Sylvester Francis, M.A., J.C.D., Ecclesiastical Pensions, XI-206 pp., 1942.
158. Guiniven, Rev. John Joseph, C.SS.R., J.C.D., The Precept of Hearing Mass, XIV-188 pp., 1942.
159. Gulczynski, Rev. John Theophilus, J.C.L., The Desecration and Violation of Churches.
160. Hammill, Rev. John Leo, M.A., J.C.D., The Obligations of the Traveler According to Canon 14, VIII-204 pp., 1942.
161. Haydt, Rev. John Joseph, A.B., J.C.D., Reserved Benefices, XI-148 pp., 1942.
162. Huser, Rev. Roger John, O.F.M., A.B., J.C.L., The Crime of Abortion in Canon Law.
163. Kearney, Rev. Francis Patrick, A.B., S.T.L., J.C.L., The Principles of Canon 1127.
164. Linahen, Rev. Leo James, S.T.L., J.C.D., De Absolutione Complicis In Peccato Turpi, 114 pp., 1942.
165. McCloskey, Rev. Joseph Aloysius, A.B., J.C.D., The Subject of Ecclesiastical Law According to Canon 12, XVII-246 pp., 1942.
166. O'Neill, Rev. Francis Joseph, C.SS.R., J.C.D., The Dismissal of Religious in Temporary Vows, XIII-220 pp., 1942.
167. Prince, Rev. John Edward, A.B., S.T.B., J.C.D., The Diocesan Chancellor, X-136 pp., 1942.
168. Riesner, Rev. Albert Joseph, C.SS.R., J.C.D., Apostates and Fugitives from Religious Institutes, IX-168 pp., 1942.
169. Stenger, Rev. Joseph Bernard, J.C.D., The Mortgaging of Church Property, 186 pp., 1942.
170. Waldron, Rev. Joseph Francis, A.B., J.C.D., The Minister of Baptism, XII-197 pp., 1942.
171. Willett, Rev. Robert Albert, J.C.D., The Probative Value of Documents in Ecclesiastical Trials, X-124 pp., 1942.
172. Woeber, Rev. Edward Martin, M.A., J.C.D., The Interpellations, XII-161 pp., 1942.
173. Benko, Rev. Matthew Aloysius, O.S.B., M.A., J.C.L., The Abbot *Nullius*.
174. Christ, Rev. Joseph James, M.A., S.T.L., J.C.L., Dispensation from Vindicative Penalties.
175. Clancy, Rev. Patrick M. J., O.P., A.B., S.T.Lr., J.C.L., The Local Religious Superior.

176. Clarke, Rev. Thomas James, J.C.L., Parish Societies.
177. Connolly, Rev. John Patrick, S.T.L., J.C.L., Synodal Examiners and Parish Priest Consultors.
178. Drumm, Rev. William Martin, A.B., J.C.L., Hospital Chaplains.
179. Flanagan, Rev. Bernard Joseph, A.B., S.T.L., J.C.L., The Canonical Erection of Religious Houses.
180. Kelleher, Rev. Stephen Joseph, A.B., S.T.B., J.C.L., Discussions with non-Catholics: Canonical Legislation.
181. Lewis, Rev. Gordian, C.P., J.C.L., Chapters in Religious Institutes.
182. Marx, Rev. Adolph, J.C.L., The Declaration of Nullity of Marriages Contracted Outside the Church.
183. Matulenas, Rev. Raymond Anthony, O.S.B., A.B., J.C.L., Communication, a Source of Privileges.
184. O'Leary, Rev. Charles Gerard, C.SS.R., Religious Dismissed After Perpetual Profession.
185. Power, Rev. Cornelius Michael, J.C.L., The Blessing of Cemeteries.
186. Shuhler, Rev. Ralph Vincent, O.S.A., J.C.L., Privileges of Religious to Absolve and Dispense.
187. Ziolkowski, Rev. Thaddeus Stanislaus, A.B., J.C.L., The Consecration and Blessing of Churches.

www.ingramcontent.com/pod-product-compliance
Lightning Source LLC
LaVergne TN
LVHW050247080826
844660LV00012B/608

* 9 7 8 0 8 1 3 2 2 3 6 4 3 *